BACK
FROM THE
DEAD

A **Newsweek** BOOK

BACK
FROM THE
DEAD

HOW CLINTON SURVIVED THE
REPUBLICAN REVOLUTION

EVAN THOMAS
KAREN BRESLAU
DEBRA ROSENBERG
LESLIE KAUFMAN
ANDREW MURR
Photographs by David Hume Kennerly

THE ATLANTIC MONTHLY PRESS
NEW YORK

A portion of this work appeared in different form in *Newsweek* in November 1996.

Published simultaneously in Canada
Printed in the United States of America
FIRST EDITION

Library of Congress Cataloging-in-Publication Data
Back from the dead : how Clinton survived the Republican revolution /
    Evan Thomas . . . [et al.]. — 1st ed.
        p.   cm.
    "A portion of this work appeared in different form in Newsweek in November 1996"—T.p. verso.
    ISBN 0-87113-689-9
    1. Clinton, Bill, 1946– . 2. Presidents—United States—
Election—1996.   3. Dole, Robert J., 1923– . 4. United States—
Politics and government—1993–   I. Thomas, Evan.   II. Newsweek.
E888.B33   1997
324.973'09'049—dc21   96-52229

DESIGN BY LAURA HAMMOND HOUGH

The Atlantic Monthly Press
841 Broadway
New York, NY 10003

10 9 8 7 6 5 4 3 2 1

CONTENTS

FOREWORD
by Joe Klein

The woman is not a "soccer mom." She is, clearly, less afflu-
ent than that. She has short brown hair, a mild Texas accent. Her husband has a mustache and a stomach; he looks
like someone who works with his hands. We see them speaking about
the death of their daughter. We see them walking hand in hand along
a country road at dusk. We see a picture of the girl, wan and thin
and smiling. Then an announcer—a female announcer—says, "President Clinton signed the Family and Medical Leave law so parents
can be with a . . . sick child and not lose their job." And then we
find out that this is not just a political ad, but a *negative* one: "Bob
Dole led a six-year fight against family leave," the announcer con-
tinues as a black-and-white shot of Dole appears. Then the mother
again, saying that Clinton understands the struggles of families. And,
finally, an almost painterly shot of the president sitting in the White
House garden with a little girl in a wheelchair, golden light—not
even Maxfield Parrish would be so blatant—streaming left to right.

This 30-second ad, which can only be described as an Empathic Negative, is a masterpiece. It may be all you need to know
about the presidential campaign of 1996. It is subtle, personal, moving, manipulative and incredibly effective. It speaks directly to the
difficulties Bob Dole had as a candidate. In mid-September Alex
Castellanos, who had the unenviable task of orchestrating the Dole
response, said, "We've counted 44,000 Clinton ads run against us,

and 97.5 percent are negative." But the Clinton ads weren't traditional Chain-Saw Massacre negatives. They were "comparative."
They sandwiched a negative message between positive images. "It's
the veneer of fact, unencumbered by truth," Castellanos said. "Bob
Dole would never be against a family leaving work to spend time with
a dying child." But he did oppose the bill. Castellanos sighed. "What
we've got here is state of the art," he said. "The negative ad of the
future."

Indeed, the Clinton ad rehearsed the themes of the summer's
conventions. They were dismissed as empty ceremonies by a whiny,
cynical press—but may be remembered as the signal political events
of the year, a perfect reflection of what Americans wanted to see in
their public square. People were sick to death of bickering, hyper-
bole and partisanship; they wanted comity, inspiration and specifics. They were more open to small, practical-seeming ideas (family
leave) than grand schemes (the 15 percent tax cut). This isn't an
unmixed blessing, of course; but it is, on balance, a remarkably healthy
development, a sign of national stability and prosperity, a reaction
against the incivility of recent years.

Frank Luntz, a GOP pollster, had a group of independent
voters watch both conventions with little machines that enabled
them to register their immediate response to each speech. The results were unequivocal. The attack dogs—Kay Bailey Hutchison,
Mario Cuomo and especially Ted Kennedy—tanked. The three highest rated speakers were Elizabeth Dole, Al Gore and North Carolina
Senate candidate Harvey Gantt (whose fourth R for students—Respect—may have been the apotheosis of what "works" politically
these days). Colin Powell would have been up there too if he hadn't
uttered one, particularly damaging phrase: "My fellow Republicans."
But Gore's speech was probably the most instructive because it was
the only top-rated effort that included partisan, "comparative" material. Remember Gore's attack on the GOP congressional leadership
and his account of the president's Oval Office vow to stand firm
against the budget onslaught? It worked because it was buffered by
the far more memorable account of his sister's death—a story some

pols and journalists found cloying, but most civilians thought moving and human. Gore managed to make the case for his boss and against the Republicans without seeming harsh or partisan: a model of the Empathic Negative.

The Clinton campaign hit something of a rough patch in mid-September. For about a week, the race seemed to be tightening. And what was causing the problem? What was the president doing wrong? He was out doing the thing he supposedly does best: campaigning. After a slam-bang first week of September, firing cruise missiles at Saddam Hussein, Clinton spent the next two weeks on the hustings. He did some presidential things on the road. He threatened Saddam again. He did an environmental photo op at the Grand Canyon. Mostly, though, it was standard political fare: energetic Clinton speeches, large and happy crowds, a bus trip, great visual images. He seemed to be doing just fine as a politician, and that was the problem. "They like him best when he's doing his job, being president," the adviser said. And they don't like politicians. Even "good" ones.

So the president was quickly ushered back to the White House. By late September, when Dole started screaming "liberal, liberal, liberal," Clinton was responding from the Oval Office. And signing bills. And holding Mideast peace summits. And strengthening his lead again in the polls. It was an important lesson: the more presidential, the more successful.

In the end, though, he couldn't resist. He careened about the country, campaigning carnivorously. It seemed more an indulgence than a necessity—a last fling, a careless abandoning of the measured presidential rhythms, the patience and discipline that had brought him back from oblivion. Bill Clinton has always run for office as if he were being chased; he seems most comfortable a stutter-step ahead of the posse. This time, the game had been way too easy. The opposition was sad and slow; the posse poky, uninterested. He appeared untouchable, sequestered in the White House, and so he came out—dashing about, nearly sleepless, flagrantly empathetic and extremely unctuous. It was almost a goad: catch me if you can.

And there was a stirring. The *New York Times* and the *Washington Post* issued endorsements that were reproaches. "His administration has been disappointing and deficient and sometimes simply tawdry," the *Post* wrote—supporting him. David Broder, that most temperate of journalists, wrote that "there is too much evidence of serious matters being swept under the rug." He pretty much predicted a disastrous second term. The *American Lawyer* examined one of the potential disasters—the Paula Jones sexual-harassment suit—and concluded the charge was far more plausible than previously assumed. There were free-floating Indonesians, a truckload of unexplained FBI files and, of course, the longstanding rumors the first lady would eventually be indicted. All of which caused only a shadow of a tightening, an electoral twinge. Not nearly enough to change his fate.

He romped. He joins Woodrow Wilson and Franklin Roosevelt as the only Democrats to be reelected this century. The posse is left breathless and frustrated, consigned to marvel at his oleaginous virtuosity. And he has been truly blessed among politicians, blessed by the nature of his opposition—George Bush, Newt Gingrich, Bob Dole (it is as if Muhammad Ali never had to fight anyone more taxing than Jerry Quarry)—and blessed by something more, a winner's luck. But even if Broder is right, and Bill Clinton does face a nightmare of a second term, the strengths and skill of this president should not go unacknowledged: left for dead in 1994, he has just completed the most remarkable political comeback of this century, and it wasn't all luck.

"I didn't lead Bill Clinton back to the 'values' issues," Dick Morris once admitted, in an unlikely eruption of modesty. "He led me." There was growth, as well as calculation, in the resurrection. There were striking moments when the president managed to transcend his weaknesses, especially his near-fatal tendency to roll over for each and every supplicant. There were moments when he had to choose a dicey, or downright unpopular, course of action, and did. Two, in particular, should not be overlooked:

The first was the decision, in the spring of 1995, to support a balanced-budget plan. Much of his staff was opposed: let the Republicans stew in their astringency, they argued. Why join them in proposing pain? And Clinton did dither. He seemed to favor balance in a New Hampshire radio interview, then danced away from it. The staff held a contentious meeting in the Roosevelt Room, divided on how to proceed. It was resolved by Erskine Bowles, the deputy chief of staff, who stood up and said, "I'm gonna go ask him." He went to the Oval Office and asked, "Are you for a balanced budget or not?" Yup, said the president—and the course was set. Suddenly, broad new strategic lines of attack were available. The debate changed from left-right to moderate-right, with Clinton commanding the middle: he wanted to get to the same place as the Republicans, only more "responsibly." This put his opponents on the defensive, as extremists, a position they gleefully embraced, shutting down the government and sealing their fate.

The second moment, far more impressive, involved Bosnia. The peace talks had broken down. The chief negotiator, Richard Holbrooke, phoned from Dayton: if the president didn't immediately call Croatian president Franjo Tudjman, the talks would be finished, the war would resume. "I've got to admit that most of us, the political types who were in the room, were against his making that call," says George Stephanopoulos. "We didn't want American troops in Bosnia for Christmas. But he didn't hesitate, and he was right. That, and standing up to the Republicans on the budget, were moments that gave him backbone. You could see him growing into the job."

Has he grown? No doubt. He's seemed more disciplined, more presidential, these past few years. Even at the end, as he bounced around the country, delivering weightless rhetorical meringues to smallish audiences, his campaign seemed more controlled and less operatically emotional than in 1992. He kept to his schedule, grew misty only on cue. The crowd in Manchester, New Hampshire, the morning of his last day as a working candidate, was tiny—a primary-size crowd. This truly was an indulgence. He admitted it was an act of nostalgia on his part. His national career had begun here. But one wonders about that nostalgia: the 1992 New Hampshire primary was exhilarating and memorable, but he didn't win it. He was, in fact, publicly humiliated; he barely survived. It was survival that he reminisced about on that last campaign swing, the famous, desperate 1992 speech in Dover when all seemed lost: "I'll be with you till the last dog dies." It had been his first Houdini turn on the national stage, and predicted much that followed. His four years in office have been a series of escape acts. It's been a marvelous spectacle, watching him run. But now the running is done. And there is nothing left for him— except to decide where, finally, he will stand.

INTRODUCTION
by Evan Thomas

This is the story of the 1996 presidential election. It tells how Bill Clinton, by shrewdness, luck and love of the game, came back from a political near-death experience to win a second term. It is also the tale of how Bob Dole, a decent and profoundly lonely man, ran one of the most hapless campaigns in modern political history. The outcome, in the end, was not suspenseful, but along the way there were many moments of courage, folly and intense human drama.

To follow the candidates, *Newsweek* created a special team. Operating outside the magazine's normal weekly coverage, four reporters spent over a year working on this single story. In return for a promise not to publish their reporting until after the election, they were given unusual access to the candidates' inner circles. The promise of confidentiality allowed them to observe the campaign in a way other reporters could not. From beginning to end, Karen Breslau followed the Clinton campaign, while Debra Rosenberg assiduously tracked Bob Dole. Andy Murr got as close to Ross Perot as any reporter possibly could, and Leslie Kaufman ably handled a variety of assignments, including the rise and fall of Newt Gingrich, an important part of our story.

This is the fourth special election project undertaken by *Newsweek*. The first three—in 1984, 1988 and 1992—were written in large part by Peter Goldman, a journalist without peer. Goldman continued to direct the *Newsweek* team in 1995–1996, and I detached myself from the magazine's Washington bureau in August of '96 to be the writer on the project. We were edited with care and skill by Kenneth Auchincloss, with a massive assist from reporter/researcher Lucy Shackelford, who somehow managed to keep it all together.

As in the past, we published a 50,000-word article in *Newsweek*'s quadrennial special election issue, which went on the newsstands the night after Election Day. We then took another month to reinterview our sources, correcting and amplifying the story. Our efforts here are greatly enhanced by the work of photojournalist David Hume Kennerly and the addition of an introductory essay by Joe Klein, the gifted political columnist. It was *Newsweek*'s good fortune to join forces with Joan Bingham at Atlantic Monthly Press to produce this book, which is, in the late Philip Graham's famous phrase, "the first rough draft of history" of the 1996 election.

1 ■ TWO DIFFERENT WORLDS

On September 2, National Security Adviser Tony Lake flew from Washington to Little Rock to brief the president on options for a cruise missile attack on Iraq. The trip was secret; Lake was hustled through a back door of the Old State House. In the kind of room where Clinton had once greeted Boy Scouts, a general from the Joint Chiefs of Staff laid out charts and maps of the Persian Gulf, showing the deployment of U.S. warships. After a few minutes, President Clinton swept into the room, flushed and excited from a political rally on the front steps. He quickly began firing questions at the national security adviser, throwing around technical terms like "target sets" and "BDAs" (bomb damage assessments). Clinton became so animated as he debated how to contain Saddam Hussein in Iraq that he might as well have been talking about how to take away electoral votes from Bob Dole in the South. Lake could tell that the president, with all due regard for the gravity of the situation and the burden of his command, was having fun.

Clinton had always enjoyed politics, but he hadn't enjoyed the presidency, at least in the beginning. The first time he had ordered a missile strike against Iraq, in the summer of '93, he had seemed tense and wobbly. He had asked up to the last minute, "Are you *sure* this is the right thing to do?" But over time, Clinton had become more comfortable in his role as commander-in-chief. He had mastered the arcana of national security and come to appreciate the

1

military for its sense of duty. He observed that soldiers, unlike congressmen, generally do what they're told.

Clinton wasn't terribly self-conscious about his growth in office. There is a wide streak of earnestness in Bill Clinton—his "Boys Nation" side, said a friend—which helps explain why he warmed to the military and came to hate the press. "Bill Clinton has less sense of self-irony than any bright person I know," the friend said. He is rarely witty, though he can be sarcastic. Badgered by his handlers in 1992 to act more "presidential," Clinton had demanded with feigned ignorance, "What is presidential?" "Less than papal but more than gubernatorial," answered campaign strategist Paul Begala. In fact, being presidential is hard to fake, even for a great actor. Some people are born to leadership, others have to learn. The fact that Clinton learned to be president, by a sometimes painful process of trial and error on the public stage, made his accomplishment that much more remarkable.

Last April, a group of Republican pollsters sat behind a one-way mirror in Knoxville, Tennessee, watching a focus group talk about Bill Clinton. The voters, mostly middle-class and middle-of-the-road, were not flattering. They called the president "slick" and "smooth," compared him to a "snake" and "Mr. Ed, the talking horse." They recalled that Clinton was a draft dodger and an adulterer and had a "loudmouth wife." And these were people who planned to vote *for* Clinton. The GOP pollsters were dumbfounded. "Why are we down 15 points?" one asked. The answer had something to do with the failings of Clinton's opponent, Bob Dole, but it may have had more to do with the way voters viewed the character issue in 1996.

Journalists and other political commentators seemed vaguely disappointed that character, by which they usually mean defects of character, did not appear to count for much in this election. But ordinary Americans have a well-developed sense of the fallen state of man. In a tabloid culture, they are vividly aware of Bill Clinton's personal sins, but, as Democratic pollster Geoffrey Garin remarked, "They *deeply* don't want this election to be about that. They want it to be about *them*." It mattered less whether Bill Clinton had flashed Paula Jones or dodged the draft or fibbed about Whitewater than whether or not he cared about ordinary people—and whether he would stand up for them against the perceived excesses of the Republican Revolution.

Voters had always given Clinton credit for intelligence and empathy. The real character question was whether he had the strength for the job. His low ratings in the first two years reflected the suspicion that he did not. He was saved in part by luck. Great politicians, like great athletes, get good bounces, and Clinton, despite his protests to the contrary, had the good fortune to preside over a period of peace and prosperity that was only marginally of his own making. But he was also rescued by his own inner fortitude. Clinton can be so sharing and caring that it is easy to forget how tough and determined he really is.

Optimism and resilience had helped him bounce back before—from a fatherless home, from political defeat, from scandal and blunder. "My god is the god of second chances," Clinton once told a religious broadcasting service. His deliverance came in the unlikely form of Newt Gingrich. It can be argued that the 1996 election was really decided in 1995, and that it was less about Clinton versus Dole than Clinton versus Gingrich—or, perhaps, Gingrich versus Gingrich. No political figure in modern time has done more to undermine the power of his message with the defects of his personality than the disastrously voluble Speaker of the House.

Bill Clinton is at heart a politician who does best when he has an opponent. Gingrich and then Dole served as perfect foils, helping Clinton to define himself in opposition to the spirit of what his ads called "Dolegingrich." Indeed, Clinton ranked with Reagan and Kennedy as a pure politician. On the stump, he conveyed certainty and purpose, a joyfulness and contagious optimism, even when he had nothing particularly new or inspiring to say.

Bob Dole conveyed a different feeling altogether. He suffered from what the professionals call "poor candidate skills." The verbless sentences, the cryptic asides, the blinking, haunted eyes revealed a politician who was uncomfortable about asking for votes. If Bill Clinton was a natural, Bob Dole was so ill-suited to the role of presidential candidate that it seems a wonder anyone let him try.

In part, Dole won the Republican nomination because there is a streak of royalism in the Grand Old Party, and Dole had waited patiently for his inheritance. But he also won by default. The Republican field was notable for those, like Colin Powell, who chose not to run. Bill Bennett, the conservative polemicist and author of *The Book of Virtues*, who had been urged by many to run a "values" campaign, begged off because he understood what he was getting into. "When Phil Gramm said to me, 'William, I'm going off to do 300 receptions in the next 40 days,' I couldn't think of *anything* I'd rather do less," said Bennett. "I thought of that movie, *The Mosquito Coast*. I mean, this guy's sort of a charming nut, and he takes his family to this horrible place. That's what it's like in a presidential run—it's like taking your family to the Mosquito Coast. Everybody has to suffer, and these are people you love."

On the last weekend of September, as Bob Dole sat on the balcony of his 12th-floor condo in Bal Harbour, Florida, he must have felt like he had come to the Mosquito Coast. With only six weeks to go before the election, he trailed Bill Clinton by 15 points. His campaign had been a disaster, a floundering exercise in muddled messages, riven by conflict and dulled by low morale. For four days, Doles sat on his balcony or out by the pool, basking in the white tropical light. Aides handed him briefing books and tried to engage him in preparing for his first debate against Clinton, only a week away. Dole tried to study the issues, but he was famously indifferent to rehearsals. Between cramming, he would close his eyes and drift off to a place where only Bob Dole has dwelled.

Dole is an ardent sun worshiper. He will go to great lengths to get a tan. His front porch off the Senate Majority Leader's office was called "the Beach" because Dole would sit there for hours, even on humid summer days, to bring color back into his face. Tanning is his one pleasure and only hobby. Such vanity seems odd in a plain and reticent man, but Dole hates pallor. He had been so pale and wasted after the war, lying helpless in a hospital bed, stinking and itching in his cast, unable to feed himself or go the bathroom. A suntan is a reminder of his survival, a measure of compensation for the shattered shoulder, the withered arm, the fist that can now only clutch a pen.

Bob Dole was a war hero, but not the usual kind. He only got into the action in the last days of the war, and then because he just missed out on a posting to an Army sports unit well behind the lines. His real heroism came after the battle, in refusing to give in to despair as he lay helpless, while other young men back from war were getting jobs and starting families. His character was not forged by commanding battalions or the shared camaraderie of the trenches. It was formed by a lonely act of endurance.

Over time, Dole learned to disguise his injury, wearing a pad under his shirt to hide his withered shoulder, folding his fingers around a pen so they would not splay uselessly. He had learned how to dress himself (slowly, with a button hook), how to memorize what he could not write down. His stern midwestern parents had taught him not to complain; war had made him truly stoic.

The result was a certain distance between Dole and his fellow men. When Andy Kohut, a nonpartisan pollster, asked voters what word came to mind when they thought of Bob Dole, the far-and-away winner was "old." It wasn't just that Dole seemed old physically. His attitude was old. Dole's stiff upper lip seemed quaint in an age when people were casually spilling their guts to Oprah or Geraldo. Dole seemed particularly out of touch to voters under the age of 40. Baby Boomer Clinton, all lip-biting soulfulness, seemed in touch with his feelings, and just about everyone else's as well. Dole just seemed crotchety, like an old man yelling at the neighborhood kids to get off his lawn.

The reality, of course, was a lot more complicated. While Clinton was perfectly capable of tearing up for the cameras and then, a minute later, privately cracking a joke to an aide, Dole had often struggled not to cry. One reason Dole resisted talking about himself and his hardships was that he was afraid he would simply dissolve. The people of Russell had seen it. When Dole had won the vice-presidential nomination in 1976, he had thanked his hometown at a rally. "I can recall the time when I needed help . . . and the people of Russell helped . . ." he had said. And then he had stopped speaking. His left hand came up to cover his eyes, and he began to cry.

Those who knew Dole from his early days, or who worked closely with him in the Senate, saw his human side. They sensed the warmth beneath his prairie cynicism, his empathy for others who, like him, had suffered. They knew that his heartland integrity was not an act. In a chamber full of blowhards, Dole was known as a great listener. He understood that politicians needed to posture, but when the showboating was over, he could get down to work.

But he had trouble asking for help. The public tends to think of politicians as puppets on a string, manipulated by their "handlers," the legions of consultants who threaten to turn modern campaigns into marketing seminars. But Dole actually suffers from the opposite problem: he won't be handled. There is a willful stubbornness to his independence. Bob Dole's god is the god of self-reliance.

He is not comfortable in an age when politicians have been so relentlessly focus-grouped, polled and packaged that every policy position, every speech, every sound bite comes out sounding like Muzak and tasting like overprocessed food. Clinton was perfectly comfortable spouting pablum; Dole clearly was not. This could have worked to his advantage if he had stuck to his plainspoken prairie integrity. But Dole's speeches were more often a strange brew of old-fashioned pandering and mordant but often incomprehensible riffs on whatever popped into his mind.

Campaigning is all about rote repetition. Dole was much too restless to stay "on message." "Be a doer not a stewer," his parents had taught him. After the war, lying in bed day after day, his wounds healing with painful slowness, he had been driven nearly mad by boredom. Dole is a great listener—but never for too long. As Senate majority leader, he liked to conduct five meetings at once, moving back and forth between them, looking for the moment when the blathering was done and the dealing had begun.

The Senate was his natural habitat; a presidential campaign was definitely not. He never mastered its arts. He never explained exactly why he wanted to be president, not to the American people and possibly not to himself. But reaching for the unattainable has long been Dole's way. He is not an impossible dreamer, but he has a kind of grim persistence. Once, Dole's mother, Bina, found him in the garage hanging from a rafter by his bad arm. He was drenched with sweat and in obvious pain. He was trying to straighten his arm so he could play basketball again. He never could, but he was going to damn well try.

Dole was accustomed to being down. He had been left for dead in the war. He had run in vain for national office three times before. Throughout, his gallows humor rarely failed. Before the first presidential debate in Hartford, Connecticut, a reporter spotted Dole high on a hotel balcony, where he had gone to soak up the sun. The reporter waved; Dole stood up and pretended to dive head first over the railing. Then he smiled, the giddy, ironic, isn't-life-absurd smile of a man who had been through ordeals even more terrible than a modern presidential campaign.

2 ■ CHARLIE'S ANGELS

f Dole's mistake was not to ask for, Bill Clinton's was to ask for too much. During his first two years in office, Clinton couldn't get enough advice. At one time or another, he solicited the opinions of New Age gurus, eminent historians, old college buddies, Hollywood TV producers, pollsters, pundits, CEOs and liberal activists, all summoned to tell the president what he should do next. Clinton's ability to talk and listen, to care and share, is a great attribute, but during the early years it had two serious drawbacks: White House meetings were never-ending, and Clinton had a tendency to agree with everyone he met. On the night of December 1, 1994, however, Clinton was not in a mood to take anyone's advice. His presidency was in tatters. The year 1992, as his aide Harold Ickes described it, had been all about "Gennifer, the draft and didn't inhale." The next two years had been worse, a series of bungles and botched opportunities from haircuts to health care. In 1994 Republican congressional candidates had run ads morphing their opponents into Bill Clinton, and the Democrats had lost control of both houses for the first time in 40 years. To dig out of the rubble, the president had assembled some of his most seasoned political advisers, including Treasury Secretary Lloyd Bentsen, Commerce Secretary Ron Brown, Trade Representative Mickey Kantor and HUD Secretary Henry Cisneros. For a couple of hours, the meeting wandered aimlessly. Then Mickey Kantor said to Clinton, "You're going to have to take clearer stands." Clinton exploded. "Goddam it," he yelled, "don't tell me about taking clearer positions. I took a clear stand on guns [banning the sale of assault weapons], and it cost us the election." He rambled on about his "tough stands" on health care and NAFTA.

"You want to talk about why we lost the election? You want to talk about why?" Clinton's face was turning purple. "Because the DNC didn't do its part. We didn't have a message." He became self-pitying. "Everyone loads everything on me, and I'm supposed to pull the whole thing. I get treated like a mule. Goddamn it, I never have time to think! Whenever I'm at my desk I end up with these lists of people to call. I'm supposed to call every junior congressman about every vote. I'm the legislator in chief. It's wasted time, because the American people don't know I'm doing this stuff. And I shouldn't have to do it. I don't have time to think." Leon Panetta, the White House chief of staff, bravely suggested that Clinton wanted to talk on the phone all the time. This produced more presidential rage. Finally the meeting broke up. Nothing had been accomplished.

Yet, looking back, Henry Cisneros realized that something important had happened, and the president's outburst had finally made it clear. Clinton had been set free by the Republican landslide. No longer would he have to spend hours soulfully agreeing with Democratic do-gooders or the old paleoliberals up in Congress, or any of the parade of party hacks who had led him astray in his first two years. The press beast would no longer be fixated on the contest of Clinton vs. Clinton. Now it was Clinton vs. Gingrich.

Typically, when presidents get in trouble they reach out to the Washington establishment. Aging "wise men" are summoned to give counsel. There is a ritual confession of error by the humbled chief executive, and the elders confer forgiveness and bland advice. When Whitewater was heating up, Clinton had grudgingly brought in Washington superlawyer Lloyd Cutler to run the disaster-prone office of the White House legal counsel. He had hired media insider David Gergen "to help me interpret Washington," as Clinton put it. But both men were gone in less than a year. Though he hid his scorn,

Clinton hated what he privately called the "fucking Washington crowd." He was not about to go crawling to them again. Instead, he turned to someone so far outside the establishment that almost no one except Bill Clinton would claim him as a friend.

Dick Morris wasn't just a hired gun, he was an outlaw. Political consultants are famous for their cynicism, but they generally work for only one political party. Morris worked for both Democrats and Republicans, sometimes at the same time. Not just moderates, but true believers on opposite sides of the political spectrum. In 1988 he almost went to work on the presidential campaign of Michael Dukakis but ended up in George Bush's camp (Bush aides were convinced that Morris was leaking their media strategy to the Dukakis team). He had been taught politics as a blood sport by his father, a New York real-estate lawyer, who had in turn been taught by Al Cohn, boss of the Bronx and father of Roy Cohn, hatchet man for Senator Joe McCarthy. Scruples were for chumps, or, as Morris liked to say as a high-school debater, "Truth is that which can't be proved false." As a grown-up, Morris's role model was Lee Atwater, the GOP strategist who knew how to drive "wedge issues" right through the American public.

Clinton's relationship with Morris went way beyond politician and political consultant. They were more like pupil and teacher —only it was hard to tell which was which. If Clinton was Elvis, Morris was Colonel Tom Parker. He was the manager who, in his own mind, had become more talented than the act. Morris's rise and fall is one of the great stories of modern political campaigning, at once tragic and ridiculous. He was a classic mercenary—demonic, brilliant, principle-free. He was mocked at the White House as a crazy person, paranoid and grandiose; some aides called him "the Unabomber." And he played a critical role in Clinton's political resurrection.

They had known each other since their late 20s, when Morris, then a young consultant on the make, introduced Clinton (his first client) to the power of polling. He showed Clinton how public-opinion polls could shape a candidate's issues—and even his beliefs.

Morris helped Clinton become the youngest governor in America in 1978. Then, as soon as Clinton got to the governor's mansion in Little Rock, he dumped Morris. In the next election, the voters dumped Clinton. Chastened, the ex-governor got back in touch with his old friend. Morris got him reelected by making him apologize to the voters for his mistakes. "When Clinton lost the election in 1980," says Democratic pollster Pat Caddell, "he sold his soul to the Devil, and the Devil sent him to Dickie Morris."

Clinton's Arkansas aides were wary of Morris. "He's an eastern sharpie," said Clinton's longtime media handler, Betsey Wright. "Mean," she added, "but God, was he good." Morris would return to Arkansas periodically, especially at election time, to keep Clinton from getting too gooey. Morris gave Clinton the idea of the "permanent campaign"—he taught him that governing and running for office were one-and-the-same. The two men shared other interests: they both craved affirmation the way a baby does milk, and they had an eye for a pretty figure. Morris once told the *Los Angeles Times* that when he saw a picture of Dolly Parton taped inside Clinton's bathroom, he knew they would get along. Still, Clinton did not accept all of Morris's ideas by any means. Many of Morris's notions were outlandish. He once suggested to another client that he produce a video simulating a Boeing 747 being blown up to show the importance of metal detectors in high schools. One of Morris's most important contributions may have been to make Clinton appear—and, more important, feel—virtuous by comparison.

Morris and Clinton fell out again in 1990. Clinton chastised Morris for paying too much attention to his Republican clients, and Morris started to walk out of the room, saying that he was going to work for Clinton's opponent. The governor grabbed the consultant by the shoulders and spun him around. A security guard had to break up the scuffle. After Clinton moved to the White House in 1993, Morris went on to make attack ads for other Republicans, portraying the president as a big-spending wimp who had "made our military a joke" and doled out taxpayer money to fund "warming huts for swimming pools in Connecticut."

But Morris continued secretly to make calls to the man he once described as "the essence of my career." Before the 1994 elections, Morris was one of the few who told Clinton that the Democrats were going to "lose big." He also predicted that Newt Gingrich would self-destruct. "Let the wave run its course," he told Clinton that December. "Get yourself in a position where you can ride the wave to your advantage." Morris, who always had an idea, had a plan for Clinton's resurrection. He called it "triangulation."

Clinton should move right, Morris said. But he needn't become a pseudo-Republican. The trick was to preempt the Republicans on issues that were truly popular, like balancing the budget and reforming welfare. Meanwhile, let the Republicans tear themselves apart over abortion, and paint them as extremists on education and the environment. It was like a triangle, he said. The Republicans and the traditional Democrats would be strung out down at the bottom, while you, the president, would float above them at the apex.

Moving to the center in an election year is hardly original advice. Far more important was Morris's urging that Clinton should ignore his handlers and the congressional Democrats. "Your advisers have become your jailers," said Morris, and the president was in a mood to listen. After the '94 elections, Morris and Clinton began talking almost every day.

Morris was bound to be hated by the White House staff. But for a time in the winter of 1994–95, they didn't even know who he was. One day in mid-December, Clinton stood in his private study and dictated, paragraph by paragraph, whole sections of a speech he was scheduled to give on national TV—a "middle-class bill of rights" that promised a leaner and meaner government. The staff was perplexed: where had this tepid Republicanism come from? "It was sort of like the ancients discovering astronomy," said Bruce Reed, Clinton's domestic-policy adviser. "It was clear that there was a powerful gravitational force, but we didn't know what it was." Major sections of the speech had sprung out of Dick Morris's laptop. The State of the Union in January was even more chaotic. Downstairs in the West Wing, the usual committee of advisers drafted the usual Democratic spiel. Upstairs in the residence, Morris was feeding the president a more centrist vision. Clinton slapped them together like a midnight sandwich dripping with jam and pickle juice. Aides ran the finished copy down the White House driveway as the president's motorcade left for Capitol Hill. The speech ran 82 minutes long and was dismissed by the Washington pundits as a mishmash. But Clinton's poll ratings notched up a couple of points.

That winter, staff members remembered, Leon Panetta began making mysterious references to "Charlie." The staffers guessed that "Charlie" was a play on the disembodied telephone instructions handed out to the winsome crime stoppers on the old TV show *Charlie's Angels*. But who was Charlie? Morris loved the guessing game. "Mystery is an integral part of power," he pontificated. He refused to allow photographers to take his picture and was rumored to use an assumed name when he checked into hotels. He commuted to Washington from his home in Connecticut, staying at a $440 suite at the Jefferson Hotel three nights a week. He compared the nation's capital to Hershey, Pennsylvania; he didn't want to work in the chocolate factory. He was fascinated by Charles de Gaulle, who avoided Paris "to gain height and space."

In March, senior adviser George Stephanopoulos guessed who the mystery man was, but Morris wasn't really outed until April, when he wrote a speech that Clinton delivered to newspaper editors, extolling the "dynamic center." Inside the White House Morris planted Bill Curry, an unsuccessful Connecticut gubernatorial candidate, as counselor to the president (Gergen's old title). Affable, verbose and earnest, Curry had an engaging, eager-to-please manner. He and Morris had spent hours together in Connecticut secretly drafting speeches for Clinton. But when Curry arrived at the White House, no one knew who he was. He was hazed mercilessly: he was shut out of senior staff meetings and his policy suggestions were often ignored. Curry said that he felt more like an extra in the high school cafeteria scenes from the movie *Grease* than an adviser to the president of the United States. He compared Morris to the "band geek who manages to capture the homecoming queen and drive the jocks into a rage."

Chief of staff Panetta was furious about Clinton's back channel to Charlie, but Morris's real foe in the White House was Harold Ickes, whose animosity ran all the way back to their days as rivals in Democratic ward politics on New York's Upper West Side. Ickes, son of FDR's commerce secretary, was an orthodox New Deal Democrat. He had paid for his liberal principles with his kidney, removed after he was almost beaten to death on a civil-rights march in the 1960s. Ickes was an insomniac with a wicked temper, and he was also famously cheap. Sitting in his frayed suit, he would pore over Morris's hotel bills from the Jefferson and fume at the numerous charges for the minibar.

Morris thought Ickes was a Stalinist. He joked that Ickes was the first man he'd ever met who liked the Communist party not for its ideology but for its pragmatism. Morris dismissed the rest of Clinton's top aides as the "thugocracy." He didn't care; he had the president's ear. In June 1995 Morris persuaded Clinton to propose reaching a balanced budget in 10 years. On the night of June 13, Morris, Curry, communications director Mark Gearan, deputy chief of staff Erskine Bowles and a few others gathered in Panetta's office to watch Clinton address the nation. The staffers were cross. They had argued hotly against the balanced-budget pledge—bean-counting was for Republicans. But Morris had triumphed. As the staffers slumped over on the sofa, Morris jumped up to turn out the lights. He wanted to dramatize the moment. The staffers just looked at each other in embarrassment. When the speech was over, Morris embraced Curry and moved to hug Panetta. The chief of staff quickly stuck out his hand in a preemptive handshake.

"It's the economy, stupid" had been an article of faith among the Clintonians ever since the slogan had been scrawled on the wall of the "war room" during the '92 campaign. Clinton's pollster, Stan Greenberg, still believed it. He insisted that the Democrats had lost Congress because they had failed to look after the "downscale voters," the lower-middle-class blacks and whites who had turned out for Clinton in 1992 but now felt disenchanted. To win them back, Greenberg believed, Clinton had to address their economic anxiety. There was one big problem with that strategy: since Clinton had been presiding over the economy since 1993, the squeeze on the middle class might be perceived as his fault.

Greenberg was not the only pollster working to reelect Clinton, however. Morris had recruited his own team, Mark Penn and Doug Schoen, a pair of Harvard-educated New Yorkers who juggled political and corporate accounts like AT&T and Texaco. Much of their political work had been abroad (Penn helped elected ten heads of state in Latin America). As Washington outsiders, Penn and Schoen were disdained by political pollsters like Greenberg, who whispered that the New Yorkers cooked their numbers. The White House staff was oblivious to Morris's polling duo, at least at first. They were denied permanent White House passes, forced to wait for admission outside the gate with the pizza vendors, bicycle messengers and lost tourists. But from their Manhattan offices, they were doing research that would change the thrust of Clinton's 1996 campaign.

As he sifted through the data at 2 A.M. one scorching July night, sweating over his spreadsheets (the air conditioning was broken), Penn worked on a contrarian thesis. The economy was not the problem. Yes, there were anxieties about downsizing, wage stagnation and the growing gap between rich and poor. But consumer confidence was actually at a 10-year high. People were mad at government and wary of Clinton, but most expressed satisfaction with their own lot.

A traditional class-war message, Penn figured, would get Clinton about 40 percent of the vote. The key to the election, as always, was the 10 to 20 percent in the middle. Penn's polling data showed that these swing voters were more worried about America's moral decline than its economy. They were upset about crime, drugs, sex and violence on TV, teen pregnancy, the growing incivility and coarseness of American life.

In working up marketing plans for corporations, Penn had probed deeply into the American psyche. He ran complex "neuro polls" that measured not only political attitudes but the way people's values and lifestyles affected their choices. He found that the typical Clinton voter was a single woman, a watcher of MTV and Oprah. She was often afraid at night and admitted to being an overeater. Clinton did well with "intuitive, feeling types" but less well with "thinking, judging, perceiving" personalities. Dole's voters tended to have kids in college, to be anti-gay and religious, to like talk radio and home improvements.

To test a "message" for a political ad, Penn and Schoen often polled in shopping malls, the town squares of '90s America. The idea behind mall testing was to catch people thinking about politics the way most Americans did—as a momentary distraction in their lives. Penn and Schoen felt that focus groups, the tool of most political pollsters, were contrived. How often did groups of 12 people sit around a room talking politics for two hours over Coke and pretzels?

With their sophisticated techniques, Penn and Schoen zeroed in on what Penn called the "swing-rich" middle—young, upscale suburban parents who were the most important bloc of undecided voters. In July 1995, Penn designed a "megapoll" that would find Clinton's "market." The survey produced one particularly disturbing finding. Parents with children leaned strongly toward Bob Dole. They associated Clinton with Gennifer Flowers and smoking (if not inhaling) pot. They just didn't trust the president to protect their children's future. "We lose the family vote," wrote Penn in a memo to the campaign.

Winning back the family vote, Penn wrote, was the key to "unlocking the electorate" for Clinton. But how to get around voter worries about Clinton's character? His answer was to stress the president's public values. "We should talk about the morality of certain actions," Penn urged during the Wednesday-night strategy sessions in the White House residence that summer.

There has always been a touch of the preacher in Bill Clinton, and the vocabulary of values came to him naturally. By the fall, his speeches were regularly drawing a moral dividing line. Republicans, he said, routinely "violated," "ignored," "trampled" and "dishonored" American values, which the Clinton administration "cherished," "respected" and "defended." So weary did White House speechwriters get of inserting "values" into every other sentence that they would sometimes just flash a "V" with their fingers at meetings when Morris or Penn started theorizing.

After values, Penn promoted a second big theme: optimism. That September, Clinton wandered back on Air Force One and held forth extemporaneously with reporters about the state of the union. People were worried about the transformation of society from industrial age to information age. That's why they were in a "funk," said Clinton. Penn groaned when he saw the headline in the *New York Times*. Funk sounded like Jimmy Carter's malaise speech—all wrong. Penn worried that Clinton had been listening again to populists like Greenberg. In fact, as Penn knew, most voters were surprisingly upbeat about their own economic future. Indeed, their quiet optimism (in contrast to the gloom emanating from Washington) looked a lot like it had ten years before, the summer after voters had returned Ronald Reagan in a landslide.

Could it be "Morning in America" again? That kind of campaign wouldn't fly, Penn knew. Americans had become too cynical, and Clinton was no Ronald Reagan. He wasn't going to get away with reciting a list of his achievements or his core beliefs. Still, Clinton ought to tap the public vein of optimism. In his effort to feel people's pain, the president was stepping on his own economic good news. Administration officials spent too much time publicly fretting over America's "problems." Robert Reich, the talky labor secretary, was a prime offender. Better, Penn suggested in a memo he sent to the entire cabinet, to talk about "achievements" and "challenges." "Failure to recognize the optimism of the electorate and to correctly revive it could be the single biggest mistake that cost us the 1996 election," Penn wrote.

At Clinton's invitation, Penn became a regular at the political meetings held most Wednesday nights in the White House residence. Clinton's top aides—who grumpily referred to these sessions as "the Charlie meetings"—looked sullen and traded glances when Morris spoke. But when Penn began discussing his values pitch that fall, even skeptics like Panetta paid attention. Penn was given a place to stash his bag and his polling data in the West Wing. It was a closet, a two-foot-wide area that could barely accommodate the beefy, rumpled six-footer. But Penn, and the politics of values and optimism, was in. Class war and economic gloom were out.

The Wednesday night political meetings in the White House were fairly small and disciplined, at least by the standards of the Clinton White House. Morris was long-winded, but the president, for a change, was not. During the first two years of his presidency, Clinton's meetings had typically been dormitory-style gabfests, with the president as chief gabber. But staffers began noticing that meetings were becoming more subdued and exclusive. Clinton wanted to know who was coming beforehand, and he routinely shut people out. He still ruminated out loud and loved all forms of policy wonkery, but he stopped making decisions on the spot. As a result, he was more likely to stick to the decisions he made. Bill Clinton was acting more like a president.

3 ■ THE GENERAL SAYS NO

is friends began to notice the change in Clinton that autumn. In mid-October Henry Cisneros traveled with him to Austin, Texas, to make a speech, and beforehand the presidential party went out to a Mexican restaurant with a group of longtime Texas supporters. Normally, Clinton would have joined— or more likely led—the joking, the laughing, the spinning of tall tales. But that night, Cisneros noticed, Clinton was just going through the motions. The president kept trying to bring his old buddies back to serious subjects, to test their reactions to what he planned to say on race and affirmative action. The Million Man March was scheduled in Washington the next day, and Clinton was worried that it might turn violent.

Race was much on Clinton's mind that fall. In July, he had tried to seek a middle ground on affirmative action, promising to "mend it, not end it." But he worried that race relations could become a major issue in the 1996 campaign. Like most Americans, he had closely followed the O. J. Simpson trial, though he was careful to avoid expressing any opinion on the case in public. Because he had no television in the Oval Office, Clinton would often slip into his secretary's office to watch the proceedings. The president was worried that an acquittal would set off a white backlash. Some advisers thought that would hurt his chances in California, where Pete Wilson had won reelection as governor in 1994 partly by campaigning against affirmative action. At the same time, Clinton was concerned that a guilty verdict might ignite black anger, possibly even urban rioting. On October 3, minutes before the Los Angeles jury was to hand down its verdict, Clinton and a dozen top aides had gathered around a TV outside the Oval Office. When the not guilty verdict was announced, Clinton stood grimly, staring at the television in disbelief. "It seemed," said one aide, "that the president was aware that everyone was watching his reaction. He seemed to be working very hard to contain himself and be presidential." But he was clearly upset. After a long silence, he muttered a single word: "Shit."

Now, two weeks later, Clinton still seemed preoccupied, Cisneros thought. The president's eyes had a distant look. Later, in the car, some of the other revelers remarked on the uncharacteristic presidential mood. "You know, he's seen things," Cisneros told them. "He knows things about the world, about people, he's seen intelligence reports that have taken him to a different place. There's no one else at that place."

The public, too, began to see Clinton differently. His openness and informality had been winning at first, but voters had been put off by the TV pictures of the chubby president huffing along in too-short jogging shorts, or discussing his preference in underwear on MTV. But as 1995 wore on, the public began to see a president who actually looked like one. He seemed to stand a little straighter; it was a matter of less waist and more chest, said one commentator. His stare was steadier, and at the same time more distant.

Some of this was pure artifice. Desperate to make their president seem more presidential, Clinton's handlers had urged him to watch old Ronald Reagan videos to study the Gipper's aura of command. The first lady had spruced up his wardrobe—the jogging shorts had to go. He began to run less, lift weights more. The midnight raids on the White House refrigerator were harder to control, but at least Clinton wasn't ballooning.

When he took office, Clinton did not even know how to salute the military, much less run it. Crises in Haiti and Bosnia gave him on-the-job training. At 6 P.M. on the night of September 13, 1994, Clinton stood in the Oval Office facing the chairman of the Joint Chiefs of Staff, General John Shalikashvili. Twenty thousand American soldiers were poised to invade Haiti in a dramatic night-time airborne assault. Long columns of paratroopers from the 82nd Airborne were lined up on the tarmac at Ellis Air Force Base, North Carolina, waiting for an order from the commander-in-chief.

The day before, some of Clinton's closest supporters in the Senate had told him that he would be foolish to invade Haiti. Worse than foolish, Clinton later told his friend, the writer Taylor Branch. He would be out of his mind. If the invasion failed, he would be able to count on all of eight votes against formal censure by the Senate. If casualties were heavy, there would be talk of impeachment.

General Shalikashvili told the president that he had 15 minutes to decide. The paratroopers needed to be loaded on their planes, the general said. H-hour was approaching. Clinton looked at the chairman of the Joint Chiefs, standing erect, rows of medals across his chest. Nothing, perhaps aside from watching old movies, had prepared him for this moment. Still, he tried to sound at once off-hand and crisp as he gave the order to load up. "Pack 'em," he said.

The airborne assault was called off after the planes were in the air, but only because the Haitian generals caved at the last moment. The American troops landed peaceably the next day. There were no U.S. casualties. Less than a year later, Haiti held its first truly democratic election since 1990.

Clinton had prevailed, in the face of warnings by some of his most astute political counselors. He had taken the same course in Bosnia. In December 1995, a few weeks after Clinton agreed to send 20,000 American troops to enforce a shaky peace agreement, Harold Ickes had this conversation with a *Newsweek* reporter:

ICKES: What the hell is the vital interest of America in Bosnia and Hercegoviya [sic]? I mean, is that a new pasta or something? People can't even pronounce it. Hercegoveeya? How the hell do you say it?

NEWSWEEK: Hercegovina.
ICKES: Yeah, right. Hello? What the fuck is that? That a new car?

Public opinion polls were just as skeptical. By overwhelming majorities, Americans disapproved of sending troops to Bosnia. But by the spring of 1996, polls also showed growing confidence in Clinton as a foreign policy president—as a commander-in-chief.

A year earlier, in April 1995, Clinton had felt compelled to insist that the president was still "relevant" in a government that seemed to be dominated by Gingrich and his Republican revolutionaries. But a few days after this rather pathetic moment, Clinton traveled to Oklahoma City to the scene of the devastated federal building, blown up in a terrorist blast. Clinton was at once sympathetic and stoic. He mourned for the dead, but he vowed to catch the killers, and he conveyed a reassuring sense that life would go on.

Looking back, commentators concluded that the public view of Clinton began to shift after Oklahoma City, where he had exhibited the take-charge determination as well as on-key rhetoric that Americans expect of a president in times of trouble. In the months ahead, as Clinton teared up in a dignified way at one funeral or another, the press would grow cynical, especially when he seemed to be able to switch his emotions on and off. But Clinton's aides were sure that he wasn't faking. They particularly saw a change in him after the assassination of Israeli Prime Minister Yitzhak Rabin on November 4, 1995. Clinton was in awe of Rabin. He regarded the Israeli leader as something of a father figure. The two men had grown close pursuing the elusive goal of peace in the Middle East, and Clinton was devastated when Rabin paid with his life. On the afternoon of the shooting, Harold Ickes and National Security Adviser Tony Lake found Clinton on the White House putting green. When he heard the news, the president began to cry. He went into his small private office and sat there. He leaned his head back against the wall. Ickes dimmed the lights and left Clinton alone, quietly weeping.

All of these experiences seemed to deepen Clinton, to lift him from the feckless swirl of his first two years and transport him to what Cisneros had called a "different place." Three weeks after Clinton helped bury Rabin, he went to Ireland on his way to visit American troops preparing to ship out from their bases in Germany into the Balkan winter. The president had used the power of his office to help broker a cease-fire by the Irish Republican Army, which seemed to present the best hope of peace for Northern Ireland in decades. In Belfast and Derry, Clinton was overwhelmed by adoring crowds, chanting his name (disconcertingly, it sounded like "Bull! Bull! Bull!" on the thick tongues of Ulstermen). It was Clinton's first experience, up close, of the enthusiasm he inspired in people from a foreign land. Senator Christopher Dodd was watching Clinton as he stood on a stage in front of thousands of screaming Irishmen. "He sort of filled out," said Dodd. "The suit finally fit."

Clinton's growth as a leader was slow and subtle, and mostly overlooked by the press. In the fall of 1995, most of the media attention was on a more glamorous figure, General Colin Powell. In September and October, Powell's publicity tour to promote his book, My American Journey, was a star turn. Powell was the anti-politician in an anti-political season, a movie screen upon which the public projected its rescue fantasies. Northern liberals saw a black man and assumed he was liberal; southerners saw a general and assumed he was conservative. By not being too specific about his mostly moderate beliefs, and by being at once disarming and coy, Powell kept the fantasy alive. At his first stop, there were 40 camera crews and a line a half-mile long. The newsmagazines put him on their covers (Newsweek twice). "If Colin Powell Had the Nerve, He Could Change America," headlined Time. The story was so fawning that Powell, who has a sense of humor about himself, told friends that it was "a major barf." A CNN poll in the early fall showed Clinton running behind Powell, 46 to 38 percent.

The White House watched the Powell phenomenon with growing disquiet. Though his aides publicly denied it at the time,

Clinton was obsessed. He was convinced Powell would run, even though Hillary and Al Gore tried to reassure him that he wouldn't. Staffers were instructed to say nothing about the general, but behind the scenes Clinton and his closest advisers were trying to figure out how to deflate Powell's mythic aura with the voters.

Commentators were comparing Powell to Cincinnatus, the general who came out of retirement to save Rome. The White House had another historical analogy in mind: George McClellan, Lincoln's famously overcautious and politically meddlesome general. McClellan had run for president against Lincoln in 1864, an act of disloyalty that seemed almost treasonous in the midst of the Civil War. "If he had run, it would have been the first time since McClellan ran against Lincoln that a commanding general ran against a president he had served," Clinton told *Newsweek* in January 1996. "I mean, think about it." McClellan had been a poor general because he had been afraid to attack, fearing that he lacked sufficient force. Powell was widely hailed as a hero of the Gulf War, thanks in part to his brilliant TV briefings. But he, too, had been extremely reluctant to commit U.S. forces, and he had pushed President Bush to cut short the war once it began.

Clinton's aides were prepared to launch the McClellan comparison with reporters and editorial writers. "We were prepared to make the case that there was something vaguely disloyal about it, that it was unprecedented," said George Stephanopoulos. "It would have made Powell more of a politician, less of a hero."

Colin Powell's flirtation was one of the great "what ifs" of American political history. Exit polls on Election Day 1996 showed that Powell would have beaten Clinton if he had run. But the polls may not mean much, since Powell never had to make his case to the people, never had to endure the inquisition of the press, never had to fend off the president's intimations of disloyalty or the right wing's assaults on his social views. Powell was vividly able to imagine the worst as he wrestled with his decision during the first week of November 1995.

The beginning of the end of the Powell presidential fantasy came on the morning of Friday, November 3, as Powell was lying in bed with his wife, Alma. She was quietly weeping and he was silently praying. Alma had never been one to mince words with her husband, and the word she used that morning at home in McLean, Virginia, was a simple "no." She told Powell that she didn't want him to run for president. The general was gloomy when he called one of his closest advisers later that morning and recounted the conversations with Alma. "I think things are going south," Powell said. He hadn't entirely ruled out a run, but he knew his heart wasn't in it.

Just a couple of days before, Powell had been boisterous and playful. "Yo!" he exclaimed to Marybel Batjer, a former Pentagon aide and member of Powell's small inner circle. "I feel great! I've got the fight!" True, there were threats from some quarters. "We're going to get your boy," a conservative senator had warned another of Powell's advisers ("Don't ever call him 'boy,'" the friend replied). Powell told intimates that he could "visualize" being president. "Leadership" and "duty" he understood: he had spent time in the Oval Office, had known and worked with three of its occupants. It was running for that office that seemed so alien and daunting.

And so his mood swung during that last week of self-examination. He was tempted by the outside political world that seemed to yearn for his clarifying grace; yet inside, close to home, the costs just seemed too high. "He'd get up for it during the day, reading his mail, talking on the phone. But in the quiet of the night, waking up in the morning, it wasn't there," said a friend who spoke with him several times a day. In the end, the decision was "personal, not political," said this adviser. Powell believed that he probably would win the GOP nomination and that if he did, he would win the election. But he lacked the passion to put himself—and his wife and children—through the ordeal of the campaign.

In the hyper world of politics, Powell's decision seemed to take forever. But in the more orderly and measured universe of Colin

Powell, where progress has always been marked by solid preparation and the steady march of efficiency reports, three weeks was not time enough to think through a life change. Between October 20, when Powell finished his book tour, and when he announced he would not run, Powell changed his mind over and over again. He tried, with all his heart, to see himself as a paradigm-shifting politician, but he never quite got past his background, and perhaps his temperament, as a careful, prudent staff officer.

Powell was "incredulous" about the adoring crowds who showed up on his book tour waving homemade POWELL FOR PRESIDENT signs. His sense of duty was stirred by conversations with three former presidents—Gerald Ford, Jimmy Carter and George Bush—not because they urged him to run (none did, in so many words), but rather because they spoke so seriously about the burden of the office. At the same time, however, Powell was bothered by what he called the "incivility" of politics. Powell was deeply offended when he heard a report (false, as it turned out) that a former colleague in the Reagan White House had taken on the task of digging up dirt on Powell's private life for the Bob Dole campaign. "Oh, God," Powell sighed to an old friend, "this is what you've got to go through." Powell regarded himself as "thin-skinned," said the friend, and he worried that he would let himself be "baited" by the far right. He also knew the press would revisit questions like his murky role in the Iran-Contra affair.

Powell fretted, too, about the logistical problems of mounting a late-starting campaign. An independent candidacy was out of the question; the general was more comfortable within the structure of a party, and he had privately considered himself a Republican since at least 1988. He had no shortage of offers of help from the GOP. Resumes poured in from would-be Powell pollsters and media consultants. But this consummate military bureaucrat was bothered that, as a friend put it, "the political game is something he knows nothing about." Two of his closest advisers, Batjer and Richard Armitage, were former Pentagon aides with little experience in electoral politics; his spokesman, Bill Smullen, was a career soldier. The expertise of a fourth, former Reagan chief of staff Ken Duberstein, came more from Beltway lobbying than running campaigns. Powell's "head-quarters" was distinctly mom-and-pop: a basement office next to the rec room at home and a computer, a fax and two phone lines in an office at the Armed Forces Benefit Association in Alexandria, Virginia. His aides later said they felt guilty they had not done more sooner to prepare for a run. But it may be that Powell didn't really want them to.

After all, the ever-cautious Powell has always attributed his success—even his survival—to his careful attention to detail. In his memoirs, he writes candidly about his fear of parachuting. Unlike the macho rangers who leapt out into the blue shouting "Airborne!" Powell admitted that he would advance to the door of the plane with "little baby steps." Powell felt he was equally unprepared for the jump into presidential politics. He was disturbed during the book tour when he was asked on CBS *This Morning* whether he favored federally funded abortions. He first said he didn't and then caught himself, saying he'd have to think about the effect on the poor. The slip reminded him that there were scores of similar questions he had yet to think through.

Professional politicians have well-rehearsed positions on even the tiniest issues. In October, Dole dared Powell to come to Iowa to talk about hog price supports. As Powell listened to Dole and other candidates, he would sometimes shake his head and say that most Americans aren't talking about arcane legislative minutiae. Powell was fascinated watching a tape of Dole at the first New Hampshire debate in October. The senator had to refer to note cards when he was asked why he wanted to be president. According to his confidants, Powell was certain he would have no trouble striking the larger themes, such as reinstilling a sense of personal responsibility in American life. At these moments, Powell felt he could rise above politics as usual—and win.

But his family resisted. On the weekend of October 28–29, the clan gathered at the McLean house. After nearly 20 moves and several wars, the Powell family was accustomed to sacrifice, but the general's approach this time was different. "All the other times he just told us. This time, it was 'What do you think?'" son Michael told a friend. Michael, a young lawyer, was favorably inclined. But Powell's two daughters, Linda, 30, and Annemarie, 26, were strongly opposed. They did not like the idea of losing their privacy. And Alma—who according to friends is not as enthusiastic about the GOP as her husband is—was adamant. She was afraid for Powell's safety and worried about giving up their quiet new life. As her husband won his stars, they had moved into ever-larger quarters, but there were always sergeants bustling around her household. Powell told one adviser, "This is the first time Alma's had her own house. She's not a general's wife anymore, and she wants to be able to do things her way."

Powell was shaken by his family's opposition. "I'm struggling," he told a close confidant. At times, the friend said, "he could hear the engines roaring. But then he'd be left alone quietly with his thoughts and he'd think, 'God, I don't know. I'm trying to force myself to do something unnatural.'"

Outside the family circle the pressure to run grew. Though Powell never discussed race as a factor in his decision, much of the country saw him as a potential racial healer. On Wednesday in the final week before his decision, GOP chairman Haley Barbour appeared at Powell's office. Barbour's message was clear: the party would welcome Powell. At the same time, Duberstein was meeting Newt Gingrich on Capitol Hill; he brought back word that the Speaker did not regard Powell as an obstacle to the Republican revolution. That night, Gingrich himself made a secret visit to Powell's house to tell the general that he would not stand in his way. Powell was enormously encouraged. He felt that GOP ideologues could be outflanked. "I think I can see my way clear" to running, he told his kitchen cabinet. "We're getting there."

But the next day, Powell learned that a delegation of GOP right-wingers was trying to scare him off with a press conference at the National Press Club. Powell was especially irked by Gary Bauer, a former Reagan White House colleague, who referred to Powell as "Clinton in ribbons." That morning Powell spoke with his cousin

Bruce Llewellyn, a multimillionaire entrepreneur. Llewellyn, who didn't know about the conservative event, was determined to persuade his cousin not to run. He appealed to Powell's sense of precision. "You can't do this thing in a haphazard way," Llewellyn told him. There was too much to do. "It will take a miracle to get it done; it's impossible," he said. The GOP doesn't even want you, Llewellyn went on. "Yeah, they're having a press conference right now to do me in," Powell replied. "That only proves my point," said Llewellyn.

Llewellyn thought he was beginning to sway his cousin. Alma pushed Powell most of the rest of the way the next morning as they talked in bed. If there was any chance left that Powell might still run, it evaporated the next day. Flying home from a speech to Pontiac dealers in Florida, Powell called a distressed Alma and learned that reporters and cameramen had staked out their house. He had to sneak in through a neighbor's backyard to escape detection. He arrived to the news that Israeli Prime Minister Rabin had been murdered. The invasion of her privacy and the assassination of a world leader were the end for Alma. She turned to another family member. "This ain't going to happen," she said.

The inner circle—Powell, Duberstein and Armitage—met Monday night in Powell's study. Alma joined the group after an hour, and Smullen was on a speakerphone. At last, the general made his decision. With little discussion, Powell also flatly ruled out a vice-presidential candidacy. "Colin, is it over?" asked Duberstein. "It's over," replied Powell, softly. Duberstein took a melancholy drive in the rain around the Virginia suburbs the next morning, looking for a place to stage the press conference. In the end Smullen lined up a Ramada hotel near Powell's office and swore the manager to secrecy.

Batjer, who lives in California and watched the announcement on TV, was startled by how tired Powell looked. He had lost eight pounds and seemed exhausted. Powell sighed when he called her afterward. "There's a lot of relief around the house," he said. Powell felt some of it himself. "How do you feel, Uncle Colin?" asked his niece Lisa Berns. "Like a weight has been lifted off my shoulders," he answered. "I'm a young man," Powell, 58, told one well-wishing politician who called him after he dropped out. "There will be other opportunities."

When George Stephanopoulos learned that Powell had decided not to run, he hustled into the Oval Office to tell the president. "Are you sure?" Clinton shot back. The day before, the president had insisted "he's gonna do it." This time he just gave a little self-mocking laugh. The White House was ordered to stay mum. "We labored hard not to seem overjoyed," said press secretary Mike McCurry. Clinton was not celebrating as he watched the evening news. "You better let everyone know there are going to be a lot of ups and downs before next year," he told Panetta. "It isn't over by any means."

4 ■ LEADER OF THE REVOLUTION

Newt Gingrich liked to say that his ambition in life had always been to be the Speaker of the House, but he had grander dreams as well. Hardly had he become Speaker when he began thinking about running for president against Bill Clinton. The two men had much in common: they were both baby boomers, policy wonks, champion talkers. They were politicians who actually cared and thought about broader themes of governance. Running against Clinton would be a way of elevating the debate to a higher level. Gingrich cherished the intense, unfiltered coverage you could only get in a presidential campaign. One to one, Gingrich believed that he would win, not just because he was a superior debater but because he was on the right side of history. He believed, said his press secretary Tony Blankley, "that he could simply make a case that was irresistible to a majority of the country that we were right and Clinton was wrong."

This daydreaming took some intriguing forms. Gingrich had read somewhere that Jack Kennedy and Barry Goldwater, as presumptive candidates in 1964, had talked about flying around the country on the same plane and pitting their opposite visions, liberal and conservative, against each other in an authentic national debate. Gingrich, said Blankley, had envisioned something like that with Clinton. Maybe they couldn't have pulled off the part about sharing the plane, but they could capture the spirit of the thing; they could seize the nation's attention by arguing "two pretty different views of the way the world works," said Blankley.

Gingrich saw himself as an epochal figure. Flat-footed and nearsighted as a boy, he had read Arnold Toynbee on the rise and fall of civilizations when other kids were out playing ball. He was a romantic; while his stepfather, an army officer, was off fighting in Korea, Gingrich watched John Wayne in *The Sands of Iwo Jima* four times in one day. Gingrich studied great leaders, hoping he could somehow absorb their aura and method of command. He particularly favored "war leaders" like Churchill and Roosevelt, Washington and Lincoln.

Even before the Republicans scored their election day upset in 1994, Gingrich had sounded out Mike Deaver, President Reagan's image maker, for tips on projecting leadership. "We're going to win in November," Gingrich announced over lunch that September. Deaver was skeptical. Gingrich wanted to see Deaver, he explained, because he saw himself as the obvious heir to Reagan's mantle of great communicator. Gingrich went on about Reagan's press strategy—always positive, anecdote-laden and disciplined on message. Deaver wanted to say it was a bit more complicated than that, but at the time he didn't want to get involved. Politicians were always comparing themselves to Reagan. What Deaver didn't yet understand was that Gingrich wasn't comparing himself to Reagan, not exactly. In "the sweep of history"—a favorite expression—Gingrich was taking his destined place at the forefront of an ideological realignment. Reagan had started the revolution. Gingrich would complete it.

For much of 1995, this didn't seem an idle boast. Most of his "Contract with America" swept through the House on a wave of "revolutionary" rhetoric. Liberalism seemed dead, and possibly the Democratic party as well. Before long Deaver, no longer so dismissive, began offering Gingrich advice. In April, Deaver persuaded Gingrich to schedule a televised "conversation with the nation." It was only a few days later that Clinton had to defend his "relevancy" at a press conference. Gingrich had almost succeeded in turning the president into a constitutional monarch, with a fancy title but without much real power.

Gingrich was in many ways an effective and disciplined prime minister. He ignored the seniority system and installed his own committee chairmen. His top men were given manuals from the army's Training and Doctrine Command; before long, they were speaking of "shaping the battlefield" and "commander's intent." A lover of aphorisms, Gingrich pretty much followed his favorite, "Listen, learn, lead." At the same time, he turned the Speaker's rooms in the Capitol into a political fairground. Photographers wondered about popping flashbulbs. In one corner, Newt's own personal historian from West Georgia College took notes, so that posterity wouldn't miss a trick. Guard dogs sniffed for bombs. Gingrich's staffers cringed when their boss would drift off into what they called "Newt World," like the day he demanded that everyone attend an all-day session with a psychoanalyst to discuss the concept of "tough love" and dependency in the context of welfare reform.

Jaded Washington—and particularly the supposedly liberal press corps—was for a time enchanted with Newt. But the public was not. Many people disliked Gingrich before they knew what he had in mind for them. It wasn't his politics; they just didn't like his style. Southerners were put off, even though he came from Georgia. He was too slick, too aggressive, too fast-talking—could anyone so ungentlemanly really be from the South? In focus groups, pollsters in both parties heard epithets like "loudmouth" and "blowhard." He shoots from the hip. He talks without thinking. He doesn't care about us. He's only concerned about himself.

Friends tried to warn him. GOP chief Haley Barbour told the new Speaker he shouldn't take a fat book contract for his memoirs, but Gingrich agreed only to forgo the advance. "You're like the kid in high school who sat in the front row of the class with the pencils in his pocket protector and raised his hand first on every question," one adviser told him. "He was usually right, but nobody liked him."

"I was that kid," Gingrich replied.

In February, just one month into his term as Speaker, a group of prominent Republican pollsters, including Fred Steeper, Linda DiVall and Ed Goeas, met with Gingrich to deliver some bad news. Steeper lived up to his nickname ("Dr. Doom") by telling Gingrich that his "negatives" were climbing and threatened to undercut his legislative victories. Gingrich seemed unperturbed. "This is momentary," he said. "We are going to fix that soon."

In early March, party boss Barbour paid Gingrich a visit. He was worried about Gingrich's poll numbers. "You can't stay down there too long, or it will become permanent," Barbour said. Again, Gingrich sloughed off the warning. He pointed to Governor John Engler of Michigan, whose numbers had cratered and whose home had been picketed when he first proposed draconian cuts in welfare. Now Engler was a rising GOP star.

Like the president, Gingrich enjoyed psycho-babble and New Agey self-absorption. But for all his self-reflection, he was remarkably lacking in self-awareness. Soon after Gingrich took over as Speaker, the Democrats began filing ethics charges against him for various alleged circumventions of the campaign finance laws and House rules. The tactics were similar to the ones Gingrich himself had used to topple Democratic Speaker Jim Wright in the the late '80s. But Gingrich refused to see that the mud might stick to him, too. At leadership meetings, he would pound the table and yell, "This is just bullshit!"

Over Memorial Day 1995, he took his annual trip to stay with Gay Gaines, a wealthy backer, at her home in West Palm Beach, Florida. Gaines lavished praise on Gingrich, calling him "the most brilliant political mind of our era." Also down for the weekend were Bill Bennett, the party polemicist most recently famous for his *Book of Virtues*, and Rush Limbaugh, the right-wing talk show host. Gaines put on some Motown tunes and the group pulled back the couches and danced. Bennett lipsynched "What Becomes of a Broken Heart," and the women did a number by the Supremes. No one openly urged Gingrich to run for president, but Bennett went on about the weakness of the Republican field. Limbaugh told Gingrich, "You are the revolution, the articulater of the dream. But," he warned, "whoever gets the nomination will take over the mantle."

Within a few weeks, Gingrich was up in New Hampshire, ritually testing the waters in the first primary state. Gingrich played coy, calling it a "moose hunting trip," and Tony Blankley, his portly, chain-smoking press secretary, dutifully wore a ridiculous "moose-hunting" outfit. Gingrich had arranged to be in New Hampshire at the same time as Clinton, and the two traded smiling barbs and bonhomie. This was it: Newt and the president, *mano a mano*.

In July, it was time for a little reality. As they sat stuck in midtown gridlock in New York, Blankley carefully broached the subject of Gingrich's negatives. Gingrich began to hold forth on his desire to have a national debate with Clinton. He was the one who led the revolution, he was the one who should take on the president. Blankley gingerly steered back to the low polls and what they meant for a presidential run. "You really can't do it," he said. "I know," Gingrich said.

Still, there was a revolution to be won in Congress. Gingrich was determined to begin the process of dismantling what he called "the liberal welfare state." Unlike earlier revolutionaries, including Reagan, Gingrich wasn't just talking about it. Gingrich's mantra was "zero in seven"—a balanced budget by the year 2002. He picked seven years not for any particular economic reason but because it seemed "mystical."

Gingrich's assault on the federal deficit spending was an honest attempt that required tough votes and eschewed the usual "smoke and mirrors" that had made budget-cutting a farcical exercise in past congresses. The Speaker was exultant when the House began passing bills in August that truly began slicing the federal bureaucracy. On the night of one particularly difficult vote, he sat with his captains around a huge garbage can filled with cold beer. Toasting their triumphs, Gingrich conjured up the Duke of Wellington conducting the peninsula campaign against Napoleon. But some of his guerrillas were getting carried away. Under the prodding of House Whip Tom DeLay, a former Texas exterminator who once called the Environmental Protection Agency "the gestapo of government, pure and simple," what began as "regulatory reform" to cut red tape turned into an all-out assault on the popular Clean Air and Clean Water Act. Republicans began to look like enemies of the environment and tools of corporate interests, who were in fact drafting much of the legislation.

Health care was an even greater political hazard. Gingrich understood that in order to balance the budget, he had to begin the painful process of restraining the growth of federal entitlement programs that account for half of government spending. In Gingrich's plan, social security was still sacrosanct, but health care for the poor and elderly (Medicaid and Medicare) was not.

Medicaid was one thing; the poor hadn't a strong constituency. But cutting Medicare was sure to enrage its over 33 million elderly recipients, who vote in disproportionate numbers. "Don't," Haley Barbour begged Gingrich. Democrats would turn on the Republicans for going after Medicare "the way the Pope hates sin." But Gingrich refused to back away from spending cuts he was sure were necessary: the Medicare trust fund was facing bankruptcy right after the turn of the century. He pointed out that he wasn't proposing to cut Medicare overall, just lower the rate of growth from about 10 percent a year to seven percent—still more than twice the rate of inflation. At first, Gingrich wanted to give a nationwide address to explain this. A pollster had provided the proper spin—the GOP was just trying to "preserve, protect, and defend" Medicare—and Mike Deaver was ready to help with the staging. But Gingrich backed away after a heated discussion with Barbour. Get a deal with Clinton first, Barbour counseled, then go on the air and take credit. Instead, Gingrich shot his mouth off in front of some reporters, predicting that the existing Medicare bureaucracy would one day "wither on the vine." It sounded as if he were talking about Medicare itself—and the Democrats were handed a devastating sound bite for a future ad.

5 ■ TARGET: GINGRICH

ne day in early September, Dick Morris burst into a "message meeting" at the White House declaring, "Medicare's a winner!" If Newt Gingrich got his way, he proclaimed, "old people will end up on the sidewalks where they'll curl up and die!" The other Clinton aides in the room tried to look serious. "Dick discovered Medicare," one staffer said to his colleagues afterward with a chuckle. "Should we tell him the world is round too?"

Bashing the Republicans for planning to cut Medicare is Democratic orthodoxy. But Morris had been handling so many Republican clients in the last few years that he was, one Clinton speechwriter put it, a "virgin" on Medicare. Morris's main push— his almost daily preoccupation—had been to get Clinton to come out for a balanced budget. From the beginning, and at monotonous length, Morris insisted that Clinton had to cut a deal with Congress or be blamed as an old-fashioned tax-and-spend Democrat. Morris didn't start paying attention to Medicare until polling by Penn and Schoen in July and August showed him that old people were passionate about protecting their benefits.

Morris may have come late to the subject, but he perceived something the old pros had missed: a chance for a preemptive strike that would hit the Republicans in the heart of their Revolution. Ickes had tapped Terry McAuliffe, the party's most aggressive fund-raiser, to pull together a huge $42 million war chest early in the year, in part to intimidate any challengers from within the party. Morris wanted Clinton to spend that money on a series of ads attacking the Republicans for cutting Medicare. "You can shove it up their ass," Morris declared. Over the objections of Harold Ickes and others who wanted to save money for the fall campaign still a year away, Morris persuaded Clinton to start spending on an "air war."

The Democrats' first commercial played on Penn's "values" theme. Called "Moral," it opened with a shot of some children raising an American flag. "As Americans," the announcer intones over swelling music, "some things we do simply and solely because they are moral, right, and good." Cut to black-and-white shots of Gingrich and Bob Dole glowering above the Capitol. "Dole and Gingrich . . ." (sinister flourish; cha-*chung*) "CUT MEDICARE" (bright red letters). The camera shifts to President Clinton in the Oval Office. "President Clinton: doing what's moral, good and right by our elderly."

Later ads became even more pointed and extravagant. They were titled "Protect," "Slash," "Cut" and "Wither." They accused the GOP of not just trying to check the growth of Medicare, but of wishing to eliminate it altogether. Republicans were portrayed as cold, heartless advocates of the rich. The Democrats protected traditional American values.

To spread the message, Bill Knapp, the campaign's media adviser, launched a stealth campaign. He wanted to reach swing voters, but he didn't want the press to pay attention. If reporters started scrutinizing the Democratic ads, the Republicans might be stirred to respond. So Knapp quietly bought time in "secondary markets," outside New York, Los Angeles and Washington. These strategically targeted ads reached millions of viewers in the fall of 1995. Morris watched happily as Clinton's favorable rating inched up with each ad, from 47 percent in August to the mid-50s by December. It was arguably the turning point in Clinton's campaign for reelection.

For the Republicans were overreaching. Gingrich had decided to try to rush his legislative program through Congress, FDR style, while his victory was still fresh and the opposition still reeling. But 1995 wasn't 1933; the crisis atmosphere was missing and a "revolution" turned out to be not precisely what the people—even many who had voted Republican—had in mind. The Medicare ads inflamed their doubts; as subsequent polls revealed, America was yelling, "Hey, wait a minute." Gingrich didn't hear it, but Bill Clinton did.

Gingrich felt stabbed by the Democratic ad campaign. He was beside himself when he met with the president on November 1. Clinton was threatening to veto the Republican budget, and a government shutdown loomed. Gingrich thought he was hearing signals—through a back channel set up by Morris—that the White House wanted a deal, but at the same time he was being clobbered on the airwaves. "I can't tell you how angry I am," Gingrich began. He was almost shaking. "You have a chickenshit operation here, Mr. President."

Clinton was intensely involved in the ads. He not only approved them but he helped to write them and knew their timing and audience. The simple, blunt message of the ads helped focus Clinton and keep him from wandering off onto other subjects or into policy arcana. Bill Clinton, responsible policy wonk, could well appreciate that Medicare costs had to be reined in. But Bill Clinton, candidate for reelection, was not above a little demagoguery. With an old actor's knack for getting inside his role, he convinced himself that he was not pandering to older voters but rather acting on conviction. When Clinton returned from Rabin's funeral in Israel on November 7, he was full of defiance for the Republican budget cuts. "I don't know if it's because I'm exhausted or what," he told the cabinet, "but I feel in my bones that this is a fight we are going to have to wage with them no matter what it takes."

Six days later, with the government scheduled to close down at midnight unless the president and Congress could reach an agreement, Clinton met again with Gingrich and other GOP leaders. He was intransigent. "If you want this budget signed, you'll have to put someone else in this chair," he declared as midnight approached. "I will not now, not ever, sign this budget. I think it's bad for America." Gingrich was stunned by the president's defiance. He had expected the White House to cave in. At a breakfast meeting two days later, he whined that the president had refused to talk to him about the budget on the flight back from Rabin's funeral in Israel. He pouted that he had been made to use the rear exit of Air Force One. "CRY BABY NEWT" jeered the *New York Daily News*. The White House gleefully released a photograph showing that the president had indeed talked with Republican leaders on the plane. Gingrich's poll numbers headed for new lows. In one congressional district in Maine, 85 percent of the voters gave him unfavorable ratings, and 46 percent marked him at zero or one on a 10-point scale. In Cleveland, the only man who ranked lower that December was Art Modell, owner of the Browns, who was in the process of moving the football team out of town.

Week after week through November and December, Gingrich drove up Pennsylvania Avenue to the White House to try to face down the president. Instead, he felt seduced. Dick Morris's back channel ran to Trent Lott, the Senate GOP whip and an old Morris client. Lott kept telling Gingrich that a deal was inevitable, that the White House would eventually fold. Thus encouraged, Gingrich thought he sensed a willingness to compromise, to rise above partisan interests. But then nothing would happen. With his sense of history and respect for the office, Gingrich would fall for Clinton's charm. Only on the ride back to Capitol Hill would he realize that he'd been had. He mournfully admitted to Leon Panetta that after his visits with Clinton, "I need two hours to detoxify."

On the way back from the White House on January 2, Gingrich finally began to accept that he had lost, that there would be no deal, and that the Republicans were being blamed from shutting down the government. He called his wife, Marianne, and groaned that he had been naive. She said she was reminded of a episode from *Leave It to Beaver*, in which Beaver gets conned out of his lunch money by a hobo. "Newt," said Marianne, "you're just being the Beaver."

One of the standard maxims of the political consulting game is "He who defines first defines last." The confrontation between Gingrich and the White House in the late fall of 1995 proved the rule. Clinton's ads had convinced millions of swing voters that the

Republicans had shut down the government, while the president had bravely defended the elderly. The truth was not so simple. Both sides were to blame for the budget breakdown. The Republicans had made a genuine attempt to solve a problem that would not go away—the unsupportable costs of federal benefit programs. They had, it is also true, recklessly voted for a large tax cut, opening the GOP to the charge that it was financing tax cuts for the rich by slashing health care for the elderly. The Democrats, meanwhile, had stalled for weeks before producing a balanced budget that was less than credible. Both sides had become hopelessly locked in. But it didn't matter. The public wasn't interested in the details.

In retrospect, Clinton scored a major victory by standing firm. But what seemed like brilliant tactics had sprung—as so often is the case in politics—in part from inadvertence. Morris himself had wanted to make a budget deal; the back channel was not a ruse. Morris's liberal foes, Stephanopoulos and Ickes, had been terrified that the president would fold. Clinton himself had no master plan; he had played the whole thing day by day. Caught between Morris pushing for a deal and his more liberal staffers lobbying against it, he was uncomfortable and unsure what to do. Alone with his aides, right after his stirring speech defying the Republicans on November 13, he had turned to Panetta and said, in an anxious voice, "Okay, Leon, now you gotta figure out the endgame." Panetta, known as a "goo-goo" (good government) type, hated the idea of shutting down the government. He had squirmed when his old Hill colleagues across the aisle tried to shame him into producing a budget with credible numbers.

Republicans suspected a Machiavellian plot in the back channel between Senator Lott and Morris. They figured that Morris had been just trying to lull them. In fact, most White House aides were furious about the Morris back channel and wanted to close it down. Only after the game was all over did they realize that the GOP had been bamboozled. "You couldn't have bought a better disinformation campaign if you tried. It was stunning. You know, Clinton's a genius," said Stephanopoulos, laughing. Two months after the press declared

Clinton the winner in the budget battle, Leon Panetta, too, was still marveling at the president's good fortune. "I could tell that this was all Machiavellian," he said and burst into laughter.

"Let's face it," Stephanopoulos said. "Gingrich saved our butt." His hot rhetoric allowed the White House to paint him and his unruly freshmen followers ("the Shiites") as extremists. On December 12, Harold Ickes remarked, "Every time Newt opens his mouth it helps us. Keep talking, Newtie. I mean, anyone with 55 to 65 percent negatives . . . Just keep flapping them lips, boy."

There were no victory celebrations in the White House. Any joy was dampened when Whitewater flared up again in mid-January, and the first lady was compelled to testify before a grand jury. It wasn't until the State of the Union at the end of the month that Clinton allowed himself to gloat a little. He got some help from Vice President Gore, whose stiff demeanor conceals a clever gamesman. As a gimmick, Gore suggested that the president single out a federal worker when it came time to recognize heroes in the gallery, a custom begun by Ronald Reagan. Gore aide Elaine Kamarck found Richard Dean, a 22-year-old veteran of the Social Security Administration who had helped rescue workers during the Oklahoma City bombing. During the government shutdown, Dean had worked without pay. The plan was for Clinton to recognize Dean, then call upon Congress never to shut down the government again. During the afternoon rehearsal in the White House theater, Gore started acting out for Clinton how best to milk the line, "Let-us-never, ever, shut-down-the-government-again." When Clinton practiced the line, droning on in the stentorian tones used by Gore, staffers dissolved into snickers. "Y'all are going to have to quit or I'm never going to get through this," the president scolded.

That night, Clinton delivered the line perfectly. The Democrats roared; the Republicans sat on their hands—even though it meant stiffing a hero. For the first time since he was elected, Bill Clinton's favorable rating moved past 50 percent and stayed there. The budget fight had been the first engagement in the presidential campaign. By exaggerating the GOP's mandate in 1995, Newt Gingrich dramatically lengthened the odds against Bob Dole in 1996.

The State of the Union marked the reemergence of Clinton as a centrist "new Democrat." "In terms of ideology," said Clinton's communications director Don Baer, "he was back to the positions he was most comfortable with. These are the ideas that got him elected in the first place." No longer did Clinton take his policy ideas and legislative initiatives from the old-line Democrats on the Hill and at the White House. A new, less liberal axis emerged within the White House staff to translate Morris's impulses and Mark Penn's polling research into a voter-pleasing "message." This was largely the creation of Dick Morris.

Baer, a balding, 41-year-old former newsmagazine editor and lawyer, had been working with Morris (secretly at first) since Clinton's controversial speech to newspaper editors in April 1995. A few months later, Morris urged Clinton to promote Baer from chief speechwriter to communications director. He and Penn also struck up a relationship with Baer's successor as speechwriter, Michael Waldman. Baer and Waldman would combine the consultants' theories and government policies into a series of high-profile events.

During his early "Charlie" phase, Morris had limited his contacts to Bill Curry and a few senior players: Gore, his chief of staff Jack Quinn, and Erskine Bowles, Clinton's deputy chief of staff. As his confidence and influence grew, Morris began reaching into the ranks of mid-level experts who generated specific White House policies on subjects ranging from television violence to tuition tax credits, teen smoking and school uniforms. Morris often appropriated the ideas of aides like Bruce Reed, Clinton's welfare and community-policing specialist; Rahm Emanuel, the point man on crime and immigration; and Gene Sperling, the budget and education expert. Though he was a traditional Democrat, Sperling had earned Morris's gratitude by guiding him through the complexities of the federal budget. More often than not, Morris rescued ideas that had been languishing in the government bureaucracy and, by packaging them as part of the "values" strategy, sold them to Clinton. Morris, said Reed, "was a great salesman."

The machinery had always been in place to reposition Clinton as a centrist, but it had remained inert during 1993 and 1994. Morris, in effect, flicked on a switch. The evolution of Clinton's stand on crime shows how the process worked. Penn's polls showed tremendous concern about crime among swing voters. Waving these findings at White House "message meetings," Morris created a market for concrete proposals by Rahm Emanuel and others, ranging from youth curfews to distributing cell phones to community watch organizations. Working with his contacts at Justice, Emanuel came up with legislation and executive orders pushing a ban on "cop-killer" bullets or establishing a national registry of sex offenders. Baer's communications shop, a windowless basement in the West Wing that looked like a cross between a flourescent-lit cave and an overstocked Ethan Allen showroom, cranked out speeches and carefully staged events. The nightly news began showing scenes of Clinton in the Rose Garden signing a bill to build more prisons or extolling his assault-weapons ban in front of a phalanx of grateful cops. By autumn, Clinton would have the endorsement of policemen's associations around the country—law-and-order cops who usually backed Republicans. White House reporters tended to treat these events cynically, as mere election-year spin. But Baer assured the president that voters didn't really listen to the skeptical commentary of the reporters. Ordinary people cared more about results, and crime statistics were dropping sharply. Even the White House liberals couldn't help but admire Morris's handiwork. By April, Stephanopoulos had to admit, "Dick does message better than anyone else."

6 ■ I'LL DO IT MY WAY

It is characteristic of the Dole campaign and its candidate that it had no clear beginning: there was never a moment or even a day when he decided to run for president. Instead, a vague restlessness, a feeling that he could win, a sense of duty and of pride all came together to make the decision for him, leaving his own volition an almost incidental factor in the equation. After more than three decades on Capitol Hill, Dole was occasionally bored. He had never quite gotten over losing to Bush in 1988—"Ronald Reagan Junior," he called him, not meaning to flatter. Like many senators, Dole felt he could look around the cloakroom or the committee room or even the Oval Office, and say to himself, "I can do better." Unlike most of the others, Dole wasn't engaging in self-deception. Dole knew that he had become a national figure. He had appeared on the Sunday morning talk shows more than any man alive. In the halls of Congress, tourists would turn and say, "There's Bob Dole!" In the weeks after the November 1994 elections, Bill Clinton looked like a one-term loser, and there wasn't any overwhelming challenger in the GOP. Passively, Dole sidled toward a decision. "Well, jiminy, maybe I could try it one more time," he would say.

Dole's sidelong approach to so crucial a choice grated on his wife Elizabeth, though she hid her frustration. She had long since learned that her husband did not like to be told what to do. Deft at indirection, Elizabeth preferred to arrange situations that would, ever so gently, prod her husband into action. But there wasn't much time. Filing deadlines were coming up. There was money to be raised, and Dole's chief competitor for the GOP nomination, Phil Gramm, was already out there raising it. As the Doles had watched the Republicans sweeping control of Congress for the first time in half a century on election night, Elizabeth had wondered aloud if Bob Dole's time had come. Dole had said nothing. By early December, she felt she had to nudge him toward a decision. Other wives might have done it across a pillow. Elizabeth scheduled an appointment.

At 9 A.M. on Saturday, December 3, Elizabeth met with Dole in his Senate office in the Hart Building. It seemed like the right time and setting. The senator's formal office was less cozy, more austere and businesslike than his majority leader's suite in the Capitol. There would be no cronies dropping by, and few staff on a Saturday morning. She could make Bob focus on the hard questions, or at least try to.

For reinforcement, Elizabeth had brought along another woman, Mari Maseng Will. An expert speechwriter and conservative polemicist, Will was used to dealing with strong-minded men. She had begun as a press secretary to Senator Strom Thurmond of South Carolina, and she was married to columnist George Will. Will arrived with a memo, a point-by-point recitation of the obstacles Dole would have to overcome in order to win. She began with the biggest one: Dole's speaking style. He rambled, he wandered, he mumbled. He ignored prepared texts and talked off the top of his head. Will could see him trying to make eye contact with individuals in the crowd, usually people he already knew. Sure, they came away with a good feeling. But the next day they couldn't remember exactly what Dole had said. That may have worked when Dole was campaigning at rural libraries in Kansas, but it would be a disaster on the national stump. Modern presidential campaigns are wild and chaotic, she said. Staying on message is everything. Did Dole understand?

He nodded, yeah.

Will added a special warning about Dole's friends in the press. Over the years, Dole had bonded with reporters covering the Hill, cracking mordant jokes and trading cynical asides. A presidential campaign, said Will, was very different. Reporters might laugh at his jokes—but they would also write them down.

Dole said he understood.

In Will's estimation, the election would center on values. Dole would have to talk about cultural decline, about fear of crime, about trash TV and religious faith. In past campaigns, Will had watched Dole edit out anything that touched on values. She wanted to make sure Dole realized that the 1996 election would turn on the very subjects Dole had been reluctant to mention.

Dole mumbled that he would talk about values, if that's what it took.

Will could see that he didn't really want to. His midwestern reticence got in the way. He disliked preaching. And the issues were so personal. They forced him to reveal himself, to be immodest. It was, Will suggested, like having to write a poem in fifth grade and then stand up and read it to the class. She remembered that feeling of embarrassment herself. Gently, she prodded Dole. "It's hard to do, isn't it, Senator?"

Yeah. But he'd do it.

It was Elizabeth's turn to speak. She wanted to make sure that Dole understood he would be playing two very different roles—Senate majority leader and candidate. She worried whether he would be able to shift from the minutiae of the Senate to articulating the big-picture themes of a national election. Could he handle both?

Yeah, yeah.

Elizabeth pressed a little harder. "Let's hear you say it, Bob. How you do it simultaneously."

Dole nodded: mmm, argh, he understood.

Now both Will and Mrs. Dole spoke. This time around would have to be different from 1988. Dole would have to delegate responsibility and not try to run his own campaign on whim. He couldn't sit on the plane with a map in his lap, deciding where to go next. There would have to be planning, discipline.

Dole said he understood, but it wasn't clear that he really did, or that he fully appreciated the difficulties that lay ahead. These two forceful women, who cared deeply for Dole and knew him well, could not have been more clear. In retrospect, the warnings and advice they gave Dole were prescient. Dole did not argue with them. And Mari Will was sure that Dole was listening; he always did, it was one of his true strengths as a lawmaker. But it wasn't apparent from his responses that he grasped how hard it would be for him to run a successful presidential campaign. At one point Elizabeth got very personal. She said that even if Dole won, he would have a very tough time. The country faced huge problems, and the press would try to destroy him. "Are you sure you want to risk that?" Elizabeth asked, in a soft voice.

But Dole showed no apprehension. He'd been through it all; he had spent his whole career under press scrutiny. He had run for president twice before. The difference this time was that he thought he could win. Dole truly believed he was the right man. "This is serious business," he would say. Who else, among the possible Republican challengers, was really up to the job? Phil Gramm, in Dole's mind, was an inflexible ideologue. Lamar Alexander was an empty plaid shirt. Pat Buchanan was a gadfly, fundamentally not serious. When Dole said, "This is serious business," his aides thought he was really saying, "C'mon, look at these other guys. How could voters choose them instead of me?"

Dole continued to be opaque about his intentions through the New Year. "I'm sort of inching along," he told Elizabeth. Then on Friday, January 6, the *Washington Post* ran a big pie chart on the front page showing Dole's approval rating at 62 percent, versus 45 percent for Clinton—a 17-point margin. Six days later, without any fanfare, he filed the necessary papers with the Federal Election Commission to become a candidate.

Bill Lacy, Dole's chief strategist, knew all the arguments against a successful Dole campaign. He had written them down in a memo back in March of '94. Dole was a "dinosaur," "mean," a "two-time loser," a creature of Washington. But Lacy dimissed them: "these aren't real barriers," he wrote. Dole was the natural front-runner because he deserved to win. The key was organization and discipline, both of which had been notably lacking in Dole's 1988 campaign. Lacy had gone back and counted a dozen different power centers in the '88 Dole campaign. Power had to be centralized, Lacy believed, in just a few top aides, experienced pros like himself.

Lacy, 42, was a mild-mannered Tennessean who had worked in the Reagan White House and in many congressional campaigns. He operated and thought like a cautious, deliberate general in a long war. He believed in overwhelming the opposition. No surprises, no tricks—just better research, better organization, and more money. Lacy loved data: focus groups, polling, surveys.

In the spring of 1995, Lacy drafted the "Dole for President Campaign Strategy 1996." He began with "Lessons from History," such as "Front runners win the GOP nomination" and "Recent GOP presidents have been 'around the track.'" Methodically, Lacy put together a seven-page binder of 83 short statements summarizing Dole's views. There was nothing controversial, new or bold in these statements. They were conservative but reasonable or at least familiar positions on immigration, affirmative action, the budget, defense.

In Lacy's mind, Dole did not need an electrifying vision to win. Experience and character counted for more, and those the senator had in abundance. He just needed a straightforward message that was sound and believable. "Everyone wants to give us the 'magic message bullet,' but I don't think we need one," wrote Lacy in a memo that February. "We need a solid message we can stick with." The campaign strategy drafted in the spring argued that Dole's beliefs could be pulled together under three umbrella themes: "reining in the federal government . . . reconnecting the government to our values . . . promoting American leadership abroad." The third was later changed to "reasserting" so that Dole could run on the "the three R's." It sounded more catchy.

Slow-speaking and amiable, with a slight southern drawl, Lacy liked meetings, lots of them. He called the top staff meetings the V-8, even after it had grown beyond eight people. V-8 sounded powerful, like a '65 Chevy Impala. Lacy wanted the Dole campaign to seem like a machine, unstoppable. "The Last Word" from his "Campaign Strategy" paper was a supposed quote from Attila the Hun: "It is not enough that I win . . . all others must lose." Lacy had taken the Attila quote off a T-shirt he had seen worn by one of his pollsters. He thought the macho line would impress the finance people who had to go out and raise money. He didn't realize that the line would be prophetic: that Dole would not so much win the nomination but survive, while his opponents lost.

When Scott Reed came aboard as campaign manager in February, Lacy handed him his March '94 memo, stressing the need for discipline and organization. "Thought you might like to see this," Lacy scribbled on the top. "We're pretty much on the model." A model campaign. No surprises. That was fine with Reed. Reed, 36, wasn't deeply concerned with vision and message. True, he preferred to have some red meat to feed the voters—he liked the idea of a flat tax, whether or not it made a whole lot of policy sense. He had worked for Jack Kemp in his '88 campaign and tried to sell Kemp's grand ideas. What Reed really cared about was getting it done. He was a detail man, a manager. Others—Lacy, Mari Will—could sit and ponder the message. Memos stayed on Reed's desk only long enough for Reed to check them off for action.

Reed was bothered from the first by Lacy's plodding style. He would stew during Lacy's endless conference calls and meetings. But Reed also liked to keep everyone happy. He was a get-along guy. Right now, in the spring and summer of '95, there was no reason to quarrel. Money was plentiful; it looked like Dole would have no trouble raising the $25 million he needed to run a primary campaign. They could afford a state-of-the-art campaign, right on the model.

To shoot the campaign's ads, Reed and Lacy were willing to pay. They chose Stuart Stevens, a hip New York adman who had written TV scripts in Los Angeles after UCLA film school. Stevens eschewed the usual Washington hacks. Working out of his loft in Manhattan, he promised the best. "You can get the guy who cut the Nike spot," said Stevens. He would take over a Manhattan production studio and make it available 24 hours a day. He set up a bank of computers—"Macintoshes on hormones"—to pull images off their hard drives. To shoot Dole's announcement speech in Russell, Stevens used a "steady cam," a camera worn as a full body suit with a mechanical arm that lets the cameraman swing through 360 degrees with the steadiness of a dolly but the mobility of a handheld camera. It was the same technique used to shoot the stair scene in *Rocky*. Stevens set about putting together a short bio of Dole's life, borrowing black-and-white snapshots from Dole's sisters. "It's a great story. Before this guy went away to the war, he was an Adonis," Stevens said one morning in the fall of 1995, as images of young Bob Dole flickered past on the monitors of his screening room. About a quarter of the film was a reenactment of Dole's war injury. Stevens hired an actor to portray the young Dole struggling to walk again. He recreated what it must have been like for Dole crawling through the tall grass of a battlefield raked with fire. Stevens, naturally, wanted to go to Italy to shoot the scene. In a rare concession to economy, he had to settle for a field in Virginia. "Bob Dole: An American Hero" lasted 13 minutes and cost $167,000.

The first real test of the Dole campaign was an August straw poll in Ames, Iowa. In one sense the poll was a charade. Anyone who paid $25 could vote, even if he or she didn't live in Iowa. It was called "Calvacade of the Stars," which made it sound vaguely like a figure-skating contest. Still, it was important. In 1975, Jimmy Carter had emerged from obscurity with a surprising showing at the Ames poll. In 1987, Pat Robertson shocked George Bush and Bob Dole and served notice of the political power of the Christian right. In 1995, Dole figured he had to win or lose credibility as a front-runner.

Dole entrusted the job to Tom Synhorst, a 34-year-old political consultant based in Kansas City. Back in 1988, Synhorst had won the Iowa caucuses for Dole, largely by making face-to-face contact with thousands of voters and organizers. Other primary and caucus states were indifferent to Dole that year, but Iowa had felt so good that Dole staffers began calling the state "the Magic Kingdom." Synhorst figured that by buying a couple of thousand tickets he could head off any surprises in the first straw poll.

With about a week to go, Synhorst realized that he had miscalculated. The Iowa Republican party was trying to fill the entire 13,500-seat auditorium at Iowa State University, and the other candidates were paying ridiculous sums to snap up tickets. Lamar Alexander had chartered a couple of 727s to ferry supporters up from Tennessee and Georgia. Pat Buchanan had forked over $37,000 on a single day to buy tickets for his supporters. Synhorst thought that by scrambling—busing hundreds of supporters in from Kansas and Minnesota—Dole could still win. But it was going to be close.

As soon as Scott Reed entered the arena on the night of the poll, he knew that Dole had problems. Dole's supporters were spread thinly around the sides. The Gramm and Buchanan campaigns had bought up the seats closest to the podium for $25 a head. Reed feared the psychological impact on a candidate expecting cheering throngs. The campaign manager pulled Dole aside and told him his supporters were out there, even if he couldn't see them.

On the afternoon of August 19, the candidates appeared onstage, spotlighted, to the blare of the Chicago Bulls fan song. Dole gave a stolid speech; he looked nervous and spoke stiffly. The applause was polite. "Where's all our people?" he asked Reed as he left the stage. He moved down into the crowd to shake hands, but few were offered. The Buchanan and Gramm supporters in the prime seats just stared at him. Dole took a cool, lonely walk down the aisle.

Synhorst felt terrible. In the men's room, he noticed a line of college kids at the sinks. They were washing off the supposedly indelible ink handstamps that indicated they'd voted—so they could buy more tickets and vote again. Synhorst was angry, not because they were cheating, but because he hadn't thought of doing it himself.

Dole ended up in a tie with Gramm—in effect, a loss. The campaign staff guiltily presented themselves to Dole and Elizabeth in their hotel room the next morning. "Here come the pallbearers," quipped Dole. "We let you down," said Reed. "This is not a reflection on you the candidate. This is a reflection on the campaign." Reed blamed poor organization. They would straighten it out and learn from their mistakes. Dole was reasonably calm. "It's no big deal," he said. "Find out what happened. I've gotta go do Face."

Synhorst realized he would have to offer to move back to Iowa from Kansas City and work full-time to atone. But the idea that the loss was a "wake-up call" for the campaign's "organization" was nonsense, Synhorst thought. True, he had made some dumb mistakes. But they didn't add up to bad organization. That was all a story cooked up to distract the press from the real problem: the campaign's message. It simply wasn't resonating. "Rein in the government"? Who were they kidding? Even Synhorst's parents, loyal Dole supporters, hadn't bothered to turn out. People didn't have a reason to vote for Dole, thought Synhorst. No amount of organization could change that.

Dole himself hated "the three R's." He thought the slogan was gimmicky and fake. What did it really mean, anyway? He felt silly speaking in alliterative bumper sticker-ese. He would say his lines, but then betray his real impatience with political ventriloquism. On Larry King one night, he fumbled around trying to spell out his message and finally said with a shrug, "whatever it is."

In fact, Dole didn't really have a vision. His midwestern pragmatic conservatism made him suspicious of big, sweeping themes or catchy slogans. Dole was conservative, but he wasn't reactively anti-government. He had seen what government could do for people, and as president, he thought he could do a good job running it. He wanted to give people the benefit of the caring community that had raised him in Russell. He did have a "little-v" vision of balanced budgets and lower interest rates, but he was incapable of spelling it out, certainly not in a 20-second sound bite.

Dole's unwillingness to stay on message drove his handlers to despair from the very beginning. "We will win if we stay on message," Lacy wrote Dole in May, plaintively underlining his words. Lacy tried to convince Dole that repetition made sense. "You know, I heard you speak on the stump in 1987 probably 15 times. And probably 14 of those times I heard you tell the same jokes," Lacy told Dole. "And you told the same jokes because they worked. You tried 'em, people laughed. It worked. Why don't you develop some real catchy lines and stick with them?"

"Got to say something new," Dole grumbled.

It didn't help that dozens of old friends—senators, lobbyists, pundits—were bombarding the candidate with advice. Dole would mix their ideas in with the official campaign themes, whether or not the two jibed. Dole's aides sometimes heard these ideas for the first time when they popped out of Dole's mouth on national television. It was almost as if Dole enjoyed defying his handlers. His independence made his aides turn on each other. "Isn't it interesting," Lacy wrote in a confidential memo to Scott Reed late that fall, "that we discuss broadcast scripts out the kazoo and show them to everybody, but none of us know virtually anything about speeches until a day or so before they are to be given?" Lacy was by implication blaming Mari Maseng Will, who ran the speech shop, but the real culprit was Dole, who would not settle on a speech until he was actually giving it.

For a while he improved. By dutifully repeating the "the three R's" with more or less consistency for a couple of months, Dole managed to silence most of the reporters skeptical of his capacity for vision. In June, he gave a highly publicized speech excoriating Hollywood for promoting trash. Dole had been reluctant to give a tough values speech and had kept his aides in suspense right up to the moment he actually said the words, "The mainstreaming of deviancy must come to an end."

But then he reverted to his wandering ways. Dole's unpredictability on the stump was born partly of his own integrity, his own inner guidance system that made him do things his way. He would agree to use a TelePrompTer for a while—then veer off into quips and jokes and dangerous asides. Elizabeth didn't seem to be much help. If anyone appreciated the need for discipline, it was Mrs. Dole, who rehearsed her own speeches down to the little laughs she would make at her own jokes. But the staff was wary of trying to enlist her to work on her husband. They knew that she did not like to play the role of conduit and guarded her time alone with Dole.

In desperation, the staff turned to a speech coach. In the late summer, Bill Lacy asked Roger Ailes, the well-known imagemeister who had made ads for Reagan's campaigns, to recommend the best speech coach in the country. Ailes sent Lacy to Jack Hilton.

A gravel-voiced man in his late 50s, Hilton had taught scores of shy, dull or tongue-tied CEOs how to win an audience. He had no qualms about being blunt with Dole when the two met in the early fall of 1995. The candidate, too, was perfectly frank with Hilton. "I hate repetition. I'm too busy to practice," said Dole. Hilton was brusque: "We have no chance to progress or succeed if you hate repetition and have no time to practice."

Dole said he was worried about sounding tedious to the media. "These people follow me around. They're going to get bored."

Hilton tried to convince Dole that the press expected him to work up a standard stump speech and stick to it.

"I know, I know," said Dole. But he still felt uncomfortable about the idea of bored reporters at the back of the ballroom. He liked to watch a few people in the audience while he spoke. He didn't like them to look bored. Hilton replied that, yes, it was good to get signals back from listeners. But he doubted that reporters were the most reliable indicators.

Dole submitted to a half-dozen sessions with Hilton over the next six months. Hilton tried to get Dole to rehearse his actual speeches, but Dole would beg off, saying that the speech wasn't ready, it would change too much before he delivered it. So Hilton had to study tapes of Dole on the stump, as well as tapes of focus groups talking about Dole. Drawing on these lessons, Hilton offered some advice. The candidate had a habit of pulling his body back and tilting his head to the left. Hilton told Dole that it would make a stronger "executive impression" if he could tilt his upper torso forward. "Soften your facial expressions," Hilton told Dole. He didn't have to smile all the time, but he didn't need to look so severe when he was concentrating. And he needed to slow his pace. "Neither you nor your audience is double parked," said Hilton.

Dole was not unreceptive. He once asked advice on where to place his disabled arm when he sat in an armchair on the Brinkley show. Hilton actually thought Dole had potential as a speaker if he would practice. He had a good voice and could appear forceful. But he understood Dole's essential reticence. Among the words Dole had trouble pronouncing was "presidency." Dole would garble the word into something like "presincy."

"Maybe," suggested Hilton, "we should run for an office we can pronounce."

Dole chuckled drily.

To win the Republican nomination, Dole understood, he would have to move to the right. Richard Nixon, his old mentor, had told him as much: you win the nomination by going right, then head back to the center to win the general election in November. Dole understood the necessity, but he resented it. He thought the Christian conservatives who dominated the party's right wing were intolerant and preachy. Dole shared the Right's nostalgia for a lost America of small-town rectitude, but he didn't like to wag his finger. Yes, he had scolded Hollywood, but only after his handlers had pushed and cajoled. Dole was particularly irritated with the right-wing groups for harassing his valued Senate aide, Sheila Burke. Dole admired Burke immensely: she was a great deal-maker with a good heart, a former nurse who could tell a senior senator where to get off—nicely, but firmly. The "wing nuts," as Burke called them, regarded her as the devil behind Dole who wanted to sell him out to the secular humanists. The senator told the *Washington Post* that he could not understand why his "friends" were "out there attacking Sheila." "I suppose," he said, "next they'll be after my dog."

The true litmus test for the religious right was abortion. Dole's voting record was consistently pro-life, but he didn't like to advertise it. During his announcement tour in March, he had never even mentioned the word "abortion." Still, he knew he would have to pay fealty to the right-to-life activists, who turned out in great numbers in GOP primaries and caucuses.

The first major opportunity came in early September. The Christian Coalition was staging its Road to Victory conference in Washington, and all the GOP candidates were coming to woo delegates. Ralph Reed, the Christian Coalition's chief and a master manipulator, called Scott Reed at the Dole campaign to deliver a threat disguised as helpful advice. Phil Gramm, he said, was planning to ambush Dole by challenging him to sign a pledge that called for a constitutional amendment banning abortion under any circumstances. "You're gonna get set up," said Ralph. Wouldn't it make sense for Dole to say that he planned to sign the pledge, too, and head off any unpleasant confrontations?

Most of Dole's advisers wanted to say yes. All of them remembered the painful moment back in the '88 campaign when Dole refused to sign a no-new-taxes pledge during a debate before the New Hampshire primary. Bill Lacy suggested that Dole make a dramatic gesture: sign the pledge at the last moment, before the delegates, saying something like, "I waited until I was before friends to take this pledge, and now that I am, I will sign it." Scott Reed was one of the few who opposed the pledge. He had been chastened by Dole's anger over an earlier campaign foul-up. The staff had returned a $1,000 contribution from a group of GOP homosexuals called the Log Cabin Republicans. Dole had not reversed the decision, but he personally did not believe in discriminating against gays, and he had been angry about the newspaper stories accusing him of pandering to the right. Reed thought that if Dole signed the pledge, it would play into a media frenzy that Reed was calling "panderama." The moniker "rent-a-Dole" was beginning to stick.

Dole, typically, gave no sign of what he planned to do. Gramm spoke on the first morning of the conference, challenging Dole to sign the pledge. Dole was scheduled to speak in the afternoon. "I'm not going to run my campaign based on challenges from Phil Gramm," he growled to Senate aides. That suited Sheila Burke just fine. She didn't want him to take the pledge.

Lacy made one last attempt to talk to Dole personally. Dole gave him the slip by going through the Senate cloakroom—no campaign staff allowed—but Lacy followed him onto the Senate elevator as he was going down to his car.

"I wish you would think about this," Lacy said as the doors closed.

"I'm not going to sign it," said Dole, giving Lacy what aides called "the stiff arm," his left arm extended, palm facing out in a forbidding stop sign.

When Dole took the stage, several Gramm supporters waved copies of the pledge and heckled, "Sign it!"

Dole waited quietly while the shouting died down. Calmly, he told the assembled Christians that he had a 100 percent pro-life voting record. When he was interrupted by more cries of "Sign the pledge!" he responded, "Don't look at pledges, look at the record, folks." When he brought Elizabeth out onto the stage, the Christians stood to applaud, not ardently, but with respect.

This was proof to Dole. You don't have to pander to succeed.

Among the friends offering Dole unsolicited advice was Richard Norton Smith, a historian and former speechwriter who had helped the Doles write their autobiography, *Unlimited Partners*. Smith worried that Dole was in danger of squandering the personal and leadership qualities that made him attractive to voters. As a candidate, he seemed so afraid of meddling and micromanaging his staff that he was letting them bend his principles. The "Log Cabin incident" was a case in point.

So Smith sat down and wrote what became known as the "Let Dole Be Dole" memo. It put bluntly what many of Dole's old friends were saying privately: that Dole's equivocating was making him downright Clintonian. Smith told Dole that he was a more authentic war hero than Colin Powell, a more authentic conservative that Lamar Alexander, and a more authentic leader than Phil Gramm. But, Smith wrote in a five-page single-spaced memo, Dole had lost his way:

"Somehow along the way your authenticity has been sacrificed in the pursuit of ideological purity. The ironic result of trying to placate the right is to undermine those very qualities of personal courage and plainspoken leadership which are among your greatest assets and your greatest source of appeal to the vast majority of non-ideological voters who want things to work . . .

"There is a difference between meanness and simple candor. . . . I don't want you to be so spooked by the former that you stay away from the latter. For one thing, people expect you to say what's on your mind. On your mind, not what some consultant or focus group tells you. . . ."

He ended with Churchill's warning about "feeding the crocodiles"—"In the end, they come after you."

Dole loved Smith's memo. He read it repeatedly and showed it to Elizabeth. Smith, he believed, had his true interests at heart. He wasn't part of the campaign, he was a historian, and he could see things more clearly than his harried, poll-driven, focus-group-obsessed campaign staff. Dole marked up a copy of the memo, signaling his enthusiasm with check marks and underlining, and sent it over to the campaign, where it was not warmly received.

Dole's handlers were even less happy in December when they learned what the candidate intended to say about Bosnia. For most of the fall, Dole had been "on message" about American involvement abroad, vowing that U.S. troops would never serve under the command of United Nations General Secretary Boutros Boutros-Ghali. Dole would string out the foreign sounding name—Booo-tros Booo-tros—in his prairie-flat voice; crowds loved his old-time xenophobia, along with his vow to make English the official language of the United States. But in fact Dole was no isolationist, and he believed in honoring America's commitments abroad. The Dayton peace accords meant that President Clinton would have to honor his pledge to send 20,000 troops to Bosnia. Dole was going to support the president, he told his staff. He pointed to his stomach. In here, he said, I know what's right. America's credibility was at stake.

"Senator," Lacy interrupted, "have you seen the polls? They're running 60 to 30 against this."

Yeah, said Dole, he had seen them, but he felt obligated. The staff shrugged and tried to figure out the best spin. Dole was satisfied. This was the way presidents had to act. His staff knew he had to win the nomination first.

7 ■ ON THE BEACH

ater, when he looked back on the short, brutish primary season in the winter of '96, Dole would feel a sense of resentment and bitterness. He had very nearly been knocked out in the first few rounds by men he regarded as lightweights. He only barely defeated Buchanan in the Iowa caucuses, the once "Magic Kingdom" that Dole had carried by nearly 20 points in 1988. In New Hampshire, Buchanan beat him. For a moment, as he was riding back to his hotel in Manchester early on primary night, when it appeared that he might lose to Alexander as well, he had considered dropping out. Beaten by Forbes in Delaware and Arizona, he had been unable to sleep after watching reporters on *Nightline* virtually write his political obituary. "My God," he said to himself as he watched ABC's Jeff Greenfield use words like "devastating," "it's worse than I thought." Only a solid win in South Carolina and then a series of sweeps on mini-super Tuesday and super Tuesday had quieted the press.

The experience brought out Dole's hard side. Gone, at least for now, was the Bob Dole who wanted to take the high road, who refused to pander to the right-wingers or turn his back on America's foreign commitments. Battered by newcomers, his years of service mocked by men he considered nonentities, Dole was resolved to do whatever it took to go the rest of the way. If it was necessary to take the low road—to go negative, to pander, even to

borrow the pie-in-the-sky promises of a figure like Steve Forbes—
then so be it.

The Forbes campaign deserves little more than a foot-
note in the history of politics. But it is worth looking
back at as an object lesson in the effects of negative campaigning. It
shows what money can do to tear down an opponent and how "going
negative" can drag all sides down into a survivalist struggle that scars
the winners as well as the losers.

Forbes's candidacy got its start as a reaction against Dole. In
the winter of 1995, Jude Wanniski, the polemicist who sold Ronald
Reagan on supply-side economics, was wearying of his efforts to con-
vert Dole to his cause. The senator refused to accept the premise that
cutting taxes would produce more revenue for the government.
Wanniski's impatience turned to anger when he read Dole's curt
dismissal of supply-side economics in a *New York Times* article on
March 5. "You see how the debt went up in the Reagan years," Dole
had remarked.

Wanniski's thoughts turned to Steve Forbes. Here was a true
believer with hundreds of millions of dollars and the willingness to
spend it on good causes. Wanniski knew that Forbes was a political
junkie who had lately begun to overcome his shyness as a speaker.
He had been increasingly active in conservative causes, not just as
bankroller but as a spokesman. Maybe he would see running for the
presidency as a grand gesture in the tradition of his flamboyant father,
Malcolm Forbes, Sr. Wanniski whipped off a fax to the publisher of
Forbes magazine: how would he like to run for president?

Forbes and his wife laughed at this call to destiny when their
7-year-old daughter Elizabeth pulled it off the fax machine in Naples,
Florida, where the Forbeses had gone for spring vacation. But Forbes
did not say no. He had been smitten with politics ever since he
trooped around door-to-door with his father on Malcolm's unsuccessful gubernatorial campaigns in New Jersey during the '50s. As a little

boy, Forbes held elections with his stuffed animals and could recite New Jersey's officeholders county by county, along with their margins of victory. Forbes had been proud to chair Radio Free Europe for Reagan and Bush during the communist collapse. At one point, he had take the board and jetted into Moscow aboard the "Capitalist Tool," the company plane. Very Malcolmesque.

Jack Kemp, Forbes's fellow supply-sider and longtime presidential hopeful, had tried to warn him about what he was getting into. "Are you ready to hold the hand of every county chairman in Iowa? To give every moment of your life to the party apparatus? Never to see your wife and kids? Because if you aren't, don't do it." Forbes had given Kemp one of his slightly goofy grins. "I'd rather write a $20 million check and have you do it," he joked. But Kemp was adamant: he had seen too much of the abuse, the rumors, the money-grubbing of presidential campaigning. But for Forbes, untested in public life, it was all new and challenging. He decided to run.

To handle his campaign, Forbes hired William Dal Col, a former Kemp aide. Dal Col had been groomed by Arthur Finkelstein, a secretive New York political consultant celebrated as one of the pioneers in the art of negative campaigning. Another Finkelstein protégé, John McLaughlin, came aboard as pollster. Forbes also hired Carter Wrenn, whose darkly insinuating ad campaigns had elected and reelected Senator Jesse Helms of North Carolina four times. Wrenn was a deep cynic. "Carter's idea of a perfect campaign is to have the candidate stay locked away at home so he won't make any mistakes and just run television ads," said GOP consultant Charlie Black, an old Wrenn crony. Wrenn didn't believe in publishing position papers. He figured that opponents would just turn them into negative ads.

Dal Col, McLaughlin and Wrenn immediately started looking for Dole's negatives. Through a series of leading poll questions, they found that Dole could be painted as a perk-loving Washington hack and pork-barreling tool of special interests. In Iowa, for instance, they found that nearly half of all self-identified Dole supporters would switch their votes when they were told: "Bob Dole voted to spend

$18 million for a subway under Capitol Hill in Washington, D.C., so senators would not have to walk from their offices to the Capitol. This subway cost $5,000 per square foot to build." This "information" was quickly turned into a negative ad.

Focus groups showed only lukewarm support for Forbes himself. "He has no animation," a woman complained. "Just no charisma." When Forbes described how he had overcome hardships in his life, like doing badly in boarding school, the participants turned the dials on the handheld approval monitors to zero. Normally, a campaign airs positive "bio" ads on its candidate to establish his character before airing negative commercials on his opponents. The Forbes campaign was airing negative campaigns on Dole four days before the Forbes bio ad was even made.

The Capitol subway ad, and equally trivial ones chastising Dole for authorizing a Florida bike path and a Colorado ski slope, bothered Forbes. "Too petty," he said. But Wrenn pushed ahead. Forbes would eventually spend $22 million on "paid media," an immense sum, far more than any candidate had ever spent on a few primaries. The main target was Dole. And the ads worked: the front-runner plummeted in the polls. His negatives tripled in Iowa and New Hampshire.

But Dole, no novice to negative campaigning, hit back. One Dole ad suggested that Forbes had been corrupt as chairman of Radio Free Europe. He put "276,000 of your tax dollars to waste redecorating the residence of a friend," charged the commercial. "This is war," Dal Col declared when he saw the ad. Another ad chastised Forbes for firing his longtime secretary because she was old. Both times the Dole ads ran, Forbes's numbers would tick down two or three points. His support would go not to Dole, however, but to Lamar Alexander, who began creeping up in the polls. So Forbes began blasting away at Alexander as well. "What is behind Lamar Alexander and his red flannel shirt?" asked a Forbes ad. "Every time Lamar moves I hit 'em. Have to do it, have to," Dal Col said, caught up in the escalating war.

The campaign hit something of a low when an activist held a press conference to announce that Forbes had a photograph by Robert Mapplethorpe, the homoerotic artist and demon of the Christian right, aboard his yacht. Forbes blamed Dole for planting the story. Actually, it was Phil Gramm.

Dole was, however, undeniably behind the thousands of anonymous negative phone calls telling Iowa Christians that Forbes was wobbly on abortion. Dal Col could see that for Steve Forbes, the lark was over. When told of the smear-by-phone campaign, the candidate's face flushed, and he began furiously tapping his feet, which was the way the gentelmanly Forbes sometimes signaled his emotions. "He was as wound up as I've ever seen him," said Dal Col. At a rally, when an audience member asked Forbes if he blamed the Christians for the attacks, Forbes snapped, "I don't think the Christian Coalition speaks for most Christians." Back on the bus, Dal Col put his head in his hands.

The day of the Iowa caucus, Dole's campaign manager, Scott Reed, decided the time had come for a peace feeler. He called Dal Col. Both Reed and Dal Col had once worked for Kemp, but now they were wary rivals.

"What do you think is going to happen?" Reed probed.

"I got you guys [Alexander, Buchanan and Dole] tight, but I am fighting to come in fourth." Dal Col paused for effect. "We think you might do third."

"Third?" Reed tried not to let the panic show. "Our polls have us at about 35 [percent]."

Dal Col let out a howl. "No friggin' way. We have you at 25."

This time Reed paused. "Look, we've been kicking the shit out of each other. We are both suffering for it. I think it is time to cool it."

"Sure, you stop it and we'll stop it," Dal Col snapped back.

"Okay." Reed said. There was another pause.

"Okay," said Dal Col.

The mutual nonaggression pact brought some civility back to the campaign. But it was the end for Forbes. Without negative campaigning, he had no way of stopping Dole. "Voters needed a reason not to vote for Dole," Wrenn said. "And we didn't give it to them." Forbes had spent about $30 million to win 900,545 votes, or $33,313.16 a vote. But he had shaken Bob Dole more than he realized.

Those anonymous negative phone calls that the Dole campaign arranged became known in the press as "push polling." The caller would say that he was simply taking a poll, but the real purpose was not to obtain the voter's opinions but to use loaded questions to plant negative information in the voter's mind. It was hardly a new technique, dating back at least to Nixon's campaigns, but it had never been used on quite the scale employed by the Dole camp.

The man behind Dole's push polling, Steve Goldberg, didn't like the term, or the charge that it was a cheap campaign trick. Goldberg, a short stocky New Yorker who looks like Detective Sipowicz on *NYPD Blue*, defended his polling technique as a legitimate campaign tool. It was, at any rate, cheap: while Dole's regular pollster, Public Opinion Surveys (POS), charged $22 an interview, Goldberg's CampaignTel charged only 60 cents for a quickie one-or-two-question call.

His techniques were not exactly scientific. He built up a large data base by randomly calling people and finding out which of them intended to vote and what they cared about. Later, with what he preferred to term "advocacy calls," he would call back voters who cared about a certain subject—agriculture, for example—and frame a question in such a way as to let them know something negative about one of Dole's opponents: did you know that Senator Gramm missed the vote on the farm bill, and would this make you more or less likely to vote for him? Goldberg could instantly pinpoint who might switch his vote to Dole. His polls thus served as a cheap nightly tracking system, as well as a kind of person-to-person negative ad.

From time to time, Goldberg would use his information to help the lesser of Dole's enemies. When Gramm seemed like the big threat in Iowa, Goldberg secretly leaked some 10,000 names to the

Buchanan campaign. Right-to-life voters were told that Gramm had lost Louisiana and Alaska caucuses, that he couldn't win, so if they didn't want to waste their votes, they should vote for Buchanan. It was a ploy that very nearly backfired.

In the heat of the early primaries, the Dole campaign was by necessity taking on a much harder edge. And Bill Lacy was not a hard man. His methodical pace increasingly exasperated more aggressive Dole campaigners like Goldberg. He wouldn't take the smallest stand without first doing a poll or a focus group, and his conference calls dragged on without decision. Scott Reed, the campaign manager, could feel his own impatience growing. As chief strategist, Lacy controlled both polling and ads. At first Reed hadn't worried about shaping the message, preferring to run the day-to-day effort, but he felt thwarted when the pollsters and admen seemed frozen in Lacy time, tentative and muddled. Reed enlisted his own strategist, Don Sipple, a seemingly laid-back Californian who was actually a driven manipulator. Sipple had come aboard against Lacy's wishes and now fit uneasily into the campaign structure, resented by Lacy's adman, Stuart Stevens.

Actually, there were two Dole campaigns: the official one, and a rump one that had started meeting secretly back in December. About once a week, Reed, Sipple, Goldberg and some others got together at a Washington restaurant (they rotated the names under which the reservations were made in an effort to be less conspicuous). At first, the dinners were a way of getting input from Sipple and letting the rest vent their frustrations about Lacy. But as the dinners continued, they became a campaign-in-exile. They allowed aides to make decisions without going through Lacy's painstaking process.

The day after Dole lost New Hampshire, frustration and distrust peaked at the morning staff meeting at the Holiday Inn in Manchester. Sipple and Stevens were interrupting each other. Goldberg could feel Lacy's leg shaking under the table. After the meeting, Sipple, Goldberg and a few others in the rump group flew back to Washington in a Cessna. (The "catered" food turned out to be a small basket of donuts, which didn't improve the atmosphere.) Swearing and grumbling, they decided that the time had come for a coup. Lacy had to go.

Goldberg took the lead. He made plans to fly to Denver that night to find Scott Reed, who had gone west with Dole. "I'm going to tell Reed to pull the trigger," said Goldberg. Goldberg was amused that he was met by a stretch limo at the airport; the campaign was already strapped for cash. It was late when Goldberg knocked on Reed's door.

"What are you doing here?" asked Reed, standing in his boxer shorts.

"I had to tell you," said Goldberg. "It's the law of the jungle. Kill or be killed." Reed stared at him. "I'm so fucking tired," Goldberg said. "I've got to find a room." Reed pulled him inside. The two talked. Reed had to get rid of Lacy, said Goldberg. If Reed didn't move first, Lacy might move against him. Or Dole would get rid of them both. The last time a Dole presidential campaign had collapsed in New Hampshire, in 1988, Dole had just left two of his top aides on the airport tarmac, with their bags.

Anxiously, Reed approached Dole the next day. Reed blamed the poor showings in Iowa and New Hampshire on lousy polling— Lacy's domain. As Reed knew, polling was a sore subject for Dole. In 1988, his pollster had assured him that he would win New Hampshire, that he didn't have to take the "pledge" promising no new taxes. Reed didn't exactly suggest that Lacy be fired, just moved aside to give Reed more control. But Dole was ready to dump him.

That Saturday night, when Dole learned that he had lost Delaware too, Dole told his political director Jill Hanson, "I'm sick of this. I want it changed. I want the pollster and the strategist fired."

Dole was willing to throw over his closest aides, if that's what winning required. When Dole's longtime Senate campaign manager David Owen had been accused of financial impropriety during the 1988 campaign, Dole had simply never spoken to him again. Dole left it to Reed to deliver the news to Lacy.

Reed called Lacy on Sunday morning. "We have a real problem," he said. Dole had "lost confidence" in Lacy. Lacy immediately
understood that he would have to bow out, but he was stunned. There
had been no warning. Reed promised to keep the story out of the
papers until Lacy had a chance to talk to Dole himself.

Of course, the news leaked first. That Saturday night, press
secretary Warfield had left a voice-mail message for another one of
the conspirators: "The torpedo is in the water. The monarch knows."
The "torpedo," of course, was headed for Lacy; the "monarch" was
code for AP reporter John King, who was often used as a designated
leakee.

Dole was apologetic when he called Lacy on Tuesday morning. "I'm sorry about the way this happened," he said. Lacy told Dole
that he had been misled. In fact, the campaign's polling had not been
askew. Lacy predicted, accurately, that Dole would win in South
Dakota, then South Carolina, then the rest of the way. "Please remember it was my strategy that got you there," he told Dole. Within
a few months, Lacy moved to Kansas to run his family candy company. He had always planned to quit politics after the campaign. He
had had enough.

By March 25, the huge harvest of Super Tuesday primaries had been gathered in. It was clear that Dole had
won the nomination. He signaled his relief by going home to Russell.
"Be kind of exciting," he told reporters on the plane. The trip was
almost canceled when a late snowstorm blew across the prairie, but
Dole insisted. As a 50-mile-an-hour wind whipped outside, the
people of Russell gathered in the high-school gym to praise their
favorite son.

Dole allowed himself a rare moment of public emotion. "It
was here I learned that doing was better than talking . . . it was here
I learned not to wear my heart on my sleeve. But I also learned to

feel deeply for my country and my family—that some things are worth living for . . . and dying for. These lessons have left their mark on me."

Afterward, a few reporters replayed clips of Dole's speech on a video editing machine, stopping the tape at key moments. "I wanted to be home . . ." Dole's voice cracked and he looked down ". . . to come to this place . . ." his lips quavered and he mashed them down ". . . and see all my friends." The reporters had never actually seen Dole get emotional on the campaign trail. Had he cried? The reporters couldn't be sure. But some of them had.

That side of Dole had been missing through most of the primary season. In most speeches, the candidate had been at once discursive and soporific. Mari Will, his beleaguered speechwriter, had run out of ways to impose discipline. At one point she worked out a "theme formula" to keep Dole on message. In Iowa, he would give three sound bites on cultural issues for every one on economic and agricultural themes ("3 x culture + 1 x economic + 1 x agriculture"). In New Hampshire, the formula was three economic for each cultural and each defense or foreign policy sound bite. Her precision was lost on Dole, who said pretty much whatever came into his mind.

Will finally gave up. Out went the 40-page tracts. She began giving Dole a few pages of talking points, one-paragraph summaries that he could glance at for inspiration. Dole promptly confounded that plan by reading the paragraphs whole, making his speeches sound even more disconnected than usual. After an especially awkward performance on the night of the New Hampshire primary—TV viewers could watch Dole shuffling through his three-by-five cards like a high-school debater—Dole abandoned the paragraph model and tried a single sheet of words and phrases. "I pretty much decide myself what I'm going to say and how I'm going to say it," he told *Newsweek* on March 10. "I don't think I need a speechwriter."

No one on the plane dared suggest otherwise. Dole's staff was intimidated by him. Campaigns are notoriously profane, but no staffer swore around Bob Dole. Campaigns are fueled by alcohol, but some staffers were afraid to drink so much as a beer around the 73-year-old senator. Left alone, and lonely, Dole needed company. The staff began looking for "grown-ups" to join him on the plane. Senators Bob Bennett of Utah and John McCain of Arizona were enlisted. "One reason he liked to travel with me was that I didn't bug him," said McCain. The former Vietnam POW felt he never penetrated Dole's inner reserve. "You never know what he's thinking."

In gingerly fashion, McCain and Bennett encouraged Dole to talk about his hard-scrabble upbringing and his painful recovery from his war wound. Dole tried, in part because he was so miffed about being cast as a Washington fat cat by his primary opponents. He grumbled that voters thought he was "born in a blue suit" and never had had to suffer or work for his position. So in March he began talking more about his triumph over hardship. Still, it made him uncomfortable. "I sorta like to hurry through it and get on with it," he admitted. Unfamiliar with the confessional form, unable to bite his lip convincingly, Dole had trouble striking the right balance. At a campaign stop in Vermont, Dole gave an overly explicit description of his war-wound recovery, describing how he had learned to go to the bathroom by himself again. At a rally on Long Island he made listeners wince with a comment about how he might have taken longer to recover because the nurses were so pretty.

Always, he was uncomfortable spouting someone else's message. At the end of March, he traveled through California with Pete Wilson, sounding themes that had worked to get the governor re-elected in the sunshine state. The trip started at the Mexican border, where Dole backed a proposal to cut off free public-school education to illegal immigrants; swung through San Quentin, where Dole praised the death penalty; stopped at Richard Nixon's grave; and ended at a mall of mostly Asian shoppers where Dole denounced affirmative action. Reporters called the trip the "Wilson Death Tour." Dole mumbled through it all and looked like he wanted to be somewhere else. He had been campaigning for three months straight. He needed a break. He decided to go sit in the sun in Florida and be alone, to make some basic decisions about the rest of the campaign.

Bob Dole had been coming to his condo at the SeaView Hotel in Bal Harbour, Florida, for the past 14 years. Elizabeth had bought the place from Dwayne Andreas, the agricultural commodities magnate who has funneled more money to more politicians than perhaps any man alive. The SeaView, a slightly faded resort, is a virtual annex of Washington. Occupants include George McGovern, David Brinkley, Howard Baker and Bob Strauss. The lobby is adorned with photos of the U.S. Capitol and the White House. The piano bar in the Emerald Room plays melodies from an earlier time.

For eleven days, Dole sat by the pool sunbathing. A photographer caught him in an unflattering pose, his shorts hiked up over his skinny thighs, his face scowling under a "Farmland" cap as he talked on a ubiquitous white telephone. Sometimes Elizabeth would join him for a while, but mostly he just sat alone, staring out to sea.

He was trying to figure out what to do next. He knew he had to do something fairly drastic. Before the primaries, his campaign research showed that voters knew hardly anything about his legislative accomplishments. After the primaries, the image was even worse: thanks to the negative ads of his opponents he was seen as a Washington hack and tool of corporate lobbyists. It had galled Dole to be pitted against men he regarded as fundamentally "not serious." On a plane trip in early March he had let his bile spill out. He was particularly offended by Forbes. "Tells everybody he's going to cut their taxes," he had muttered. "Get a life." At a debate, he had even refused to shake Forbes's hand.

Slowly Dole began to turn over in his mind a plan of action, a dramatic stroke that would shock the political world. He had been cast as a Washington insider. Well then, he would leave Washington. Not just give up his job as majority leader, as many had urged, but depart from Capitol Hill altogether. He would resign from the Senate. Show that he was really serious, that he was willing to sacrifice everything. Freed from the demands of running the Senate, he would be ready to experiment, try new ideas. Maybe even a big tax cut.

Dole made this plan alone. He did not tell his Senate colleagues, and he did not inform his most trusted aides until he had made up his mind. Apparently (according to Dole's own recollection, but not Elizabeth's), he didn't even tell his wife.

Don Sipple, the strategist brought in after the coup against Lacy at the end of February, couldn't believe the sorry state of the campaign. There was no money; it had all been spent on the primaries. There was little useful research on Clinton, and no real plan for taking on the president in November. Then in April, everyone, including the candidate, went on vacation.

In his garrulous way, Newt Gingrich made a pass at rallying the troops. In mid-March, over bourbon with senior party officials in the Speaker's office, he suggested a "total party effort" to shape a unified message. He was a little vague about what this "Team GOP" might do, but he clearly envisioned a large role for himself. As Dole plunged in the polls, Republican leaders were getting nervous. Fred Steeper, a GOP pollster, felt that Dole had to make his case before Labor Day—in fact, before the Olympics at the end of July—or risk falling too far behind. But no one could agree on what a winning message might be. By mid-April, even the normally ebullient Newt was looking worried.

Nothing improved when the candidate returned from Florida. He was supposed to look leaderly running the Senate—the so-called rotunda strategy—but instead he looked like a tedious Washington insider, spouting legislative arcana. Desperate for a diversion, pollster Steeper cast about for some way of showing that Dole was more trustworthy than Clinton, and seized on a focus-group question that asked, "Who would you rather have as a guardian for your children—

Clinton or Dole?" Few of the housewives in the focus group seemed to trust the president. The staff advertised this finding to reporters, but Dole botched an opportunity to hammer it home on *Meet the Press*. He was asked by a compliant pundit why people trusted him more than Clinton with their children. It came from a focus group, Dole said. Couldn't explain why.

Dole himself was feeling frustrated. The Democrats were tying him in legislative knots. Their proposal to raise the minimum wage was dominating the floor and the headlines. As Dole left the Senate floor one day, he was barraged by questions from reporters. "Minimum wage? What about the minimum wage?" Dole staggered into his office, closed the door, and complained to his old friend the lobbyist Tom Korologos: "I'm so sick and tired of the minimum wage I can't stand it." Korologos was worried about Dole. He said that Dole's colleagues were suggesting that he step down as majority leader. "I hope you don't," said Korologos. "You ain't gonna, are you?" Dole simply stared at him.

On Monday, April 22, the author Mark Helprin stopped by Dole's Senate office. Helprin was an unusual man, at once a literary figure who wrote fabulist novels and a conservative foreign policy expert who wrote hard-line op-ed pieces for the *Wall Street Journal*. He had written a flattering editoral about Dole in January. On his own initiative, Helprin had agreed to help draft Dole's acceptance speech for the GOP convention in August. Dole had been touched by Helprin's first draft, an elegant invocation of a simpler time, America before the 1960s.

Helprin was led onto the leader's porch, "the Beach," where Dole was sunning himself. The author did not know Dole well, but he was not shy about giving advice. Why don't you leave the Senate, he asked shortly after they shook hands.

"Pull up a chair," said Dole, who was gazing west, down the Mall. "If I'm going to run for president, I'm going to run for president."

The next day, Dole let Scott Reed in on his secret. "I'm thinking of resigning," he said. "What do you think?"

Reed could barely contain his joy. He had been getting blamed by the pundits for Dole's stalled campaign. He resented the fact that he couldn't control the candidate, who spent most of his time in Washington under the dangerously moderating influence of his Senate chief of staff, Sheila Burke. Reed tried not to show how happy he was, lest his enthusiasm cause Dole to change his mind. But as soon as he had left Dole's private office, he scrawled a list of all the reasons why Dole should quit:

Bold/unpredictable
Burst of energy
Shake DC insider
Free from Senate
Engage in campaign
Screws up Clinton strategy
Redefines Dole
Better control of message/not Senate

To be judicious, he also wrote down some of the cons:

No longer leader
Diminished? Depressed/Alone
Loss of platform?
Running from problems
Money shortage—need to keep moving

The ayes clearly had it. He called Dole later that day and told him that resigning was a very good idea. He immediately began making plans, though one thought nagged him as he lay awake that night. Dole's life was the Senate. Would he be depressed by the loss of that anchor? Could he adjust to a new routine, to the rigors of constant campaigning? Would he become the Dole of 1988, constantly second-guessing his campaign manager?

Over the next few days, Helprin and Reed became what Reed called "midnight phone pals." Helprin would fax drafts of a speech announcing Dole's Senate resignation to Reed's private number when no one else was around. Reed would scoop up the pages and bring them to Dole. Helprin struggled to match his flowery prose to Dole's no-frills style. "Can't say that," Dole would grumble. "Don't want to say that."

In his circumspect way, Dole tested his plan to leave the Senate on a group of old-guard Republicans who acted as self-appointed consiglieri to the GOP nominee-to-be. Worried about the widening gap in the polls, Nick Brady, Bush's Treasury secretary, had sought out a breakfast with Dole in early May. Get a few friends together, talk things through, Brady suggested. Dole's old pal Bob Ellsworth wasn't sure Dole needed more free advice, but Dole said sure, bring them on.

The graybeards—Brady, Bush's Defense secretary Dick Cheney and Bush's pollster Bob Teeter—met over breakfast in Dole's Capitol office with Ellsworth (who had been Nixon's political director), Dole and Reed. Everyone had cold cereal except Dole, who ordered hot oatmeal. "Where's the hot oatmeal for us?" asked Ellsworth.

Dole began by subtly probing his friends. Should he get out on the road more, move away from the Senate? He never went as far as to say that he was thinking of giving up the leadership, much less leaving the Senate. But the group was unanimous: get away from Washington. The picture of Dole squabbling with other lawmakers was all wrong. Even the camera angle on C-Span was bad—it was aimed down from above, making Dole look like a small fixture on the Senate floor. Dole needed to get out and campaign, the old hands counseled. Leave the Senate details to others.

It was exactly the reaction Dole was looking for, though he told his friends nothing.

The awkward subject of Newt Gingrich came up. Should Dole distance himself? Dole was getting that advice from his Senate colleagues. Some of his own political staff referred to Gingrich's Team GOP as "the amphibian group" because they regarded Gingrich as vaguely reptilian. But Dole himself was loyal to Gingrich. "Newt's a good guy," Dole said. "I like Newt." He thought Gingrich had helped him and supported him through the primaries.

His advisers acquiesced. But maybe he could appear in fewer pictures with the Speaker.

The day before Dole was scheduled to make his surprise announcement—amazingly, the secret held even after a few key staffers had been told—Jack Hilton got a call from Scott Reed. Reed told him to be on the 7 A.M. shuttle to Washington. He didn't say why.

When Hilton arrived at campaign headquarters, he was handed the speech. Hilton read it to Dole the way he thought it should be read. "I have done it the hard way," he said, drawing out the words of the highest impact line.

"I have done it thehardway," mumbled Dole.

"No," said Hilton. "The . . . hard . . . way." Hilton tried to coach Dole on reading from the TelePrompTer, which Dole still regarded with suspicion. The machine had failed him several times during the campaign. Like most speakers, Dole kept a paper copy on the lectern in front of him, but because of his bad arm he couldn't easily turn the pages.

Hilton could tell that Dole was moved by the speech. His breath caught, his eyes welled as he practiced. Hilton was thrilled. The speech coach had worked on Dole to stop calling himself "Bob Dole" like some freshman congressmen who was trying to boost his name recognition. "You know what I like most about this speech?" Hilton asked. "The word 'I' is in it 49 times." Dole laughed. Hilton had also tried to cure Dole of his other speaking foibles, like his unfinished sentences and constant use of the word "whatever." These were among ten tips Hilton had written down and ordered Dole to tape on his refrigerator. But he had no illusions that Dole would actually follow the advice.

Later that morning, when Dole told his staff, they stood and applauded. Dole was overcome and began to cry. "I just wanted you to know . . ." he began and broke down again. Tears were flowing liberally through the room full of longtime loyalists. Sheila Burke went to get tissues and came back with a towel. "It's not the end," Dole said. "It's the beginning. I think we're going to make it. I'm upbeat," he continued. He gestured at Elizabeth. "Slept like a baby."

When it came time to give the speech, Dole choked up several times. He tried to focus on the TelePrompTer screens so he wouldn't break down. It was the best speech anyone had ever heard Bob Dole give.

The next morning, Dole got up and went to open the Senate. He was supposed to leave for the "bright light and open spaces of this beautiful country," but it was hard to let go. He walked around the leader's office that would soon not be his, and looked out at the Beach where he would no longer be able to bask. "I'm outta here," he finally said, and got on a plane for Chicago.

8 ■ THE YELLOW OVAL

Bill Clinton admired Bob Dole. He had told aides that if he lost, he would rather lose to Dole than any of the other Republican candidates. "Dole," he said, "would make a better president than the rest of those jokers." He appreciated Dole's statesmanlike decision not to play politics on Bosnia, and he had found him reasonable and responsible during the budget standoff. At one point in the negotiations over the government shutdown, he had even phoned Dole to tell him, "I don't want to do anything that would hurt you in the primaries." This solicitude was not altogether altruistic, of course. Clinton also liked Dole because he thought he could beat him. It was rather like Jack Kennedy's attitude toward Barry Goldwater. When a White House aide had objected to letting Goldwater appear before the cameras during a Rose Garden ceremony in 1963, JFK had said, "No, let him be. He's all mine."

When he locked up the Republican nomination in March, Dole was 8 points behind in the president's polls; by the time he resigned from the Senate in May, he had fallen 15 points behind. To keep his staff from getting complacent, Clinton kept muttering, "Greg Norman, Greg Norman, Greg Norman," after the golf pro who had blown a six-stroke lead in the last round of the U.S. Open. "Excited?" James Carville, Clinton's flamboyant '92 campaign manager had exclaimed in early May. "Hell, you work for Bill Clinton, you go up and down more times than a whore's nightgown. Nuttin' to be excited about yet."

By the spring of 1996, the Clinton campaign had found a routine and a rhythm. Egos were as large as ever, and they often clashed, but the campaign was no longer riven by the backbiting and suspicion that had marked the early "Charlie" period. In part, the competing camps had been brought together by the prospect of victory. They still quarreled over the means, but confidence ran high, even though the old hands warned against overconfidence. The inner workings of the Clinton campaign showed an edgy mix of alertness, cockiness and ruthless purpose.

Clinton aides couldn't believe their good luck when Dole returned to the Senate in March to wage a "Pennsylvania Avenue campaign" against the White House. The match-up was perfect: Senator vs. President. "He wants to be Son of the Senate," said political director Doug Sosnik. "We're gonna go on being President. He can worry about amendments and cloture. We're gonna go overseas and have a summit." Under Morris's stage management, Clinton was in full presidential mode. Dole's camp, by contrast, couldn't even package their primary victories. "Why are they celebrating in a Washington hotel ballroom with him reading from a bunch of three-by-five cards?" Sosnik wondered as he watched the news. "That's the visual of the day?"

If Bob Dole wanted to appear at the side of Newt Gingrich, the most unpopular political figure in America, that was fine, jeered the Clinton aides. If he wanted to be associated with the institution responsible for the longest government shutdown in history, so much the better. Al Gore suggested that Dole and Gingrich belonged together like Bonnie and Clyde. Clinton's team was baffled by Dole's behavior. Why hadn't he quit the Senate earlier and gone on a campaign blitz bashing Clinton's character? They couldn't understand his apparent inertia, the long Florida vacation, the desultory campaigning between legislative squabbles in Congress. "Welcome to the Sitzkrieg," said Ron Klain, Vice President Gore's chief of staff. Clinton's aides had laughed at the visuals of Dole sunbathing in his too-tight shorts as he worked the phone by the condo pool. "Not your average American on vacation," scoffed Doug Sosnik.

William Knapp, one of Clinton's top two admen, braced for an assault that never came. "They should be hitting us harder," he said in April. Along with Hank Sheinkopf, a blunt former New York cop who was the campaign's attack-ad specialist, he geared up a rapid-response operation. But there was nothing to respond to. The Dole campaign was giving Clinton a free pass. Instead, Dole was concentrating his energies on passing legislation, worse than a waste of time in the view of Clinton's political team.

George Stephanopoulos, who could be scathing when he was in his partisan mode, thought that going back to the Senate was "the single dumbest mistake you can make. Sitting there being a legislator is one of the single most unattractive things to a regular person." Stephanopoulos's scorn set the tone for the White House political team. The Clintonites felt they had successfully turned the Senate floor into a trap for Dole. "Dole has elected to conduct his campaign in the single most uncontrollable, unscheduable, unmanageable forum in public life," Klain and Sosnik wrote in a March 15 memo plotting ways to ensnare Dole. The Democrats proceeded to box Dole in with the bill to raise the minimum wage. "It's almost a shame it worked so quickly," Stephanopoulos said when Dole finally quit the Senate. "It was all going so well."

On the afternoon of May 15, President Clinton's top admen, Knapp and Bob Squier, sat in their tastefully high-tech office on Capitol Hill, watching Bob Dole finally give up his congressional career of more than three decades. Perpetually tanned, fond of quips, Squier was a smoothie around town, a fixture at Georgetown cocktail parties who, as a sideline, dabbled in literary documentaries on Hemingway and Faulkner. Knapp was an irreverent, wisecracking workaholic. Together, they had made the brutally effective ads accusing Gingrich and the GOP of selling out the elderly on Medicare.

Squier and Knapp were appalled by the "visuals" of Dole's resignation speech. If Dole was trying to convince voters that he was a man of the people—"a Kansan, an American, just a man"—why was he surrounded by a bunch of middle-aged pols in suits, with a shot of the Capitol dome looming behind them? And what idiot let Gingrich get in the same frame while Dole was making the most important speech of his career? Gingrich had been dragging Dole down in the polls for at least six months. Knapp and Squier had been doing their best to marry the two in the ads they made for Clinton: in the voice-overs, the announcer would say "Dolegingrich" as one word, as in "the Dolegingrich cuts in Medicare." And if Dole was such a "doer," the man who could get the job done, how come he was abandoning his post and leaving the gridlock behind? Dole had not finished declaring his independence from Washington before the two men began thinking of how they might be able to portray him as a quitter.

That night, at the political meeting in the Yellow Oval Room on the second floor of the White House residence, Dick Morris began, as always, by asking his pollster, Mark Penn, for the latest numbers. Penn had done a quickie poll of 400 voters in the afternoon, and the results were encouraging. People had been moved by Dole's performance, but they weren't more likely to vote for him. "It's not a vote getter," Penn said. "It's more of a 'so what?'" Morris then held forth in his colorful way. Dole's quitting was "like a military funeral at sea," he said. "There will be a huge memorial. There will be lots of attention. It'll be glorious. Uplifting. Then the coffin will slip beneath the waters, the waves will wash over it, and the boats will sail on."

Clinton, who tended to overlook Morris's fanciful metaphors, sat impassively in his wingback chair. He had been surprised that Dole was not just quitting as majority leader. "Really?" he had asked when Stephanopoulos gave him the news that morning. "Wow." He was not nearly as confident as Morris about the futility of Dole's move. Al Gore, too, was wary. Dole had always been predictable and cautious. Now he was making a risky and unexpected move. The vice president had long worried that the White House was underestimating Dole.

For the next few days, the president's staff looked at the polling to see if Dole had gained "traction." At first, they laughed derisively at Dole's clumsy costuming—pinstripes getting aboard his plane in Washington, blazer and khakis when he emerged in the heartland. Morris continued to scoff. "We're going through more Dole resignation scenes than there are death scenes in a Wagnerian opera," said Morris. "He'll go out in the country and resign, he'll go to Russell and resign, he'll come back to the Senate and resign." To remind voters of Dole's true home, the "oppo" team at party headquarters manufactured thousands of "Dole/Gingrich '96" buttons, which were handed out at rallies to unsuspecting Republicans.

But on Monday, after Dole's first weekend on the road, Morris and Penn began detecting signs that Dole was gaining, if only slightly. Dole's favorable rating, stuck for weeks at a dismal 40 percent, had started to creep up, to 48 percent. It was important to keep Dole below 50 percent, the ceiling for unsuccessful challengers in the past. What's more, voters were starting to use words like "effective," "decisive" and "on my side" to describe Dole, words that made him seem like a leader. Morris wanted Dole to stick in voters' minds as a legislator: petty, process-oriented, mired in the details. Voters were also beginning to pay attention to Dole's life story. Penn found that 77 percent now knew that Dole was from Kansas and that he had been badly wounded in World War II.

Looking at the numbers, Morris flew into a state approaching hysteria. He called Clinton and told his client that he needed to make a major decision. The president summoned a special session of the political team in the Yellow Oval on the night of Thursday, May 23. Morris repaired to his laptop and composed an agenda in agitated language and upper-case emotion. "DOLE IS ESCAPING FROM THE CELLAR . . . WE ARE LETTING HIM DO IT," he wrote. Maybe Dole's gains looked modest, but they could be leading indicators of trouble unless the Clinton command got over its caution— "THE CREEPING CANCER OF THIS CAMPAIGN"—and went negative fast. "Dole is about to break this race wide open and slash our lead to single digits," Morris wrote. "We must not let him."

Squier and Knapp had already produced his weapon of choice, a 30-second ad titled "Empty." At the meeting, Knapp punched it up on the video screen. The ad opened with a shot of a cluttered desk top and an empty chair, with the Capitol looming in the background. The camera panned past a black-and-white portrait of a scowling, Brylcreemed, 45-year-old Bob Dole. "He told us he would lead," intoned the announcer as the shot widened to show packing boxes. "He told us he was a doer, not a talker. Then he told us he was quitting, giving up. Leaving behind the gridlock he helped to create— and all he offers is negative attacks." Cut to bright shots of a studious Clinton, hard at work in the Oval Office. "Meanwhile, the real work goes on: balancing the budget, protecting Medicare, education, the environment, reforming welfare, cracking down on violent crime." A parade of gauzy images marched by: an old lady smiling in a hospital bed, cheery schoolchildren, a healthy family tromping through the forest and jut-jawed police officers.

Squier turned up the lights. The president turned back in his wing chair to face his advisers. For months, the meetings in the Yellow Oval had followed a predictable pattern. They would begin with Morris's somewhat manic monologues. Using reams of polling data, his feet barely touching the floor as he sat on an overstuffed pillow, Morris would rattle off a stream of ideas, some dreadful, some goofy, some inspired. Then Squier or Knapp would screen the latest ad. Clinton and Gore sat at the front of the room; an ever-larger group of White House advisers and staffers squeezed themselves onto the delicate silk sofas that lined the room. Gore tended to slouch way down in his chair, his long legs stretched straight out in front, with his hands in his lap and his chin on his chest. From the back of the room it looked as though the vice president was taking a nap. But whenever Morris's recitations got too tedious, Gore would pipe up. "Hey, Dick, could you go over that again?" The line would inevitably provoke a round of giggles, since Morris had the annoying habit of repeating himself almost robotically—some likened him to a human tape recorder—whenever anyone new entered the room.

Every now and then Ickes, Stephanopoulos or Panetta would challenge Morris's analysis, but more often than not White House staffers would trade covert smirks and snickers when they thought

Morris had gone too far. The president, sitting in his wingback chair, his glasses perched on his nose, leafed through the voluminous agenda that Morris handed out each time. If the mischief became too obvi- ous, he would cast a disapproving glare at the offending staffers. "It was always like, 'Come on, kids, knock it off. Stop picking on your brother,'" said one regular in the meetings.

On this evening, the discussion was unusually spirited. Morris and Squier began by arguing that voters were starting to buy Dole's campaign bio: a hardscrabble kid from the heartland turned war hero turned bold citizen challenger of the shifty, liberal, duplicitous— perhaps even criminal—Bill Clinton. They were forgetting about a "35-year gap," said Squier drily. "It's filled with pretty pictures, but Dole doesn't appear to have had a job in all those years." The voters needed to be reminded of what Dole had been doing in that time and what he was walking away from now.

Ron Klain agreed. "We've taken too much of this," said Gore's chief of staff. "It's time to whack back." Stephanopoulos, who had formed something of an entente cordiale with Morris over the past two months, also agreed. But Ickes, eternally hostile to Morris, resisted, with support from Panetta and Commerce Secretary Mickey Kantor, Clinton's campaign chairman in '92. Going negative would just provoke the media. Reporters, ever eager to even the horse race, would say the White House was panicking. "Why do we need to do this?" Kantor and Panetta asked. "The guy's a national hero. Let him retire in peace." Voters hated negative campaigning. How could Bill Clinton, draft dodger, accuse Bob Dole, war hero, of being a quitter? Wouldn't Clinton just be accused of trying to deflect attention from Paula Jones's sexual harassment law suit and Whitewater?

Clinton listened to this debate in silence. When he had lis- tened enough, he gave a two-word order: "Buy it."

It was one of the few times his advisers could remember Clinton authorizing an ad in front of the whole group. Usually, he met with Ickes the next day to give his decision. Actually, Clinton had made up his mind before the meeting, when he had talked to Morris earlier in the day. But he liked these meetings; he was pleased that everyone could have their say. Dole, he thought, could never run such a collegial, smooth operation.

"Empty," dubbed "the Quitter" by the press, aired for five days in 51 percent of the country. Dole's favorables stopped climbing. Clinton's remained stable, more than 10 points higher. He was 17 points ahead in the horse race. Going negative had worked. As he looked at the numbers on Monday, May 27, a chilly, rainy Memorial Day, Morris was exultant. "If we keep this up, we're going to be in a landslide," he crowed. Penn replied, "With numbers like this, we can almost afford to take a day off."

Morris and Penn kept their optimism to themselves, mindful of Clinton's incantations about Greg Norman. More seasoned staffers knew that good news never lasted for long in the Clinton White House. Sure enough, the next day, May 28, Whitewater blew up again.

9 ■ MASTERS OF DISASTER

Just before five o'clock on Tuesday, May 28, White House staffers got some news they had been dreading. Three of the president's old friends had been convicted by a federal jury in Little Rock on fraud charges related to Whitewater. Jim and Susan McDougal, who had made the original investment in Whitewater with the Clintons, appeared headed for jail, along with Clinton's successor as governor, Jim Guy Tucker. The details of the case were complex and obscure, but the outcome meant that Whitewater wasn't going away before the election. The special prosecutor, Ken Starr, could now try to "flip" the McDougals and Tucker and make them testify against the Clintons. Clinton sat at his desk, looking sad and subdued when Stephanopoulos and press secretary Mike McCurry told him the news. "Don't be in the bunker," said Stephanopoulos. Clinton said, "I need to think about this for a few minutes."

The mood was uneasy two nights later at the political meeting in the Yellow Oval. Penn tried to be reassuring. He had been reporting for months that Whitewater was not a vote-mover. "The voters just don't care," he told Clinton. On character, Dole had Clinton beaten hands down. But it didn't seem to matter. As long as Clinton embraced public values the voters cared about—as long as he was tough on crime and drugs, down on TV violence—voters would forgive or forget about his personal life. Morris and Penn had created a strategy to "immunize" Clinton against character attacks by the GOP. Republican ads on womanizing or the draft or "slick Willie" would be countered with Clinton's record on banning assault weapons or supporting school uniforms or calling for a V-chip in TVs. Penn's slogan was "public values trumps private character."

The Whitewater verdicts in Little Rock had not changed that, said Penn as the political team slouched down on the silk sofas. They had not affected the president's credibility. The convictions had, however, given new life to the special prosecutor Starr. Until now, voters had been willing to grant the presumption of innocence to Starr's targets. The White House had had some luck painting Starr as the tool of Republican interests. But voters did understand the word "guilty," even if they cared little about the legal tangle of Whitewater.

"Get to the point," snapped Clinton. Lectures about the public-relations aspect of Whitewater always made him irritable. He was sullen about Morris's "public values" strategy. "You still have to defend the man," he would say. And he was worried, said Stephanopoulos, that Starr ("that son of a bitch") would indict Hillary "for no good reason."

"There's no change for your credibility, Mr. President," Penn responded quickly and carefully. "But the convictions do give Starr enhanced credibility."

As usual, the discussion in the Yellow Oval had danced around the topic of scandal. Only Morris, obnoxious and, in the eyes of other advisers, overly familiar with the president, could easily say "Whitewater" in front of Clinton. Other aides would refer euphemistically to "character attacks" or "other stuff." Paula Jones, the Arkansas woman suing Clinton for sexual harassment, was almost never referred to by name.

But Whitewater was never far from anyone's mind, even at the best of times. It had a way of returning to spoil the moment. The word "Whitewater" had come to mean "everything bad"—any petty scandal, even ones that had nothing to do with Arkansas land deals, fell under its rubric. The topic consumed hours and hours of the Clintons' time and much of their money. Clinton bitterly complained that he would not be able to afford Chelsea's college tuition because of his legal bills. "It's a horrible parallel, but it's like the term 'AIDS,'" said Stephanopoulos. "AIDS isn't any one thing, it's everything. It can kill you, but it can also be chronic and let you go on for years."

To campaign consultants like Morris, Whitewater was an abstraction, a problem to be spun. But to the White House staff and the Clintons it was a permanent affliction, a disease that sapped their energy, clouded their thinking, threatened to turn the most trivial or innocuous acts into a grand jury subpoeona. Bruce Lindsey, Clintons's closest personal aide, was a well-organized man who used to keep track of things by writing himself notes on a card he carried in his breast pocket. The cards were creamy white, embossed with gold and topped with the presidential seal—badges of honor, at first. On them, Lindsey would meticulously organize his day. He would jot down reminders, phone calls, scheduling notes, even the punch line to a joke he might want to tell his friend Bill Clinton as they unwound over an evening game of hearts aboard Air Force One.

By 1996, he had stopped. "I don't write anything down if I don't have to," said Lindsey, pulling a clean white card from his breast pocket. "Who can afford it?" As Clinton's closest confidant had painfully learned (Lindsey had been named as an unindicted coconspirator in one of the Whitewater cases), even the most innocuous scrap of paper can wind up displayed on a projector in a Senate hearing room or splashed across the pages of a newspaper.

Junior aides had become equally wary. The vice president's press secretary, Lorraine Voles, was shocked to find her notes from a 1993 conversation with a newspaper reporter blown up as a sinister-looking graphic on *Nightline*. She had merely been writing down a reporter's questions about the travel office affair, but since the words "travel office" appeared, she felt compelled to turn over her notebook to a congressional committee. Moderately paid aides like Voles, who was a deputy press secretary at the time, racked up thousands in legal fees.

The staffers with the most to lose worked for Hillary Clinton. All but one of her 13 senior staffers received a subpoena at one time or another. Her chief of staff, Maggie Williams, had spent her career as a do-gooder before coming to the White House, mostly working for liberal think tanks. This earnest 41-year-old black woman spent more than a year's salary on lawyers to represent her before various investigating committees. Had she spirited Whitewater-related documents out of deputy White House counsel Vince Foster's office on the night of his suicide? Witnesses said yes; Williams, backed by a lie-detector test, swore no. She said she just sat on Foster's sofa that night, weeping for a dear friend.

Williams was accompanied to one confrontational Senate interrogation by her mother. "Ma, this is a waste of time," complained Williams. Her mother, who could remember the noble role played by the federal government during the civil rights era, admonished her to respect the institution. "You will say, 'Senator,'" instructed Mrs. Williams. "You will be polite." To make sure, Mrs. Williams sat in a chair right behind the witness's chair. Whenever Maggie appeared even slightly querrulous under the barrage of often abusive questioning, Mrs. Williams would give her daughter's chair a swift kick. For a long time, Williams could not talk about the depositions, the testimony or the legal bills without crying.

The steadfastness of Hillary's staff was admirable. "Hillaryland," the suite of offices occupied by the first lady's staff in the Old Executive Office Building, was about the only part of the White House that did not leak. Mrs. Clinton was able to command great affection and loyalty by playing the role of a warm den mother to her mostly young assistants. She could be silly, wearing a Christmas necklace of flashing lights; or corny, exclaiming "Okey Dokey Artichokey!"; and sometimes a little prudish, admonishing some of the women on her staff for wearing too short skirts. She could be cozy, asking about their boyfriends. She could also be demanding, calling them in the middle of the night with trivial questions that could have waited until morning. She was able to convey her own sense of mission and purpose, even her spirituality. But she was a disaster at the art of damage control. In a town where the first rule of scandal is get it out and get it behind you, Mrs. Clinton equivocated, stalled, stonewalled and thus prolonged Whitewater.

It was hard to tell why. Was she really hiding something? Or was she just embarrassed to be seen having tried to make a fast buck? In 1992, the Clintons had campaigned against the excesses of the '80s, the get-rich-quick schemes of the Reagan era. It would hardly do for Mrs. Clinton, advocate for the rights of poor children, to look like a greedy yuppie who had tried to use her husband's office to cash in on land deals and cattle futures. Or maybe Mrs. Clinton really believed what she said: that her private financial matters were none of the press's business. For whatever reason, Mrs. Clinton was behind most of the decisions that kept the White House from taking the course of openness.

The starkest example was her opposition to a plan advanced in the late fall of 1993 by presidential adviser David Gergen. A creature of the Washington establishment brought in to counsel the president, Gergen was known in the White House as the Cat in the Hat, both for his slinky feline posture and felicity, and because like Dr. Seuss's cat, he kept coming back. Gergen had the novel idea of simply inviting the *Washington Post* over to the White House and opening up the Whitewater files. Gergen predicted that the *Post* reporters would drown in the minutiae, then bore their readers with an unreadable five-part series. But Hillary strongly objected. She had a lawyer's resistance to turning over anything she didn't have to.

Hillary reinforced her husband's suspicion of the press. In the early days of the '92 campaign, the Clintons had enjoyed the company—and support—of some of the top Washington political writers, who tended to be Ivy League-educated and to share the Clintons' neo-liberal New Democratic beliefs. Gennifer Flowers changed all that. The Clintons began to view reporters as sleaze merchants. When Clinton arrived at the White House, he glanced down into the pressroom. "Smells like a gym down there," he said.

The Clintons made a half-hearted attempt to woo the local press mandarins, the columnists and commentators from the nets and newsmagazines, the *New York Times*, the *Washington Post*, and the *Wall Street Journal*. But they failed to appreciate that though reporters can be seduced by a White House dinner invitation for a while,

stronger forces inevitably come into play. The strongest is a phenomenon that might be called the Scandal Death Watch.

Most Washington reporters aren't really interested in digging
up scandals. There is a small cadre of investigative reporters who pore
over documents (usually slipped to them by congressional staffers).
But most of the high-priced journalistic talent is more interested in
watching the endgame—not the crime, but the cover-up. The spectacle of public officials stonewalling is a reliable ratings-booster.
Reporters assume that eventually the facade will crack and the offending public official will be denied confirmation or fired or driven
to resign. But the waiting game is juicy, full of ritual intrigue and back-
stabbing and human pathos. Even columnists who tend to be sympathetic, who generally defend the officials under fire, would be at a
loss without that juice.

In recent years, first ladies have become favored targets,
perhaps because they can't be summarily dismissed. Nancy Reagan
received terrible notices as Queen Nancy until she learned how to
mock herself, dancing in secondhand clothes to the tune of "Secondhand Rose" at the press corps' annual prom, the Gridiron Club show.
Hillary invited scrutiny by playing an active policy role, most notably in the failed attempt at health-care reform, and by championing
combative political tactics—she was constantly urging her husband
to "fight back." Even her ever-changing hair styles fueled the journalistic fires. She claimed to be bewildered by all the attention, summoning up the unfairness of it all by quoting one of Chelsea's favorite
nursery rhymes: "As I was standing in the street / As quiet as could
be / A great big ugly man came up / And tied his horse to me." But
then she would allow herself to be photographed by the *New York
Times Sunday Magazine* in a white organdy gown for a piece on her
search for spirituality.

Hillary had a devoted following, especially among working
women. But her negatives often ran higher than her husband's. When
Whitewater flared up, her standing plummeted to dangerous lows.
During the winter of '96, when she was summoned to testify before
the grand jury, she lost 15 points in one week. White House aides
worried that the first lady would drag down the president.

It was Harold Ickes who came up with a solution. He may have lost out to Morris in the struggle for Clinton's ear, but his wary—some would say paranoid—personality was well-suited to the role of campaign guardian. Ickes had successfully warded off a primary fight by insisting on a massive war chest to intimidate any challengers from within the Democratic party. He had persistently warned that the Republican Congress would use its subpoena power to harass the White House, and Al D'Amato's Whitewater committee had proved him right. Ickes had personal experience with scandal: as a New York lawyer whose firm represented unions alleged to have mob ties, Ickes had spent a year and a half disentangling himself from an ethics investigation before he could join the Clinton White House.

Ickes's approach to Whitewater was to try to isolate the scandal. He could see that the press corps' obsession with Whitewater was, as White House spokesman Mike McCurry put it, "polluting" the daily briefings in the pressroom. McCurry wanted the entire subject to be "walled off," allowing him to stay on message. Ickes's first step was to hire Jane Sherburne, who would work exclusively on Whitewater. She and Ickes created a separate Whitewater unit sealed off from the rest of the White House.

Sherburne became known around the White House as "Whitewater Jane." Her office was the former White House barbershop in the basement. The barber's chair was removed, but the mirror on the wall remained. There was also a fax machine used to communicate with the independent prosecutor and congressional investigators. (In true Washington fashion, document requests and subpoenas tended to arrive around 5 P.M. on Fridays. Information deemed damaging to the White House went out after 6 P.M., too late for the evening news.) A box of tissues was placed prominently on Sherburne's desk. They were often needed, Sherburne said, as she guided dozens of White House employees—often interns subpoenaed because they had opened mail or taken phone messages—through the intricacies of congressional and grand jury testimony.

Sherburne's main client was Hillary Clinton. For the first lady's grand jury testimony, Hillary and Sherburne decided on a "head-held-high" strategy. After testifying, the first lady would make a statement to the horde of reporters in front of the courthouse, claiming to have "appreciated the opportunity" to tell the grand jury her side of the story. Just before she went outside, Hillary jotted some notes of what she planned to say. Before she stepped in front of the microphones, she handed the slip of paper to Sherburne, who stuffed it in her purse. Several days later, at her daughter's 13th birthday party, Sherburne was horrified to find the first lady's handwritten notes still crumpled in her handbag. She tore the paper up and threw it away. As she watched her daughter Elizabeth celebrating with her friends, Sherburne had a change of heart. She fished the first lady's note out of the trash, smoothed the wrinkled fragments of paper and taped them together. Then she handed the bedraggled note to the teenager as a gift. "This is a piece of history," Sherburne told her daughter. "It's partly because a first lady has never been subpoenaed before. But it's really because this is a reminder of a woman I admire and I want you to admire also. This sort of sums up what she's been through."

As a damage-control spokesman, Ickes and Sherburne tapped Mark Fabiani, who had proved a master as chief of staff to Los Angeles mayor Tom Bradley, defending the mayor against a string of unproved ethics violations in the late 1980s. At first Fabiani would have nothing to do with the job. He already had a cushy post as a top official at HUD. But Ickes, in his blunt way, made Fabiani an offer he couldn't refuse. "When you're on a team," Ickes told Fabiani, "you play the position you're most needed in. If you don't do that, then you aren't part of the team."

Fabiani's office was tucked over on the top floor of the Old Executive Office Building, across from the Africa directorate of the NSC, about as far from the center of West Wing power as possible. Fabiani's intense, irreverent deputy, Chris Lehane, jokingly dubbed Room 488 the Arsenal of Democracy, and he and Fabiani called themselves the Masters of Disaster. Lehane filled his office with artifacts and memorabilia, like a bottle of Whitewater cologne and a glossy photo of the Whitewater alternate juror who showed up every day in a Star Trek uniform. The walls were lined with Whitewater cartoons, and the floor was piled high with pie graphs and charts showing the hundreds of hours and millions of dollars Congress had spent on fruitless investigations.

Mike McCurry was delighted with the arrangement. He simply referred Whitewater questions to Fabiani, whom he called "my garbage man." The Arsenal's basic approach was to drown reporters. Instead of the Administration's usual practice of withholding information, Lehane and Fabiani bombarded them with it—documents, testimony, phone and beeper logs, favorable press clippings, GOP misstatements. Shrewdly, the damage controllers counted on the essential laziness of the press corps. "When we first set up shop, it was like the Gold Rush," says Fabiani, laughing. "We'd tell reporters that we had something to show them and they'd come flying over here like we were giving out free samples. Now, when we call to show them something, your hear this, 'Uh . . . I'm pretty busy today.' So we just messenger it over."

Fabiani's basic story line was: sure, the Clintons or their aides might be guilty of poor or emotionally clouded judgment (the original Whitewater investment, removing files from Vince Foster's office) or mismanagement (Travelgate and Filegate) but not of criminal behavior. The real villains are D'Amato and Starr, one a partisan fronting for the Dole campaign, the other a partisan masquerading as an "independent" counsel, all part and parcel of the Republican-driven, anti-Clinton scandal machine.

In the last week of June, Whitewater, as broadly defined by the Clinton camp, seemed to be breaking out all over. In Little Rock, two good-old-boy buddies of Clinton were on trial by the special prosecutor for funneling illegal contributions to Clinton's 1990 gubernatorial campaign; White House aide Bruce Lindsey was named as an unindicted coconspirator. On Monday, a new book by *Washington Post* investigative reporter Bob Woodward revealed that in 1995 Mrs. Clinton, wounded by scandal and defeat, had turned to a new-age guru who prompted her to conduct imaginary conversations with the late Eleanor Roosevelt. The tabs and late-night comedians immediately began hooting over "Hillary's séances." On Wednesday, a pair of hapless White House aides, Craig Livingstone and Anthony Marceca, were summoned to Capitol Hill to explain what they had been doing with the private FBI files of hundreds of federal officials, including many top Republicans from the Bush administration. "Filegate," with its Nixonian overtones, threatened to become a scandal that voters could understand, even if Livingstone and Marceca had more in common with Abbott and Costello than Haldeman and Ehrlichman.

On the phone late one night with White House counsel Jack Quinn, Clinton fumed over how to handle the file flap. If he summarily fired Livingstone, he complained, he would be accused of being unfair to his employees, as in Travelgate. But if he waited for due process to take its course, the story would stay in the news for days. Either way, Clinton felt, he would lose. Quinn listened and tried to calm down the chief executive. Quinn had given up a cushy job as Gore's chief of staff to become White house counsel (Clinton's fourth) in November of 1995. He had been horrified at first by the scandals left unresolved by his predecessors and by the new ones that erupted on his watch. The FBI files, especially, "were a goddamned disaster," Quinn said. "Sometimes you think people planted little bombs here. You open up a drawer and they just blow up. Sometimes I think this place is booby-trapped." There were also arguments with the Whitewater damage-control team. Quinn, the top White House lawyer, often disagreed with Sherburne and Fabiani's legal strategy, especially their propensity for releasing White House documents. But Quinn, a tough Irishman who was shrewder at scandal management than some of his predecessors, was tenacious and humorous (he kept a framed "Get Out of Jail Free" card signed by Al and Tipper Gore on a table in his office). Quinn counseled the president that it was better to take the heat from the media than dump Livingstone. Quietly but firmly, he advised Livingstone to fall on his sword and quit.

On June 28, the Masters of Disaster were confronted by a threat from yet another quarter. The front page of the *Washington*

Times trumpeted the sort of headline the president's men had always dreaded: CLINTON'S WEE HOUR DASH TO A ROMANTIC TRYST. The president, the story alleged, had been sneaking out of the White House at night, under a blanket on the backseat of a car driven by Bruce Lindsey, to rendezvous with an unnamed starlet at the Marriott Hotel. This account came from a new book called *Unlimited Access* by a former FBI agent named Gary Aldrich. The agent's memoir of his five years on the White House detail included tales of gay group sex in the White House showers, dildoes and drug paraphernalia hung from the White House Christmas tree, rampant gender-bending, pear-bottomed men and square-shouldered women, hair that was too long, skirts that were too short—a veritable cesspool of modern depravity.

George Stephanopoulos read the newspaper account—and slightly more respectable versions in the *New York Times* and *Washington Post*—with a sensation he associated with bad motel food in New Hampshire and screaming headlines about Gennifer Flowers, the bimbo who had almost ended Bill Clinton's political career before the first primary in 1992. Stephanopoulos had an almost too-keen appreciation of the modern media food chain. First come the lurid accounts in the supermarket scandal sheets, like the *National Enquirer*, which gladly pay for stories. Then come the tabloids and the less responsible press like the *Washington Times*. Then the tidal wave: toned-down stories full of denials in the establishment press, tut-tutting by talking heads on the weekend shows, and the killer blow, the TV news mags like *20/20* and *60 Minutes*, which reach tens of millions of voters.

A fierce partisan who thinks in terms of kill-or-be-killed, Stephanopoulos had been one of the creators of the Clinton War Room in the '92 campaign. His rule of survival was never to let a news cycle pass without hitting back. By Friday, June 28, Stephanopoulos knew that strongly worded denials would not suffice. Aldrich was already booked on *Larry King Live* and *Dateline*; even the august David Brinkley had invited him on his Sunday talk show.

Stephanopoulos got up from his desk in the West Wing and walked the six blocks to ABC News headquarters off Connecticut Avenue. He demanded to see Brinkley's producers and launched a fierce assault on Aldrich's veracity. This guy can't prove a single allegation! He's completely discredited! How could you have such an unreliable source on your show? The ABC producers suggested that Stephanopoulos come on the show, too.

Slightly mollified, Stephanopoulos next called on Room 488, the Arsenal of Democracy. He wanted to know everything about Aldrich. Was he just a shill for the Dole campaign? It didn't take too many Nexis searches by Fabiani's shop to find some interesting links. Aldrich's publisher, Regnery Press, specialized in right-wing causes. Regnery had published books by a lobbyist for the National Rifle Association and a less-than-flattering portrait of Clinton as governor of Arkansas called *On the Make*. It turned out that Aldrich was being represented by Matthew Glavin's Southeastern Law Foundation, which had close ties to Newt Gingrich, and that his PR was being handled by Craig Shirley, a conservative activist who had handled publicity for Paula Jones, the woman suing Clinton for sexual harassment. Shirley, it appeared, was also a part-time adviser to the Dole campaign.

Stephanopoulos called Clinton, who was meeting with the chief executives of the G-7 nations in France. Clinton wanted to make sure that Stephanopoulos would tie in the Dole campaign when he went on the Brinkley show to blast Aldrich and his book. "Can we get documentation on this?" Clinton asked. The Arsenal of Democracy immediately put together a press packet helpfully pointing out Aldrich's GOP connections. The packets were sent out in time to make the Sunday papers.

Like most Washington conspiracies, the story of Gary Aldrich was actually more silly than sinister. Aldrich, who favors pressed white shirts, had been shocked when the Clintonites first arrived at the White House in their short skirts and with their sometimes slovenly manners. In his time on the White House detail, he had become accustomed to Republican haberdashery and politesse. What really irritated Aldrich was the disrespect the young Clinton aides seemed to show toward their guardians in the Secret Service and FBI and just about anyone in a uniform. On one occasion, Aldrich claims, he was kept waiting for 30 minutes outside the office of press secretary Dee Dee Myers while she chose her lunch menu. His revenge was that new weapon of less-than-devoted servants the world over: the tell-all memoir.

As a former agent, Aldrich was required to get the book cleared by the FBI, however, so he needed a lawyer. He turned to Jay Stephens, a former U.S. attorney with a partisan profile (a Reagan appointee, Stephens had considered running for the GOP Senate nomination in Virginia). It was Stephens who sent Aldrich to Regnery Press. Over lunch at the University Club in August 1995, publisher Al Regnery was somewhat skeptical when he heard Aldrich outline his book. "The bottom line is this won't put any-one in jail," said Regnery. He later encouraged Aldrich to add more salacious details. "This is the stuff that sells," he told Aldrich.

As it happened, Aldrich had already been approached by another author with an interest in President Clinton's sex life. David Brock, a writer for the right-wing *American Spectator*, had gained notoriety by getting Arkansas state troopers to tell tales of then-Governor Clinton's dalliances in various backseats and hotel rooms. Brock hoped Aldrich could update the story from a White House angle. But when the two met for lunch in June 1995, it was Brock who did most of the talking. Brock said that he had heard from a friend who heard from a friend who worked at the Marriott that the president had trysted there—maybe with a celebrity. Another rumor had the president slipping out of the White House at night under a blanket over his head.

Brock decided that Aldrich wouldn't be much of a source—too far out of the loop. But Aldrich, in his quest for more juicy stuff, called Brock and asked him if he had "any proprietary interest in the Marriott story." Brock replied, "No, it went nowhere for me." Instead the story went straight into Aldrich's book.

Brock didn't give it any thought until he saw the *Washington Times* headline trumpeting Clinton's *Newsweek* reporter Michael Isikoff later that day. Isikoff had been pressing Aldrich for his sources, and the FBI man told him it had been "a journalist." Isikoff, a veteran investigative reporter who knew all the players in and around Whitewater, guessed the journalist was Brock. Isikoff read Aldrich's description of the source to Brock: "a highly educated, well-trained, experienced investigator who is conducting his own investigation of the Clintons."

"Yep," said Brock. "That's me."

By Sunday, word of the *Newsweek* scoop was making the Washington rounds. George Will, a regular on the Brinkley show, called Brock at his home Sunday morning before going on the air and learned himself of the extemely shaky provenance of Aldrich's allegations. The former FBI man did not know it, but he was walking into an ambush.

Stephanopoulos couldn't believe his good fortune when he arrived at the ABC studios on Sunday morning. There, standing with Aldrich, were Craig Shirley and Matthew Glavin, the two men who, Stephanopoulos believed, had close ties to the GOP. "Dolegingrich" had accommodated the White House by stepping out of the shadows just in time to be exposed by the truth tellers from the Arsenal of Democracy. Stephanopoulos had been accompanied by Chris Lehane, the deputy Master of Disaster in Room 488. Lehane took one look at Shirley and Glavin and cracked, "Thank you, we've got our first sound bite."

Sensing a fiasco, Shirley asked the ABC producers to move them to a different waiting room. The clean-cut Lehane taunted Aldrich as the FBI man left makeup: "Is my hair too long for your taste?"

On the show, Aldrich was mercilessly interrogated by George Will, who exposed the book's dubious sourcing. As a shaken Aldrich left the set, he passed Stephanopoulos going to take his turn. "Liar," hissed Stephanopoulos. The presidential aide wasted no time:

STEPHANOPOULOS: . . . We have to look behind Gary Aldrich to see why this is happening.

DAVID BRINKLEY: Well, why? Tell me why.

STEPHANOPOULOS: Here's what I think. I mean, it's no accident. In the studio today with Gary Aldrich is an adviser to the Dole campaign. . . .

Stephanopoulos went on to tick off Shirley's work for the tobacco lobby and the gun lobby and to describe Aldrich's other handlers. "So you have a smear campaign conducted by Republican party operatives," he went on, full of appropriate moral indignation.

With help from the Masters of Disaster, Stephanopoulos had managed to turn a potentially disastrous scandal into a shameful Republican plot in less than 72 hours. Actually, there hadn't been much of a plot. Craig Shirley had helped out in the Dole campaign, finding some right-wing surrogates to speak for Dole during the primaries. But Dole's top advisers kept Shirley at arm's length, finding him too extreme. Aldrich said he knew nothing about the GOP ties of his advisers and resented the implication that he was somehow used.

The character attacks made headlines in June. Aldrich's book jumped on the best-seller list and stayed there. But Clinton's standing in the polls was unaffected. By early July, Clinton and his team began to breathe easier, even to joke a little about subjects once forbidden. One evening after Dick Morris had finished reciting polling data on voters' approval of Clinton's foreign policy performance, McCurry stood up and began a dramatic reading. His text was "Bill Clinton, Ambassador of Love," from *Harper's* magazine. "Clinton's foreign policy shows that he is a better lover than any president in U.S. history," McCurry began.

"Hey," said Clinton. "Gimme that."

Clinton, his reading glasses perched on his nose, became engrossed in the article, which went on to compare Clinton's hesitance to use force abroad to his supposed skills in bed. "For once, here is a president who delays his own climax to coincide with that of his mates . . ." the article stated. Later, Morris scolded McCurry for distracting Clinton from the task at hand.

But the Yellow Oval discussions were definitely taking on a lighter tone. After the flap over Hillary's imagined conversations with Eleanor Roosevelt, Penn had polled on whether the first lady was really talking to spirits, or whether she was just seeking a deeper understanding of the problems faced by earlier presidential wives.

Penn displayed the results for Clinton on the overhead projector in the Yellow Oval. Thirteen percent thought Hillary was trying to talk to the dead. Almost 80 percent went for the more benign explanation. Eleven percent were undecided.

Penn was about to whisk away the display when Clinton interrupted. "Hey, leave that up there," the president said. "That's more than a hundred percent."

"Yeah, we got the paranormals," someone cracked from the silk sofas.

"Well, they're our voters," Clinton shot back. "I told you I was expanding my base."

10 ■ WHATEVER

By the spring of '96, the Dole campaign was so broke that it was scheduling outdoor events in order to save the rent on a meeting hall. The Republican party did come up with $5 million to air Dole's bio ad, "The Story," in 20 cities. GOP focus groups had been only lukewarm after viewing the video. They liked the fact that Dole smiled and seemed warm, but "he's not telling me what he's going to do as president," complained one man. Others didn't want to hear about Dole's war wounds. They accused Dole of "playing on our sympathies, asking for pity"—a judgment that would have made Dole wince. Tony Fabrizio and his polling team began mockingly referring to the video as "Pityquest." The verdict of the polls was even more disquieting. Dole was actually doing worse with people who saw the ads.

Clearly, the $30 million Democratic ad blitz against "Dolegingrich" had taken a toll. The members of one focus group referred to Dole as "Newt's uncle." "We've got to make this guy seem compassionate," said pollster Bob Ward. Maybe they could do it with his choice of vice president. Somewhat wistfully, Ward began refer-ring to the still-unnamed veep nominee as "she."

In June, the campaign tried to come up with a catchy slogan. After endless discussion, Dole's advisers settled on "A Better Man for a Better America." The campaign also selected "message mod-ules" that were supposed to summarize the themes of the campaign.

"More opportunities. Smaller government. Stronger and safer families." At about the same time, the Clinton/Gore campaign went up on the Internet with its own home page. Fabrizio called Ward. He asked if he had seen the Clinton/Gore web site.

"No," Ward said.

"Log on," said Fabrizio. "Are you working late tonight?"

"Yeah."

"Screw it. Go out and get drunk."

As soon as Ward logged on to the web site, he could see why Fabrizio had recommended the bottle. The Clinton/Gore themes were almost identical to theirs, including such phrases as "strengthen America's families," "take back our streets from crime, gangs, and drugs" and "making government work better and cost less." Ward could understand what the Democrats were up to: both sides were finding the same results in their polling and research. The difference, Ward thought, was that Clinton used his polling and research. The Dole people ignored theirs.

T he campaign was definitely drifting. Dole had failed to take advantage of the emotional lift from his resignation speech in May. Because his staff had been caught by surprise, there was no plan to follow up on it. Dole ended up wandering aimlessly around Florida the weekend after his resignation, vacationing as much as campaigning. There was no attempt to coordinate the "air war"—the paid ads—with the "ground war"—Dole's speaking schedule. The schedule drove the message, instead of the other way around. If Dole was supposed to appear in Milwaukee, then someone would think up something for him to say there. And then there was the old problem: Dole's contrariness, born of resistance to the PR gimmickry of modern campaigns, often drove him to ignore whatever message his handlers tried to feed him. On May 21, Dole was scheduled to make a no-nonsense speech on welfare reform in Fond du Lac, Wisconsin. The speech was supposed to advocate mandatory drug testing for welfare recipients. But when the speech was leaked to the press before it was shown to Dole, he was irritated. Worse, a *Boston Globe* reporter pointed out that Dole's grandparents had been on welfare. Would they have been forced to take the tests? Dole was furious. He called headquarters to denounce the speech. "I hate it," he said.

On June 12, Dole and Elizabeth embarked on a three-day swing through the heartland that was supposed to unveil the new "Citizen Dole." (His campaign plane was no longer "Leader's Ship"; from now on it was "Citizen's Ship.") Campaign aides told reporters, "If you go on one trip this month, this is the one."

The trip was a disaster. Dole left out his best lines bashing Clinton as a '60s liberal and, as usual, he wandered from the prepared text. "We went through a tough primary. Spent all our money," he said, prompting a round of stories (fueled by the Clinton campaign) that his campaign was now exceeding the federal spending limits. Instead of concentrating on Citizen Dole, he reminisced about the Senate. "I understand the government does good things. I'm not out to destroy it," he said. He mentioned that on his first morning as an ex-senator, he had phoned his old Capitol office and gotten a recorded message. He joked about being out of work. "I'm going around the country to see where they have the best unemployment benefits," he said in Toledo. Resigning from the Senate left "sort of an empty feeling," he admitted to the voters. "It's like taking a cold shower. It will take a few days of withdrawal pains."

To the despair of his handlers, Dole was clearly homesick for Washington. Typically, he grew rebellious. Like a little boy, he willfully refused to do what he was told. He flirted with the TelePrompTer in Overland Park, Kansas, and abandoned it altogether in Louisville, Kentucky. On the plane to Toledo, he joked to reporters, "Don't worry very much about what I say; we're just trying to get good pictures."

Dole couldn't understand why the reporters, his friends when he had been a senator, no longer laughed at his jokes, or if they did, twisted his attempts to be offhand into serious stories. Asked how he planned to resolve differences in the party over abortion, Dole shrugged and said, "Piece of cake." He was just kidding, trying to make light of the hard job of unifying angry right-to-lifers and pro-choice moderates. But the next day the *New York Times* built a whole story around the comment. The reporters on the plane, Dole groused, had not "an ounce of humor." He would not have been amused to know that reporters were calling his plane "the Sinking Ship."

That wasn't the worst. As he and Elizabeth cruised down the muddy Ohio River aboard the steamer *Belle of Louisville*, a local reporter asked if the FDA should regulate tobacco as a drug. Dole wondered aloud, "Is tobacco addictive? To some people smoking is addictive. To others they can take it or leave it." The press accounts immediately made Dole into the tool of Big Tobacco or a retro figure or both. Dole felt he was just being honest and personal. He had once smoked and quit. He didn't think that he had been addicted—what was nicotine after all the morphine shots he had taken to numb his war wounds? Stubbornly, he refused to back off. "We know it's not good for kids. But a lot of things aren't good." He mentioned milk as "one of those things," thereby creating a new flap.

The Democrats gleefully piled on. Dole was soon dogged on the campaign trail by "Buttman," a succession of Democratic volunteers wearing a cigarette costume. The press played along. Dole was exasperated with a *New York Times* story on June 29, "Dole Re-Asserts His Doubts That Tobacco Is Addictive." That's not what I'm trying to say at all, Dole grumbled. He felt he had been intentionally misquoted.

That weekend, Dole was embarking on a feel-good tour with Elizabeth to promote their book, *Unlimited Partners*. The line-up was squishy soft: *Live with Regis and Kathie Lee*, an interview on the *Today* show with Katie Couric. Before Dole went on the *Today* set, his communications director, John Buckley, warned that if tobacco came up, he should answer, "I have nothing more to say on that."

Dole was tired; he had been on the road for two weeks. He was expecting softballs from Couric, "America's Sweetheart" of the morning shows. But Couric pressed him on tobacco. Still stewing over the *Times* article, Dole silently fumed. The press was making Buttman into a national celebrity. But how about the fact that the Democrats took contributions from the tobacco companies? Dole's brow darkened, he became surly. He attacked Couric and the rest of the media for being "biased." He suggested that Couric was violating the campaign finance laws by "sticking up for the Democrats." He further suggested the NBC and Couric were hypocrites because they, too, took tobacco money. He even attacked former Surgeon General C. Everett Koop, a political icon, for challenging his views on smoking. Elizabeth looked pained while her husband self-destructed beside her. "Let's talk about the book," she suggested, smiling bravely, trying to take control. But Dole and Couric went back to arguing about tobacco.

The time had come for a refresher course from Jack Hilton. Arriving at Dole's Watergate apartment on July 14, the speech coach was blunt. "It's got to stop," he said: Dole could not sail off from his basic message to get into silly arguments with reporters. Dole protested that he had been brought up to answer when asked. You don't have to be rude, said Hilton. But "you're never going to get a message through to the electorate if you allow yourself to be dragged all over the landscape." Couric's questions had been legitimate, even if the interview was supposed to be about the book. Attacking the "liberal media" just sounded mean-spirited and defensive, even if the press was disliked by the public. Couric had gotten Dole to agree that Surgeon General Koop had been "brainwashed." Dole had been suckered. Tobacco wasn't worth fighting over. "Why spend your face time with the public on that?" Hilton demanded. Dole just listened.

Dole, for once, behaved. On *Larry King Live* the next night, he smiled and looked relaxed. Elizabeth seemed to calm him, touching his arm affectionately from time to time. Watching TV, Hilton worried that Elizabeth, relentlessly on message as always, was perhaps a little too articulate. At moments, Dole seemed mute beside her.

By July, morale in the Dole campaign had reached new lows. The inevitable leaks began. The Team GOP gatherings with Newt Gingrich and Haley Barbour were suspended altogether. "There would be fistfights if they held those meetings," said one Dole aide. Gingrich was in a huff, complaining that the Dole campaign wouldn't listen to him. Barbour was sick of hearing Republicans all around the country complain about Dole. At headquarters, paranoia was rampant. When was the next purge?

The campaign manager, Scott Reed, tried to stay focused. He made an effort to catch leakers by setting traps, giving different tidbits of information to different staffers, then waiting to see which ones emerged in print. "When I catch them, I will fire them," he vowed, though in the manner of most leak investigations, he never did. Reed told himself that campaigns have peaks and valleys. He was getting the blame now, but with some luck he could wind up the hero. He set his hopes on three events that, he believed, would turn the campaign around: the economic plan, the vice-presidential nominee, and the convention in San Diego.

One serious problem was that the campaign now had no strategist. Don Sipple, the image maker brought in to replace Bill Lacy after the February purge, hadn't much use for Reed. By June, he had set up a separate company, New Century Media, to produce Dole's ads. Reed asked pollster Fabrizio to take on the strategist's job, but Fabrizio demurred; his experience was all from state and local elections, not presidential campaigns. Fabrizio also felt cut out; he thought his research was being largely ignored. Months later, Fabrizio would kick himself. "I knew what the data said," he admitted in October. "I knew what the problems were." He could see that Sipple's attempts to make the campaign turn on character were doomed to fail. The campaign was not about character, but about delivering the goods to voters. Instead of talking about Dole's war wounds, Fabrizio felt that Dole's ads should extol his achievements over the years, tell people how Dole had worked to save social security and about his record on women's issues such as domestic violence. This is what the swing voters really cared about, Fabrizio believed, and unless Dole spoke to the needs of women, his gender gap would be huge. But Fabrizio decided to be a team player and go along. He didn't want the campaign to have to endure another shake-up.

Fabrizio spent some of his time sparring with the GOP's self-anointed idea man, Newt Gingrich. At the convention, Gingrich wanted to stage a mock signing of the welfare bill, with Dole signing a dummy bill as president. Gingrich was trying to show that the welfare reform bill that Clinton finally agreed to accept was actually a GOP bill. Fabrizio thought that was a terrible idea. Why make the point that Clinton had moved to the right and was acting like a conservative? Also, Fabrizio was determined to keep Gingrich off the same stage as Dole. "We're listening to a man who, other than Perot, has the highest negatives of anyone in politics," Fabrizio argued. "Why don't we just get fountain-of-youth advice from Jack Kevorkian?" Fabrizio finally prevailed; the convention planners agreed to keep Newt offstage during the convention.

On July 11, Dole pollster Bob Ward traveled to Milwaukee to moderate a round of focus groups. He asked, "What are you seeing about the presidential campaign?"

The swing voters mentioned the headlines. Filegate. Tobacco.

"Is this going to affect your vote?" Ward asked.

No, the voters said. It really wouldn't.

Why?

The voters said the controversies were politics as usual. Clinton can't be trusted, they said. His people are political operatives. This is nothing new.

"What do you think of Clinton?" Ward continued.

He'll say anything and do anything.

"Then why do you still plan to vote for him?"

He's not doing a half-bad job, the voters said. Character doesn't really matter.

Ward wasn't surprised. The discussion only confirmed what polling had already suggested. Americans had come to have low expectations for their presidents. As long as they didn't screw up the world or the economy, they were okay. The bureaucracy seemed to churn along no matter who was in the Oval Office. Since the Cold War ended, people were far less concerned with who was sitting next to the red phone. Dole, Ward thought, would have had a much better chance if people were still worried about nukes.

Dole had once worried that he was too old to run. When his campaign collapsed in 1988, an aide had tried to reassure him, "Don't worry, you can run in '92." Dole answered, "That's about how old I'll be." With his tan and his lightly dyed hair, Dole felt he looked young and vigorous enough in 1996, but voters were not so sure. Senior citizens were among the most critical. They knew their own limitations and wondered how Dole kept going. The campaign tried to bluster past the age issue, suggesting that Dole was healthier than Clinton and implying that the president was covering up something by not fully releasing his own health records. But everyone in the campaign was aware that Dole's age was dragging him down. When adman Stuart Stevens first shot Dole's bio film in Russell, Kansas, in August 1995, focus groups that saw the film kept wondering: who are all those old people? Some caustically asked if the film was an ad for a nursing home. Dole looked reasonably well, but his friends looked decrepit. Stevens ended up cutting them from the final version, instead using footage of Elizabeth extolling her husband.

Dole added to the problem with ocassional remarks betraying his age. Pop culture, to him, meant Glenn Miller. His efforts to appear hip to youth were mostly a flop. He tried to talk to Dartmouth students about the movie *Animal House,* which was inspired by a Dartmouth frat, but he forgot that most of the students listening to him had been toddlers when the movie was released. When he made the mistake of visiting the Rock and Roll Hall of Fame in Ohio, a reporter asked him for his favorite rock group. "We didn't visit that part," said Dole. At a rally in Portland, he was asked if he liked Hootie and the Blowfish. Dole looked blankly for a moment and then finally gave an honest answer: "Anything that gets me votes."

Republicans win when the subject is taxes—or so goes Republican orthodoxy. The logic is not subtle: Republicans want to cut them, and Democrats want to raise them. The modern models are Ronald Reagan, who won two terms by putting money back in the taxpayers' pockets, and George Bush, who was thrown out of office for violating his own "no new taxes" pledge. Dole knew the history as well as anyone, but he had a problem: his own history.

Dole believed in lower taxes, and he voted for the Reagan tax cuts in 1981. But as chairman of the Senate Finance Committee, he was the one who had to clean up the mess afterward. The massive 1981 cuts opened a gusher of red ink because spending was not cut to the same degree, and Dole and other responsible legislators were left trying to stanch the flow. Dole was perhaps the most responsible. He led the passage of a $250 billion tax increase in 1982 and had the courage—some would say the foolhardiness—to try to nip the annual cost of living allowance for social security recipients in 1985. President Reagan nixed that attempt at fiscal prudence, and other Republicans taunted Dole. Newt Gingrich called him the "tax collector for the welfare state."

Dole's political instincts were at war with his good-government scruples. To win the GOP nomination, Dole knew that he could not afford to be outflanked on the tax issue. In 1995, Dole embraced a $245 billion tax cut proposed by Gingrich and the House Republicans. But he was hardly a true believer. "The good news is that a busload of supply-siders went over a cliff," Dole liked to joke. "The bad news is that there were three empty seats." If the tax cut stood in the way of getting a deal that would produce a balanced budget by the year 2002, Dole was perfectly willing to make some compromises.

In November, as the budget negotiations were heating up, Dole waffled on *Face the Nation*. "Will the tax cut be $245 billion?" he asked rhetorically. "I'm not certain at this point." He was forced to retreat the next day and publicly reaffirm his devotion to cutting taxes. But he didn't mean it; for the good of the country—and to break the embarrassing budget deadlock—Dole would have, without hesitation, traded tax cuts for spending cuts in a backroom deal. With Clinton and Gingrich dug in, it was Dole who finally declared, "Enough is enough," and forced an end to the government shutdown in January.

The Republican primaries gave Dole a refresher course in the wisdom of posing as a tax cutter. Dole may have scorned Steve Forbes's flat tax as "snake oil," but he saw that it won votes. A record of fiscal responsibility, no matter how worthy, didn't seem to be much of a vote-getter. As Dole sat in the sun in April, recovering from his battering in Iowa and New Hampshire, he understood that he would have to come out for a tax cut, and a big one, to win in November.

The dilemma was how to propose a big tax cut and still look credible. Dole knew that the Democrats would mock him for a deathbed conversion. Instead of Bob Dole, paragon of prairie virtue, he would seem positively Clintonian in his expediency. Any tax cut plan, Dole knew, would have to also balance the budget. The numbers, he told his aides, had to add up. To help write such a plan and lend it an aura of legitimacy, Dole called on a panel of economists from institutions like Stanford, Harvard and the University of Chicago. In sober academic language, Dole's advisers produced papers calling for a half-trillion dollar tax cut over six years to boost economic growth. The tax cuts would at least help pay for themselves. Supply-siders claim the miracle of "feedback": tax cuts increase economic growth, which in turn produces more tax revenue, paying for the tax cuts. Dole took what he saw as a more responsible position, claiming a feedback return of only 30 percent. That still meant that Dole had to find roughly another $400 billion in spending cuts to make the numbers add up. His economic advisers were a little vague about how that might be done. Their suggestions included such devices as selling airwaves to broadcasters and the ever-popular "closing of loopholes." For public consumption at least, the big-ticket items—social security and Medicare—were not to be touched.

Remarkably, given their animosity during the primaries, Dole turned to Steve Forbes for advice. On May 22, Forbes came to Dole's private office in the Capitol. All smiles, Dole complimented Forbes on the effectiveness of his attack ads on Dole as a "Washington insider." Dole understood, he said, the need to take dramatic steps to shed that image. "All they know about me is that I'm a senator and wear a tie every day," said Dole. "I've got to do something bold. I've got to do something big." He was thinking about a tax cut—15 percent across the board.

Forbes was taken aback at Dole's new line, but he enthusiastically joined in. Why not just repeal the tax hikes of 1990 and 1993? That would get the ball rolling, said Forbes. The problem was that those increases had fallen mostly on the rich. Repealing them might look like trickle-down economics of the most flagrant kind. Forbes countered by suggesting that middle-class taxpayers should be able to deduct their payroll taxes for social security. Too complicated, argued Dole's people. Senator Spence Abraham joked that the campaign buttons would have to read "AGI – FICA"—adjusted gross income minus the social security payroll tax deduction. It would be much simpler, argued Abraham, just to cut taxes 15 percent across the board.

This debate, and endless wrangling over timing and scale, rattled on for weeks. Dole had originally contemplated announcing his economic plan in June, but the schedule kept slipping. Some of Dole's handlers suggested that he wait until after the convention. Better to undercut the Democrats with a splashy announcement on the eve of their convention in late August, suggested Mike Murphy, one of Dole's consultants. Murphy, a maverick whose long blond hair fell over a balding pate, thought that the campaign was panicking. "We all want to release the tax plan now because we're getting our brains beat in," said Murphy. He proposed that Dole hold off and ride a whistle-stop "Tax Cut Express" across the country. John Buckley, the communications director, exploded that Murphy was crazy if he thought Dole could get through his own convention without announcing a plan. "We are teetering on the edge of farce here," Buckley seethed.

The debate continued in a conference call a few days later. "You guys want to announce the tax plan, half-assed, in the middle of the Olympics, with no ad money to support it," shouted Murphy.

"Mike, look on the front page of the *New York Times*. Do you see the Olympics there?" Buckley demanded.

"I'm like a swing voter. I don't read the fucking *New York Times*," Murphy retorted. "I watch television. It's all over television."

At each meeting, Dole's advisers would search his face for a hint. Did he favor rolling back the earlier tax hikes? Or making the 15 percent slash? Dole would narrow the options to these two—and then add in six more. His aides began grumbling that he was at it again, dithering and procrastinating when bold action was called for. "We've plowed this ground 10,000 times. Why are we doing this again?" moaned an exasperated adviser during one late-night work session only two weeks before the convention. There were the usual leaks and recriminations. But Dole bided his time. To him, this was just like cutting a deal in the Senate. You listen, listen some more, find the middle ground. Dole's equanimity allowed him to rationalize the whole exercise. He wasn't betraying his deficit-hawk principles to bribe the voters with a tax cut. He was searching for a responsible compromise.

Yet Dole's hesitancy may have been influenced by some private misgivings. The clearest sign was his long-running minuet with Senator Pete Domenici, the earnest chairman of the Senate Budget Committee. Dole and Domenici had been through the budget wars together, urging colleagues to make hard but fiscally responsible votes. Dole very much wanted Domenici's support and his respect. He risked losing it with a $550 billion tax cut. "As you prepare your economic plan, you are aware that your credibility is at stake," Domenici warned Dole in a private memo on June 25. The veteran deficit hawk was dubious about the tax cut. "Neither of us over the years have been able to produce credible spending cuts of the magnitude that would be required to balance the budget by the year 2002 and execute such a tax plan," Domenici wrote Dole.

Yet in the end, Domenici came around and supported the full tax cut. How Dole managed this was subtle, a matter of winks and nods and unstated assumptions. The biggest assumption was that in the end, Dole would do the right thing, no matter what he promised to get himself elected. Domenici was encouraged that Dole's economic plan called for a constitutional amendment requiring a balanced budget. Such a straitjacket would force fiscal responsibility. Domenici also knew that Dole would be willing to make the tough choices—to cut Medicare and maybe even social security. For the record, and in all his campaign statements, Dole insisted that he would balance the budget without touching those sacred cows. But privately, he signaled Domenici otherwise.

On August 1, only three days before the economic plan was announced, Domenici and Dole were still fretting over how to squeeze the last $200 billion out of the budget. If entitlements like Medicare and social security and the Pentagon budget were put off-limits, it would mean cutting all other spending by some 30 percent. That might mean slashing whole departments and gutting popular programs like the National Weather Service. "Senator," said one of Domenici's aides, "I don't need to tell you how difficult that is given what we've been through in the last few years."

"There are other ways to get there," said Domenici. He said that Congress could rein in spending on entitlements by trimming the annual increases in social security and Medicare. As usual, Dole just said nothing. But he winked.

When the plan was finally announced on August 5, the reception was skeptical. Reporters asked what had happened to Dole the old deficit-hawk. Even the *Wall Street Journal* editorial page, a cathedral of supply-side faith, wondered whether Dole was being overly optimistic in his assumptions. The early opinion polls registered disbelief. Most people dismissed the plan as pure politics. The Dole campaign, in response, cited the 1993 gubernatorial campaign of Christine Todd Whitman, whose pledge to cut New Jersey taxes by 30 percent initially had been laughed at—but who had been elected and then delivered on her promise. How would you explain Dole's sudden willingness to embrace tax cuts? a reporter asked Steve Forbes. Forbes smiled his goofy grin and replied, "It shows he has a great capacity for growth."

At the Fairmont Hotel in Chicago, Dole trotted out his panel of academic worthies. "They don't endorse pie-in-the-sky packages," he said. He seemed to be convincing himself as much as his audience. When Dole chose Jack Kemp, a leading supply-sider, to be his vice-presidential nominee four days later, Dole himself started to sound like a true believer. "Fifteen percent," he began trumpeting, adopting a peculiar form of numerology. Fifteen had been Kemp's number when he played football. Yes, and there were 15 letters in the names Bob Dole and Jack Kemp added together. Fifteen letters in the names Elizabeth and Joanne (Kemp's wife). Giddy campaign staffers kept coming up with new and more arcane numerological signs. It was all a little far-fetched, rather like Dole's economic plan.

11 ■ APPOINTMENT IN SAN DIEGO

During the first two years of the Clinton administration, the press heaped derision on the White House for its clumsy and indecisive appointment process. Reporters would have been just as scornful if they had known the inside story of Dole's selection of a running mate.

His vice president, Dole regularly declared, should be a "10." Not an unknown or a compromise or a favorite son, but someone who was ready to take over as president "on day one." For months, Dole had wanted Colin Powell. The retired general had seemed like the one candidate who could change the dismal electoral equation. "Everyone else is third," said John Buckley. "There is no second."

Powell, however, had said he didn't want the job. In back-channel conversations, Powell's advisers warned Dole not to offer Powell the veep spot; the general would just reject it. Finally, Powell agreed to see Dole at a fund-raiser for Senator John Warner of Virginia at the suburban home of Ken Duberstein, a skilled Washington fixer who was close to Powell. Powell and Dole met in Duberstein's "ego room," lined with photos of Duberstein with various Washington personages, on the evening of June 8.

The two men talked about a variety of subjects—national security, affirmative action, the congressional agenda. Powell was coolly genial, Dole respectful. Dole did not mention the vice presidency, and so Powell never had a chance to say no. But he did talk about his wife Alma's fear that if he ran for office some crazy person would try to shoot him. Dole picked up on the general's body language: he was being pleasant enough, but he never sat forward in his chair, the way a politician does when he really wants something. When the two men emerged after half an hour to smile for photographers, Dole had changed his mind. Forget him, Dole later told Scott Reed, he's off the list. According to Reed, Dole had found Powell too liberal. After listening to Powell talk, Dole wondered whether Powell was a true Republican. Scott Reed felt oddly relieved by the decision. They couldn't afford a running mate who wasn't 100 percent with the program. But if not Powell, who?

The Dole campaign had erected a thorough, if cumbersome, process to help Dole choose wisely. There were flip charts and flow charts, decision trees, check-off lists, a vetting process designed to expose the smallest foible. Rod DeArment, a Washington lawyer and old Dole adviser, had designed a questionnaire with more than 60 entries. It incorporated the search criteria for the presiding bishop of the Episcopal Church (the church was good at ferreting out sexual pecadillos) and lessons learned the hard way by earlier candidates. There were detailed questions on business investments (Geraldine Ferraro, Hillary Clinton), drug use (Bill Clinton), military record (Clinton, Dan Quayle), "bimbos" (Clinton, Gary Hart), and hired help (Nannygate).

In April, Dole had asked his old friend Bob Ellsworth to run the search process. "I trust you and I've known you a long time. Plus, you don't talk to the media," Dole said to Ellsworth. A veteran of the Washington wars, Ellsworth was privately skeptical that Dole would find his "10." Dole wanted someone who was in his early 50s, yet ready to govern; Ellsworth thought there was no such person. Dole was also interested in finding a nonpolitician. Ellsworth steered him away from CEOs. "It's like Michael Jordan going off to play baseball. It doesn't work," he told Dole. Dole said he wanted someone who could help him win. "That hardly ever happens," said Ellsworth. Dole would be lucky to find someone who didn't drag him down.

"Gimme some names," Ellsworth said finally.

"You know the names," said Dole, but he mentioned a few anyway. Powell, Dick Cheney, Christine Todd Whitman.

"How about a conservative Democrat?" asked Ellsworth. He mentioned David Boren of Oklahoma and Bob Graham of Florida.

Dole shook his head. "Nunn," he said. He liked the chairman of the Armed Services Committee.

In the end, the list of about a dozen names consisted mostly of governors: John Engler of Michigan, Tom Ridge of Pennsylvania, Jim Edgar of Illinois, George Voinovich of Ohio, Tommy Thompson of Wisconsin, Carroll Campbell of South Carolina. A couple of senators: Connie Mack of Florida and Don Nickles of Oklahoma. An elder statesman: James A. Baker, who had been secretary of Treasury and State in the Reagan-Bush administrations. All good men, but none of them seemed likely to make the difference on November 5.

O n the morning of July 5, Dole met with his vice-presidential search team on the roof of his campaign headquarters behind Union Station. Dole missed "the Beach," his Senate balcony. Now he had to make do with a view of some railroad tracks and a parking lot. As Dole sunned himself, Ellsworth ran through the usual prospects one more time.

"We ought to figure out a way to get Elizabeth on this list," said Ellsworth. "She's number one on everybody's list," said Dole. Everyone laughed, but they weren't kidding. Except for the fact of her husband's name at the top of the ticket, Elizabeth Dole was an obvious choice. A woman who could close the gender gap, but who was pro-life. A two-time cabinet officer who was articulate, attractive, and never, ever, off-message. Governor Whitman of New Jersey was in many ways equally appealing, but her pro-choice views were anathema to the religious right. With Perot in the race, warned pollster Tony Fabrizio, Dole had to choose a pro-life veep or risk losing Christian conservatives to a protest vote. Elizabeth, on the other hand, was a star attraction at prayer breakfasts. In early July, the campaign had actually looked at the Constitution, which makes it difficult for the president and vice president to come from the same state. Maybe Elizabeth could change her residence.

Later that month, Scott Reed and party boss Haley Barbour went so far as to sound out Ralph Reed at the Christian Coalition. Careful always not to alienate the religious right, the Dole campaign regularly touched base with Reed and his boss, evangelist Pat Robertson. Before the primaries, Reed and Robertson had been dead set against Colin Powell. "If you pick Powell," they had warned Dole that winter, "it's over." The party would be torn apart. In May, a delegation from the religious right had come to pray with Dole—and remind him to choose a pro-lifer.

Dole respected Ralph Reed, a pragmatist who served as a clever mediator between the true believers and the more expedient world of Washington. Dole wanted Reed's political judgment, as well as his blessings. As it happened, Reed was reading *The System* by David Broder and Haynes Johnson, an account of the collapse of Hillary Clinton's health-reform crusade. The book showed how Hillary had first eclipsed her husband, then dragged him down. Putting Elizabeth on the ticket with Dole "would be a big mistake," said Reed. "She would be fabulous, and that's the problem. People would start grumbling that the ticket should be reversed." The campaign did go so far as to include Elizabeth's name on a list of possible running mates in its polling. She did well enough; people liked her and thought she was qualified for the job. But they choked on the idea of a husband-and-wife team. It was too much like a monarchy—"she wouldn't have passed the smile test" was the way Scott Reed put it afterward—and she was quietly dropped from the list.

On July 30, with the convention less than two weeks away, Dole was riding with party activist Bill Bennett in Hollywood, on the way to making another speech bashing the entertainment industry. Bennett told Dole that he had heard Senator Nickles of Oklahoma was on the short list. "I think he's a good man," said Bennett.

"Well, what about you?" Dole asked.

"Um, I'm a pretty good man," said Bennett.

"For this," Dole added. The question was as close as he had gotten to asking someone to be his running mate.

"No, no, don't do that," Bennett said. "Not now, maybe later. No, thank you very much, sir."

Dole persisted. "Well, we need to win this thing, you know. Catholics," Dole grunted. "Call you tomorrow."

Bluff and forceful, Bennett was marvelous polemicist, with a gift for eloquent laments on the moral decline of America. As Education secretary and drug czar under Reagan and Bush, he had first-rank experience with hot social issues. The press liked him. But Bennett feared that he would be a tempting target if he ran for vice president. The author of *The Book of Virtues* was bound to be held to an impossibly high personal standard. Bennett was a good family man. But he had once been a hard-partying graduate student at Harvard. He had even dated Janis Joplin. Who knew what old photos might still be floating around? Bennett refused to fill out DeArment's questionnaire.

Dole was running out of time. Still, there was one name they hadn't really considered. Jack Kemp was in many ways ideal. Almost alone among leading Republican politicians, he had standing with African Americans. An advocate of saving the inner city through the power of free enterprise, he was optimistic, attractive, energetic. He could close Dole's perceived compassion gap. And as one of the original apostles of supply-side Reaganomics, he was the perfect man to sell Dole's tax cut.

The catch was that Kemp, whose career began as a quarterback for the San Diego Chargers and the Buffalo Bills, had never gotten over wanting to play that position. He talked about being a team player, but as HUD secretary during the Bush administration, he was always trying to call the signals, disrupting cabinet meetings and refusing to follow the White House line.

Kemp had also been a source of exasperation to the Dole campaign. To give himself cover against the flat taxers on the right,

Dole had made Kemp the head of his tax commission in April 1995. Dole wanted some vague promise to create a "fairer, flatter" tax system sometime in the future. But dogmatic as ever, Kemp kept insisting on a single, specific tax rate. He refused to endorse Dole; worse, he backed Steve Forbes instead. As he was about to endorse Forbes in early March, Kemp called Scott Reed, who had once worked for Kemp as his chief of staff, to tell him the news as a matter of courtesy. Reed exploded. "Why are you fucking me?" screamed Reed, who is normally controlled. "You're fucking yourself and you're fucking me!"

In characteristic fashion, Kemp aggravated the wound. At an Iowa fund-raiser, he said, "I love Bob Dole. I just hope our party doesn't come across sometimes as a party of grumpy old men." On July 9, at a pro-Israel fund-raiser, Kemp was asked, "Why should we support Dole in the coming election?" Kemp answered, "I can't give you a good reason." His wife, Joanne, standing beside him, softly protested, "Aw, c'mon, Jack." "No," Kemp charged on, "Dole hasn't done enough to make his case to you."

Now Kemp was in political exile, not even consulted on the making of Dole's tax plan. He felt neglected and depressed; he told friends that he was in "the wilderness." So he was a little taken aback when he heard from his old subordinate, Scott Reed, on July 23. Reed was just fishing. If Dole approached him to be veep, was Kemp interested?

"I'd like to talk to Bob," said Kemp. He wasn't sure if this was a serious feeler.

Reed coolly informed him that wasn't the way things worked. "You're not talking to Bob. That's not the way we do this. Nobody's talking to Bob," he said, emphasizing the first name that he, Scott Reed, never used. To Reed, and to any other staffer, Dole was "Senator." Kemp, on the other hand, was "Jack."

"You talk to me, you talk to the [vetting] team," Reed told Kemp. The chilly conversation ended. Neither man called back the other.

But less than two weeks later, on August 4, Dole's thoughts turned back to Kemp. "What about the quarterback?" he said. Pollster Fabrizio was lukewarm. His polls gave Kemp only a one-point edge over Senator Connie Mack. Kemp couldn't deliver a state, wouldn't attack Clinton, and wasn't disciplined. Still, the campaign should at least bring him back on board to sell the economic plan, which was being announced the next day. John Buckley, another Kemp alumnus (he had once been Kemp's press secretary), was assigned to make the call.

"How are you?" asked Buckley.

"How should I be?" Kemp responded. He sounded dejected.

"We're coming out with a plan you're gonna love," Buckley told him. It would include a big tax cut. To Buckley's surprise, Kemp choked up on the phone. He had felt frustrated and ostracized.

"Help us sell it," Buckley asked.

"I'm a team player," said Kemp. He was; he plugged the Dole plan on CNN, the next day on *Today*. Dole watched approvingly. Despite his dark-side reputation, Dole had learned not to hold grudges in the Senate. Lose a vote today, get it back tomorrow. Dole knew that Kemp could unite the deficit-cutting and supply-side wings of the party. He told Scott Reed to go see Kemp.

"Are you up to this?" Reed asked when they met in a hotel room. "Can you be on the team? Can you be a number two on the team?"

Kemp was bursting with eagerness. "I can do it, Scott. I can do it. I can do this."

Kemp and Dole finally met that night at a borrowed apartment at the Watergate. They talked frankly about their differences, but as usual, Dole was indirect about what he wanted. He did not offer Kemp the job.

By morning, when Kemp met secretly with Reed and Buckley in a van in the parking lot of the Key Bridge Marriott in Rosslyn, the quarterback was feeling ambivalent. How could he work with Dole? he wondered aloud. Why should he give up his comfortable life? His income from the speaking circuit was more than $500,000 a year.

Learning of Kemp's reluctance, Dole decided to use an old Washington trick. He called conservative commentator Bob Novak and leaked that he was considering Kemp. Sure enough, Novak broke his scoop within minutes on CNN. Within minutes after that, the Republican faithful gathering in San Diego were buzzing about Kemp. Dole knew that Kemp would hear the roar of the crowd.

Dole was also forcing his own decision. If Dole did not pick Kemp now, the letdown would be huge. As one Republican told Scott Reed: "If you're not bringing Kemp to San Diego, you better bring Colin Powell or you might as well not come."

And yet even then, Dole had not made up his mind. Or at least he wasn't telling his aides. As reporters gathered in Russell, Kansas, where Dole planned to announce his running mate on the Saturday before the convention, he dithered one last time. There was the religious right to worry about. Christian Coalition head Pat Robertson and Kemp had tangled bitterly when they were running against each other for the GOP nomination in 1988. Dole had not called Robertson to pacify him about Kemp, and now Ralph Reed was warning that Robertson was "bent out of shape."

Dole's aides were not absolutely sure he would go through with it. He still had not told Senator Mack that he was not his choice. Mack was, in effect, on standby. Kemp, stuck on an airplane, wasn't available at the agreed-upon time for a phone call from Dole. Dole continued to worry about Kemp's positions on immigration and affirmative action, which were far more positive than the GOP platform. And he was confronted at the very last moment with rumors of a personal indiscretion in Kemp's recent past—tales that very nearly sank his chances that night. The campaign had not thoroughly vetted Kemp's history for potential problems; it wasn't until reporters started asking about the latest gossip that Nelson Warfield finally went to Dole, assuming that he had already been briefed on all the rumors. He hadn't been. Neither had Elizabeth, who was even more upset than her husband; the new tale, coupled with others that had followed Kemp for years, seemed to suggest a pattern of behavior if they were true.

With the choice hanging in the balance, Dole sent Reed and Warfield to an RV parked outside Dole's house—Reed to put the question to Kemp, Warfield to act as witness. Kemp emphatically denied the rumors. The two aides went back inside and worried the problem some more with the Doles. Warfield thought any potential damage was "sustainable." Dole ultimately agreed; finally, with contradictory rumors flying and the press holed up in a fetid basement in Russell's American Legion hall, he placed The Call to Kemp at 10:06 Friday night.

Dole recounted a story from his own vice-presidential campaign in 1976. During a swing through Minnesota, he had made a policy pronouncement on milk price supports. Word came quickly from President Ford: there was only one guy at the top of the ticket, and he would be the one making policy. Kemp seemed to get the idea. Dole made the offer; Kemp accepted. And Kemp himself called Ralph Reed and prevailed on him to mollify Robertson.

The next morning, the 1996 GOP ticket had breakfast together at Dole's childhood home in Russell. Dole took Kemp down into the cramped, dark basement where he had lived as a boy when the family had to rent out the ground floor to make ends meet. Dole warned Kemp about the loose carpet on the third step. Emerging for their first photo op, the two men waved. Reporters who had traveled with Dole gasped when Kemp put his hand on Dole's back to guide him in another direction. They all knew: you don't touch Dole.

Kemp could not believe Dole's generosity. After all the words that had passed between them, he was astonished that Dole would reach out to him, rescue him, really, from the political wilderness. Kemp, a brawny man given to bear hugs, was bothered that he couldn't embrace Dole without hurting him. "I can't even put my arm around him," he told his aides as he sat around his hotel room in San Diego. At their appearances together, Kemp had been leaping on the stage and whipping off his suit jacket, as usual, only to notice that Dole was struggling but unable to remove his as well. Kemp broke down as he talked about his running mate. "I can't believe the courage this guy demonstrates every single day," he said. Together, the new partners flew west, to San Diego.

The Republicans were haunted by memories of the 1992 convention in Houston. The party had seemed harsh and intolerant; some of the speakers, particularly Pat Buchanan, had come across as phobic. San Diego, the party leaders vowed, was not going to be a repeat performance. Instead, the GOP wanted to project an image of inclusiveness.

Abortion was an obvious stumbling block. The party platform would surely call for laws to protect the unborn, just as it had ever since the Supreme Court legalized abortion in the early '70s. Still, the party leaders wanted to appear tolerant of different beliefs, especially to attract women voters. At the same time, the GOP could not afford to drive off the Christian right—possibly into the arms of Buchanan, who had the potential to lead a messy walk-out. All through the summer of 1996, party leaders wrestled behind the scenes with a way to finesse the abortion issue. In the end they succeeded—but not before Bob Dole had created some embarrassing and probably unnecessary headlines.

The first step toward pacification was to make Henry Hyde, a congressman well-respected by both pro-lifers and pro-choicers, the head of the platform committee. In May, Scott Reed dispatched an aide to rummage through earlier GOP platform planks, looking for some tolerance language that could paper over differences between the different wings of the party. The staffer found some suitably innocuous language in the 1980 platform ("we recognize that members of our party have deeply held and sometimes differing views on issues of personal conscience"). That seemed about right to Reed. Who could argue with a plank that Ronald Reagan liked?

In early June, Dole began publicly dropping hints that the party was heading for a more tolerant stance on abortion. The press predictably interpreted these remarks as signs of waffling, and the campaign was under pressure to issue some kind of clarifying statement. Reed was in a difficult position. The party moderates wanted the tolerance language in the abortion plank itself. But the right-to-lifers were opposed. You can't "tolerate" murder, they argued. And why single out abortion? Why not put the tolerance language in a separate plank of the platform or in some kind of preamble? Reed tried to fudge this dispute. With Dole's approval, Reed had the campaign issue a statement, in time for the evening news on June 6, declaring that the GOP platform would include some language on tolerance— but conveniently avoiding any mention of where this new language would go. The press clips in the morning were positive, including a news analysis by R. W. Apple of the *New York Times* praising the GOP's judiciousness. The party leaders felt the abortion issue was behind them. John Buckley even allowed himself to declare, "We can win this election."

Dole's aides knew they were still walking a tightrope, however. They were afraid of what Dole might say. He wanted the tolerance language in the abortion plank, not off in some preamble. The point was abortion. Why pretend they were also talking about trade, or gun control, or term limits? Although he had used abortion as a weapon in his rough reelection campaign for the Senate in 1974, the subject made him uncomfortable. His own daughter was pro-choice. Besides, Dole disliked having to kowtow to the religious right, even though he usually accepted the necessity.

It took Dole all of three days to spoil the campaign's premature sense of relief. On June 10, he told CNN's Candy Crowley that the tolerance language would be in the abortion plank. What's more, his position was "nonnegotiable." Buckley and Reed were crushed. Curses flew around the room as the campaign staffers watched Dole change his position on TV. "Get me a transcript!" someone yelled. Aides muttered about being "blindsided" by their own candidate. As usual, Dole had simply refused to be handled. The hairsplitting was too cute for him. "Got a little bit out ahead of me on this," he told Reed.

Henry Hyde was threatening to quit, and spokesmen for the religious right were in a high state of outrage. The only good news was that Dole was being attacked on national TV for being too tolerant. Clearly, a deal had to be cut before the August convention blew up. Reed persuaded Dole to look for a compromise in terms that he knew Dole would understand: "You don't have the votes to win this one," Reed told his boss. Dole finally agreed to a separate tolerance plank.

But a lot of damage had already been done. The moderates and religious right continued to squabble, their fights overshadowing the tax plan when it was announced in early August. Dole was fed up with the whole issue. Asked about the platform in an interview as the convention began, Dole announced that he hadn't even read it.

Most voters shared that attitude; platforms have long since ceased to be a meaningful part of American politics. But the convention itself did matter: for the average person, it was the first chance to take a real look at Dole, to measure him as a man and not just the familiar talking head on television. It was crucial to make him seem warm and humane. The job of making that happen fell in large measure to Elizabeth Dole.

Bob Dole's aimless campaign had been acutely frustrating to his wife. Elizabeth's approach to her work was diametrically opposed to his. She liked order and schedules. Memos never sat on her desk for long. But Dole would keep them for weeks, rereading and underlining them, slowly and often inscrutably working toward a decision, which he then usually felt free to reverse. She would memorize her speeches word for word. Dole preferred to wing it. She was relentlessly on message. He had no message. He liked to ad lib and was all too willing to answer a reporter's question. She would turn cold if the questioning turned personal and once had a press secretary fired partly because she left her alone in an interview. Elizabeth (the staff knew better than to call her by her childhood nickname, Liddy) was appalled at the intrusiveness of the press. She was mortified when reporters speculated that Dole's prostate operation had affected his sexual performance. Despite her May Queen smile, Mrs. Dole was intensely private. She would arrive at work, go straight to her office and close the door. Dole would wander the halls, asking random staffers, "How's it going? What's happenin'?"

Mrs. Dole wanted to help her husband, but she wasn't sure how. She worked incredibly hard for him, traveling at least four days a week (no press allowed on the plane). The day after Dole resigned from the Senate, Mrs. Dole was working the crowd in a parking lot at the Lodge of the Ozarks in Branson, Missouri. Even though it was 11 o'clock at night and she had been on the road all day, her lipstick shone, her hair was soft and waved, her smile was gracious, if fixed. Gamely climbing over mulch and bushes to reach well-wishers, she apologized in a Carolina drawl for her "boardinghouse reach" into the crowd, never once teetering back on her black high-heeled pumps. She was tireless and perfect. When she appeared on a daytime talk show called *Leeza*, it was hard to tell the hostess from the guest.

In her effort to be prepared, Elizabeth insisted that an aide write up a list of "common questions" (why does Dole want to be president? what is his position on abortion? on gun control?) and compose complete answers to each one. She memorized the document and used it to respond to Larry King, where she ended up outshining her husband. Later, she was hurt by reports that staffers no longer wanted the couple to do joint appearances.

Whatever her misgivings about the campaign, Elizabeth felt she had to operate by indirection. She could never barge into a staff meeting and upbraid her husband, as Hillary Clinton was reported to have done to the president on numerous occasions. She preferred to work on Dole through his aides and advisers. She felt that Jack Hilton, his speech coach, was a little too laid back. Try to spend more time with the candidate, she urged. Hilton shrugged that Dole was a "reluctant dragon." Hilton, in turn, asked Elizabeth to try to work on Dole. But she demurred; that would be too confrontational. Instead, Hilton gave Elizabeth a list of speaking dos and don'ts to pass along to her husband.

She did have some quite specific criticisms of the campaign operation. Why wasn't there more money for ads? Where were the "adults"? Where were the political sages, the Bakers and Deavers who had gotten Reagan and Bush elected in the 1980s? In May, it had been Mrs. Dole who recruited Donald Rumsfeld to play the role of senior adviser. A 62-year-old businessman who looks a little like Woodrow Wilson, Rumsfeld had held a variety of senior posts and cabinet jobs in the Nixon, Ford and Reagan administrations. He was disciplined and tough-minded, if not particularly visionary. But he didn't want a hands-on job, and he had no more luck bringing order to the Dole campaign than anyone else. Mrs. Dole was embarrassed when her criticism of the young and inexperienced staff leaked into the press. She protested to Scott Reed, with whom she got along well, that she had been misinterpreted. She wanted to send each staffer a personal note, but Reed stopped her. The notes would just leak.

Though she was not officially in the campaign chain of command, staffers made sure to check with her first. "See what Elizabeth thinks," Dole would mumble, even if he didn't always include her in his own decision-making. She persuaded Dole not to forget two-wage-earner families and working women in designing his tax plan and thought up one of his favorite speech lines ("veto Bill Clinton"). But she didn't feel comfortable trying to impose a theme or basic message on her husband.

As the convention approached, Elizabeth Dole decided that perhaps she could lend a hand more directly. If only people knew Bob, she would say. To help them know him better, she would tell the delegates—and the national audience beyond them—his story of suffering and redemption, the personal story he was too embarrassed to tell himself. She was, as ever, well prepared. Her plan—to leave the podium and work the convention floor, chatting with delegates like a kind of GOP Oprah—had all the spontaneity of a sorority tea dance. She had spoken with a lapel mike hundreds of times at local Red Cross chapters, as well as on the campaign trail. She actually felt more comfortable without a podium separating her from the audience.

Elizabeth's aides were nervous. The campaign was not known for the smoothness of its events, and the logistics of Elizabeth's stroll

President Clinton at the White House

Taking in the Election Night fireworks in Little Rock

The Clintons and Gores, Election Night in Little Rock

The Gores in Tennessee

Head to head

Clinton at a West Palm Beach rally

El Paso, Texas

Fiftieth birthday party at the Waldorf-Astoria Hotel, New York City

Clinton   Dole

Last day of campaigning in Iowa

The president campaigns in Florida.

Clinton campaigning in Longview, Washington

Clinton with a child cancer survivor

Clinton at a Tampa church during the last week of the campaign

Last week of the campaign: A little girl sings the national anthem in Union, New Jersey.

Clinton at the last campaign rally, Sioux Falls, South Dakota, November 4

A pensive Hillary

Clinton's nemesis, Al D'Amato, in the Oval Office

Peter Morgan/Matrix

Dick Morris and his wife, Eileen McGann, speak to the press outside
their Connecticut home.

George Mitchell prepping
Clinton in Saratoga, New York,
for the first debate (with Leon
Panetta)

After the first debate, Hartford,
Connecticut

The San Diego "town hall" debate

Chief of Staff
Leon Panetta
and White
House
photographer
Bob McNeely

Clinton on
Air Force
One, waiting
to disembark
for yet another
event,
Lexington,
Kentucky,
November

Campaign bus
with Bruce
Linsley,
Longview,
Washington

The power of
the
presidency:
Clinton
arrives in
Denver on Air
Force One.

Waiting to announce the signing
of the Welfare Reform Bill (with
George Stephanopoulos)

The president in Long Island after
the TWA crash

At ease in the Oval Office

Bipartisan meeting in
the Cabinet Room at
the White House, last
meeting

First daughter

Clinton and Gore watch election returns at the State House in
Little Rock.

Barbra Streisand, Election Night in Little Rock

Senate Leader Dole surrounded by reporters as he walks to his office
from the Senate Chamber in February

Dole in his Senate office in January 1996

Dole's last week as
senator

Dole with adviser Don
Sipple in Dole's office
prior to the State of the
Union response (Sipple
was later fired)

Gingrich and Dole talk to Clinton for forty minutes regarding the budget (in Dole's office).

Dole takes a last look at his Senate office after resigning.

Dole's last day in the Senate, with the governor of Kansas, in Dole's office

The day Dole left the Senate: Trent Lot and Senator Strom Thurmond in Dole's office

Last days in the Senate

Dole campaigns in Concord, New Hampshire

January: two faces of Dole in New Hampshire

The Doles in San Diego in the last two weeks of the campaign

The Republican Convention

Dole arrives at an El
Toro, California, air base
during the California
campaigning.

Bob and Liddy in
Washington, D.C.

A Dole supporter in Russell,
Kansas

Dole faces a Clinton supporter in
San Diego.

Dole talks to Clinton on his last day in the Senate.

Dole with his senior campaign staff in the D.C. headquarters. Left to right: Vin Weber, Don Rumsfeld, Jerry Jones, and Scott Reed.

Colin Powell at the Republican Convention

Dallas: Perot picks Pat Choate as his running mate.

Dole boards his campaign plane.

were daunting. Mari Will, who was still informally advising Mrs. Dole (she had given up her thankless job as campaign communications director), foresaw a nightmare scenario as delegates in elephant hats rushed Mrs. Dole as she came down to the floor. The technicians were worried that her lapel mike would fail because there was so much radio transmission in the hall. Mrs. Dole didn't want a handheld mike— she wanted to be able to reach out and touch people during her talk. But three handheld mikes were made ready, just in case. She was a little apprehensive about the 12 steps down to the floor, so a railing was installed. But she turned down offers to pace out the speech in advance. She just needed to know where every one would be, and she told the networks what path she would take, so cameras could be placed in the right positions.

When she ascended to the podium on Wednesday night, the normally bustling and noisy convention hall grew hushed. Her lapel mike did fail once she stepped down to the floor level, but she grabbed a replacement so smoothly that many reporters speculated the failure had been staged to show off her poise. The "Dole Stroll" was a hit.

Her husband was proud of her success—and for once he practiced to ensure his own. Still, there were some lengths to which he wouldn't go. An eighth-floor room at the Hyatt had been equipped with TelePrompTers and a model of the convention-hall podium; Dole called it the "torture room" and spent hardly any time there. He preferred to prepare for his speech by sitting on his hotel balcony, tanning himself and eating a bowl of chocolate ice cream. It was always hard for Dole to accept anyone's help, even when he needed it most, and now that prickliness began to chafe on his relationship with his speechwriter, Mark Helprin.

Helprin was a romantic. In his own mind, Dole was another Cortez. Like the 16th-century conquistador who scuttled his ships after arriving in the New World so his troops would have no choice but to follow him inland, Dole had abandoned his safe haven in the Senate. Helprin wanted Dole's acceptance speech in San Diego to burn with the flame of bold endeavor, to evoke a time of braver deeds and purer hearts. "Let me be the bridge to an America that only the undeserving call myth," Helprin wrote in an early draft. "Let me be

the bridge to a time of tranquillity, faith, and confidence in action."
He had flown to Kennebunkport to show the speech to George Bush,
who read it aloud one afternoon after lunch. The former president
heartily approved.

Dole, not surprisingly, objected to some of Helprin's flowery
language. At first, Helprin didn't mind. Dole was a Gary Cooper figure; Helprin respected his astringency. The novelist-speechwriter
could see that his first draft was too ripe, too emotional for Dole to
deliver. "Isn't that too much?" Dole would say. "Wouldn't that be
going too far?" The candidate also wanted to soften some of Helprin's
hard lines. The "undeserving" Americans who could not see Dole's
earlier, better America became merely "unknowing."

But as they worked on the speech through July, Helprin began
to bridle at Dole's changes. Helprin was proud of his reputation at
the *New Yorker* and the *Wall Street Journal* for being difficult to edit.
Editors wouldn't dare move a comma without his permission. Now,
when Dole wanted to change "the republic" to "the nation" to make
his speech less lofty, Helprin bristled. Of course, this was Dole's
speech, but the whole world knew Helprin was writing it.

And Dole began to grow irritated with Helprin. The author
would follow him as he trolled the hallways at headquarters, lobbying to preserve parts of the speech. Dole would give him "the stiff
arm," his typical forbidding gesture. "I'm giving the speech—not you,"
Dole would mutter. Dole ordered Helprin to add passages on crime
and education, on his role in legislating social security, food stamps,
and the Americans with Disabilities Act. Then he decided this
sounded too much like a laundry list, so he told Helprin to take some
of the programmatic sections out. Later, he reversed direction again,
adding bits on terrorism, trade and foreign policy. Dole was also uncomfortable with a barb at Hillary Clinton's book, *It Takes a Village*.
Helprin wrote pointedly that it takes a "family" to raise a child. Dole
didn't want to be seen as attacking the first lady, though he felt better when Senator Kay Bailey Hutchinson used a similar line in her
convention speech and seemed to get away with it.

Most of all, Dole was unhappy with Helprin's tone, which
he found too preachy, a sort of eat-your-peas sermon on the need for

sacrifice. His political instincts told him to be upbeat, positive, for-ward-looking. But as usual, Dole was unable to discuss his objections in a way that produced a coherent result. Without telling Helprin, he brought in his old Senate speechwriter, Kerry Tymchuk, to draft a new ending. Tymchuk had read a bootlegged copy of the speech and was horrified by the harsh tone. He thought the text was mi-sogynistic. Women, already wary of Dole, would flee across the wid-ening gender gap. Tymchuk was also dubious about all that "bridge" language, hearkening back to the past. Shouldn't Dole be more fu-ture-oriented? A backward-looking vision by a Republican candidate who was more than 70 years old would be a dream come true for Democratic image makers. Tymchuk shared his concerns with Sheila Burke, Dole's old Senate chief of staff, and Richard Norton Smith, author of the let-Dole-be-Dole memo. They in turn appealed through the back channel to Elizabeth, who forwarded their suggestions to Dole.

Their concerns were well-founded. Rule one of campaigning is to talk about the future, not the past, particularly if age is a factor in the campaign. Indeed, over at the White House, President Clinton's speechwriters had already written a line about a "bridge to the future" in the draft of the acceptance speech that Clinton was scheduled to give in Chicago at the end of August. The contrast with Dole's "bridge to the past" could hardly fail to play in the president's favor.

Typically, Dole compromised without telling anyone. Instead of bypassing Helprin's bridge to the past, he added a detour at the end of it. Tymchuk and Smith wrote a new ending in which Dole pronounced himself to be "the most optimistic man in America." The sunny, forward-looking peroration hardly squared with the elegiac, backward-looking beginning. But the author of the first part never discussed the matter with the authors of the second.

In his San Diego hotel room, Helprin was furious when he learned his speech was being rewritten behind his back. He decided to pack his bags and go home. When Dole called on him for some more help on Tuesday afternoon, two days before the speech, he had gone swimming with Peggy Noonan, Reagan's old speechwriter.

Tracked down after he returned from Coronado Beach, Helprin told John Buckley, "I just can't do it."

"If you leave, things will get ugly," said Buckley.

"What do you mean? Is that a threat?" said Helprin.

"I'm just trying to protect you," said Buckley.

"From what?"

"From being seen as a huffy prima donna who is having a hissy fit." (Buckley says he never used the term "hissy fit" and that he spoke to Helprin after he learned that the speechwriter was talking to reporters.) Helprin left anyway, provoking a raft of stories that the speech was going badly on the eve of the convention.

To measure the convention's impact on voters, the campaign filled two rooms with citizens, one in Denver, one in Atlanta, and asked them to register their reactions by twisting a dial. The needle started at 50; readings at 80 and 90 were considered exceptional. Colin Powell's speech Monday night rocketed toward 100. Elizabeth Dole's walk-and-talk hit readings almost as high. Dole's speech received 60s and 70s—good but not great. It was enough, though, to give the campaign a much-needed sense of momentum. As the delegates disbanded, the campaign's internal polls showed Clinton's lead cut to three points. The Dole team was ecstatic. They were back in the election.

There were a few doubters. Alone among Dole's pollsters, Fred Steeper had been through every presidential campaign since 1972—including Bush's failed campaign in 1992—and the experience had hardened his natural pessimism. "Dr. Doom" believed that Dole needed to be ahead after San Diego to have a shot at beating Clinton in November. The Democrats were sure to get their own bounce in Chicago. The week after San Diego, Steeper predicted that Dole would be down by 10 points by Labor Day. No modern presidential candidate who was that far behind at the beginning of September had ever won.

On Labor Day, Dole was down by at least 10 points in almost every media poll. On September 5, three days later, his own polls showed him 20 points behind, his lowest level yet.

12 ■ THE MORRIS DANCE

On August 19, his 50th birthday, Bill Clinton sat in the front of Air Force One, reading Stephen Ambrose's *Undaunted Courage*. The night before he had been feted at a huge fund-raiser/birthday party at Radio City in New York. The CIA's briefing in the morning had been a gag: the spooks reported that Moscow had gone on alert after detecting an "unidentified heat source" in midtown Manhattan (the blaze of candles on Clinton's birthday cake) and that the leader of a rogue African nation had defected the night before on *Larry King Live*. The CIA also thoughtfully listed the ages of leaders around the globe, to make Clinton feel younger by comparison. Clinton had spent most of his birthday with Chelsea, Hillary and the Gore family, helping to rebuild a black church burned down in Tennessee. Now, he put aside his book and his papers to talk to a reporter about his decision to sign the welfare bill that had been passed by Congress at the end of July.

There had been tremendous opposition from some of his oldest friends and closest aides. Marion Wright Edelman, the social activist who had gone to law school with Hillary, pleaded with Clinton to veto the Republican bill, which ended welfare as a federal entitlement program. She warned that children would starve as a result. Both George Stephanopoulos and Harold Ickes had urged the president to take a stand, to make a political virtue of facing down the GOP. But Dick Morris had urged the president to sign the bill—

to show that he was a centrist at heart, to demonstrate to swing voters that he was willing to take a hard line and put the poor to work.
Unknown to most of the others, the first lady was also privately counseling Clinton to sign the bill. If the bill hurt the poor, she advised
her husband, then he could fix it in his second term. The important
thing was to get reelected first.

On July 31, Clinton had called together a dozen advisers and
cabinet members to help him decide. A slight majority urged him to
veto the bill. Liberals, led by HHS Secretary Donna Shalala, argued
that the bill was deeply flawed. Bruce Reed, a softspoken veteran of
the 1992 campaign, made the argument for the centrist new Democrats. He reminded Clinton that when the Republican Congress
started talking about welfare reform in 1994, Gingrich had framed
the debate in terms of orphanages and cutting off aid to teenage
mothers. Faced with White House opposition, the Republicans had
moderated their position and had already taken out the most objec-
tionable provisions in their bill, Reed said. They were unlikely to offer
anything better in a second term. Clinton agreed. And if the Democrats won back Congress, the president said, they would be unlikely
to produce any sort of welfare-reform legislation at all. "We made a
promise to the people in 1992 to end welfare as we know it," Reed
concluded. "This bill isn't perfect, but it keeps that promise. We would
have a hard time explaining to the American people why we didn't
do it."

After a couple of hours, Clinton said, "Okay, listen, I've
worked on this for 16 years, I'm going to go into my office and make
up my mind." Summoning Gore and Leon Panetta into the Oval
Office, he announced, "I'm going to sign it." Looking back at that
decision on the Air Force One flight two weeks later, Clinton said
that he had not lost any sleep over it. "When I first became president," he said, "I was always worried that I would have to make big
decisions based completely on other people's advice. I was afraid, you
know, that I'd get hit with some great foreign policy crisis before I
had a chance to get my sea legs. But this was an area where I well
recognized the need for enormous humility. Nobody's been able to

solve this problem, and I might be wrong. I just believe that it is worth the risk." As the president's plane soared along on a summer's evening, Clinton seemed content.

There were times, his aides thought, when Bill Clinton acted more like a campaign consultant than a president. No detail seemed too trivial for the chief executive. He would edit his own fund-raising mail. He could tell you how many copying machines there were at campaign headquarters, and he wanted to know who was traveling on each campaign trip and at which hotel they were staying. He could spend hours analyzing polling data, screening commercials, debating the pros and cons of negative advertising. He loved to chew over the '92 precinct returns while watching the '96 primary results. He even wrote some of his own speeches, usually refining them in the back seat of his limousine on the way to the event.

And there were times when Dick Morris acted more like a president than a campaign consultant. Here was a man who could announce to a receptionist at a dentist's office that he was "running the country," who, when asked at a dinner party if he had anything to do with bombing the Serbs answered, "Well, I didn't fly the plane," who could—in the presence of others—scold the president for making decisions without consulting him first. Morris bragged that he operated under "Hillary rules": if Clinton could tell his wife, he could tell Morris.

By the summer of 1996, White House aides had become accustomed to seeing Morris scurrying along, his leonine head and squat, barrel-chested torso balanced on short legs, his manner at once fidgety and nervous and utterly self-assured. He rarely made eye contact, instead conducting conversations with staffers while squinting at the tiny screen of his Casio handheld computer. "Let's see where we are on this," he would say, jabbing at the keys with his index finger. If he wasn't fiddling with his Casio, he was talking on his cell

phone, and sometimes doing both at once. A young aide trailed behind to take commands. When he entered a room, he would introduce himself to people he had already met several times: "Hi, I'm Dick
Morris, the president's political adviser."

He expressed everything with an air of certainty that others
found insufferable. "I'm not arguing what I think," he would say when
challenged, "I'm arguing what I know." He quoted Bob Dylan and
mused about the "Hegelian synthesis." When he described his trade-
mark theory, triangulation, he was just as likely to allude to the French
parliament as Gingrich's Congress. He thought Clinton might pick
up a trick or two from the pomp of the French presidency. His "gloire
de France" modes led the White House speechwriters to call him "De
Gaulle" behind his back. Most White House aides just called him
"Dick."

At meetings, he would ask with archaic politeness, "May
I be seated?" But he didn't hesitate to talk back to the president.
After one meeting in the Yellow Oval, he had blown up at Clinton
for appointing Evelyn Lieberman as deputy chief of staff to replace
Erskine Bowles, who was leaving to run a venture capital firm. "I
thought we had a mutual consultation agreement," Morris scolded
the president in front of the others who stayed behind. "You've gotten everything so far," Clinton snapped back. "Your pollsters, your
media team." Referring to Bob Squier's close ties to Gore, Clinton
continued to bristle: "Hell, you've practically turned the vice president into your employee. Everyone's on a team around here but no
one's on the president's team." Clinton sulked. Stung by Clinton's
criticism, Morris bolted Washington the next morning. The day
after that, he secretly signed a $2.5 million book contract with
Random House to tell his version of the campaign.

Morris was obsessed with control. Though only a political
consultant, he thought nothing of calling subcabinet officials and,
in the name of the president, demanding action on his pet policies.
Within his own staff, he wanted to know who was meeting with
whom, even socially, and what they discussed. He threw tantrums if
he suspected a staffer of talking to a reporter, but met secretly with a

stream of journalists in his suite at the Jefferson Hotel. Once, when he spotted two reporters chatting, one on the way out from seeing Morris, the other on the way in, he joked, "Gentleman callers in a brothel don't talk to each other." He loved codes and conspiracies. When talking on his cell phone, "A" was the president, "B" was Hillary, "C" was Chelsea.

White House staffers laughed at Morris's behavior between their spasms of outrage. But they also paid attention. They could see the results in every tracking poll. Over the past year and a half, Morris and his pollster, Mark Penn, had found a way of talking to the swing voters—the young marrieds with children who were worried about the declining morality and civility of American society. These people didn't trust government to come up with grand schemes, and they thought Congress was a hopeless sinkhole. But they were grateful for small, concrete steps that might improve the quality of their lives. Morris was fascinated with executive power. Presidential statements and commissions could succeed where haggling with Congress could not. Throughout the spring and the summer, Clinton made headlines with his pronouncements supporting school uniforms, teenage curfews, V-chips to screen out smut on TV, tobacco ad bans, and tuition tax credits. Even if the media ridiculed his proposals as petty and dubbed Clinton the "mayor-in-chief," the strategy was working. Young suburban parents—"soccer moms," in the new political vernacular—were responding. By summer, Clinton's personal- and job-approval ratings were in the low 60s—record territory for this president. At campaign headquarters and in the White House, people began whispering the word "landslide."

Morris's great gift, said White House aide Bruce Reed, was "to imagine things that others thought were unthinkable." Back in the spring of 1995, the man called "Charlie" had seemed delusional to most White House aides. A Democratic president who could embrace a balanced budget, shove crime and welfare down the Republicans' throats and win a landslide victory only two years after his party had lost control of Congress for the first time in 40 years? Impossible. But Morris's ability to fantasize and fashion a wildly different reality had won over a small group of Clintonites (Vice President Gore, White House counsel Jack Quinn, deputy chief of staff Erskine Bowles, director of communications Don Baer, domestic policy adviser Reed). "It's not easy to get the government to do things," said Reed. "That's what Morris was incredibly good at. He had this way of ignoring obstacles that stopped other people. I'm not even sure he saw them." Over time, others came around. Stephanopoulos and Panetta accepted him grudgingly by the spring of 1996. Only Harold Ickes remained an unalterable foe, but he knew Morris had Clinton's ear.

When some of Morris's dreams became real, he dreamt up even wilder ones. His overreaching became increasingly laughable. In February, when he learned that anti-tobacco activist Victor Crawford was dying, he urged Clinton to rush to his deathbed for a photo op. "When should we do this?" asked Panetta, with mock seriousness. "Quickly!" Morris answered, oblivious to the sarcasm. "He's dying!" Another time, Morris proposed a rating system for violent toys. White House staffers gave up after they couldn't figure out how to classify squirt guns.

In early August, George Stephanopoulos called Morris to tell him about a major scientific discovery. Analysis of a meteorite that had fallen to earth from Mars showed fossilized evidence that life had once existed there. "This is going to break and we need to respond to it," said Stephanopoulos.

"This is huge. Huge!" Morris responded. Life on Mars was futuristic, millennial, spiritual—just the story for the man who would lead the nation into the 21st century. It was so obvious: Clinton = future; Dole = past. Mars could be Clinton's New Frontier. "I've got it," he blurted to Stephanopoulos after a couple of seconds. "We announce a manned mission to Mars."

Stephanopoulos sighed and hung up, but Morris started working his cell phone. He placed calls to the technological experts in Gore's office (the vice president was a fan of the space program). He called NASA, he called the rest of his team, he called anyone who would listen. "We need to get on this!" he bellowed. Between poring over poll results and viewing ads, Morris thought nothing of tugging on the levers of the federal government to get immediate authorization for a manned mission to Mars. He invoked the summer hit movie, *Independence Day*, about a president who fights off space invaders. Life on Mars was the ultimate triangulation, he argued. Clinton as leader of the Earthlings, boldly going where no Democrat had gone before. Morris thought Clinton should schedule an Oval Office address on the subject. A mere candidate, like Dole, could not announce a mission to Mars. But a president could. "People will get this," Morris insisted. "This is really big. Huge!"

The only real thing that was launched was another round of Dick Morris jokes. "Dick, we've got good news and bad news," went one. "The good news is that we've agreed to go ahead with the manned mission you proposed. The bad news is: you're the man. How soon can you be ready?" Stephanopoulos cracked, "There's life on Mars. Dick's proof."

Morris became especially agitated during the Republican convention in San Diego. He was impressed by Elizabeth Dole's performance and worried when Dole's favorable ratings rose into the 50s in Penn's overnight tracking polls. For the first time since the race began, Clinton's lead dropped into single digits. Morris began fretting that his handiwork was becoming undone. Now, with the Democratic convention approaching, Morris wanted to dictate every detail of proceedings. Without consulting anyone, he banged out speeches for Hillary and Gore. His language, always florid, was becoming rococo. For a section on children's issues in the first lady's speech, Morris wrote, "Bloom, little ones, wherever you are planted." Upon reading Morris's draft, Harry Thomasson, the Clinton friend and Hollywood producer brought in to stage the Chicago convention, drawled, "Dick's gone bad. Someone's gonna have to put him down." Some of the other consultants began wondering if it was time to relieve Morris of his command, just like in World War II navy movies.

A few days before the convention, Morris showed up in Gore's office with an unsolicited draft of the vice president's speech. Instead of dropping off the speech for Gore to study at his convenience,

Morris planted himself behind an old wingback chair and began to orate. The dimunitive consultant bounced up and down behind the chair, bellowing as if he were addressing a packed convention hall. When he got to the applause lines, he excitedly thumped on the side of the chair. Eager to spare the White House antiques, Gore and others applauded dramatically whenever Morris started slapping the chair. After Morris left, Gore turned to his slack-jawed advisers. "Well," the vice president said, "that was entertaining." He threw away Morris's speech.

Morris was furious when he didn't get his way. He cussed out Ron Klain, Gore's chief of staff, over the speech that paralyzed actor Christopher Reeve was to deliver on the first night of the convention. He fought so angrily with adman Bob Squier over the keynote address to be given by Indiana governor Evan Bayh that the two men stopped speaking to each other. He sparred with Harold Ickes, who refused to listen to his harangues and threw him out of his office. Inevitably, the spats spilled into the press. "Top Strategist Losing His Grip on Campaign," headlined the *Wall Street Journal* as the Democats headed for Chicago. No one knew it at the time, but Morris had bigger problems brewing with a less reputable paper.

Morris's home in Washington was "the King Suite," a $440-a-night bedroom and drawing room at the Jefferson Hotel, six blocks from the White House. The suite was tastefully appointed with faux antiques and oil paintings of 19th-century European pastoral scenes. It was one of only two suites in the hotel with a balcony. Beginning in August 1995, Morris had been visited there on a regular basis by a $200-an-hour call girl named Sherry Rowlands. In July 1996, Rowlands called on the editors of the *Star*, a supermarket tabloid based in Tarrytown, New York. She described in detail Morris's fondness for fondling and licking Rowlands's feet, how he liked to read foot-fetish magazines, and how, on one occasion, he paraded around the hotel room "on all fours, like a dog." Never reluctant to show off, Morris let Rowlands listen in on his phone conversations with the president. During one discussion, according to Rowlands, Clinton became irate at Morris's suggestion that he cut Medicare to make a budget deal. She quoted the president as saying, "Aw hell, Dick, I don't want to wake up in the morning and see a whole bunch of cripples in wheelchairs chained to my front gate."

Morris lavished champagne and gifts on her, but as she explained to the *Star*'s editors, she became put off by his tastes and his indiscretions. Morris would describe his petty feuds with Stephanopoulos and Ickes. "She came to be quite offended by the way he was acting—and how childish they [the White House staff] all were," said Richard Gooding, the *Star* writer assigned to the story. "She told me, 'I think grown-ups ought to be running the country.'" Her motives in coming to the *Star* were not entirely patriotic. Unlike mainstream news organizations, the *Star* pays for news. Rowlands may have read reports that in 1992 the *Star* paid Gennifer Flowers some $200,000 for her story of an affair with Bill Clinton.

The *Star*, with 2.5 million readers, calls itself a "responsible tabloid." The paper's editors wanted some proof. Rowlands turned over diaries she had kept, her private key to the King Suite, and a copy of a check signed over to her by Morris. She even told them about the discovery of life on Mars—a secret, she claimed, "only seven people in the world know about." Still, "we wanted to see it with our own eyes," said Dick Belsky, the paper's news editor.

The paper and the hooker joined forces on a memorable sting. Rowlands had a Yorkshire terrier named Bijou (French for jewel; the name was Morris's idea). On the evening of Thursday, August 22, four days from the opening of the Chicago convention, Rowlands brought Bijou to the King Suite for a little romp. She found Morris agitated about the convention. She listened in as Morris called the editor of *Time* magazine, Walter Isaacson, and told him, in a moment of rare modesty, that he didn't want to upstage the president by being on the cover of the magazine. "You don't have my permission to put me on the cover!" bellowed Morris. (*Time* did it anyway.)

Rowlands opened the door to the terrace to let Bijou scamper out. Morris followed, hugging and kissing Bijou's owner as they sat outside in the warm twilight in their bathrobes. Several floors above, a *Star* photographer started snapping pictures.

Hillary Clinton would seem to be Dick Morris's exact opposite. What did an earnest, left-leaning, do-gooder first lady have in common with a cynical consultant who was determined to reposition her husband to the right? The answer, of course, was pragmatism. It had been Hillary who placed the call to Morris in 1980, when Clinton was defeated as governor of Arkansas after only one term, begging him to come back and salvage her husband's career. Likewise, the first lady was glad to have Morris return to the fold after the GOP sweep in 1994 made Clinton look like a one-termer. Still, Hillary's respect for Morris did not extend to affection. She viewed Morris like "an electric appliance," said an aide, to be plugged in, used and then returned to the shelf.

Morris was equally cold-blooded in his assessment of Mrs. Clinton. He saw her as a useful lightning rod. Whitewater, Morris told the president, was Hillary's legal problem, not his political problem. Besides, voters liked seeing Clinton spring to her defense. It seemed manly. Whenever Whitewater flared, Morris would repeat, "It doesn't move the numbers." He was oblivious to the emotional anguish caused by the headlines and subpoenas. Morris was more interested in Hillary as a prop. He pushed for a "softer look" and urged her to wear "jewel" colors like jade and lapis, more pastels and dresses instead of suits.

Hillary would just roll her eyes. She was perfectly capable of changing her own hairdo (the only "fun benefit of the job," she joked). But she made sure to listen to Morris's strategic advice. She did not attend the political meetings in the Yellow Oval—her presence might be misinterpreted—but she sent her chief of staff, Maggie Williams, to take notes, and she received private briefings directly from Morris.

She was intrigued by Morris's distinction between public values and private character. During one of their private briefings, as Morris explained for the umpteenth time how voters would judge Clinton by his performance, not his reputation, Hillary laughed wistfully and said with a trace of sarcasm, "Can you do that for me, too?"

Hillary seemed to live in two irreconcilable worlds. On her foreign trips, she was revered as something close to a saint—a guardian of human rights, children and womanhood. As she traveled around the United States, thousands of women came out, teetering on folding chairs in crowded halls just to catch a glimpse. She was a role model and a heroine. But back home in Washington, she was still written about by the press as a pushy yuppie overachiever. Prosecutors and investigators hounded her. The miasma of Whitewater would dissipate and then come wafting back. In early January, just as she was about to go on book tour to promote *It Takes a Village*, a memo by a former White House staffer turned up implicating her in Travelgate, and her long-sought law firm billing records were suddenly discovered. "Saint or Sinner?" asked a *Newsweek* cover story. "This is like the Twilight Zone," she moaned. "What next?" A few weeks later, author Jim Stewart's Whitewater narrative, *Bloodsport*, was excerpted in a *Time* cover story. The red M in the *Time* logo seemed like two horns rising from Mrs. Clinton's head.

The president's usual reaction, in moments like these, was to turn purple, explode, blame someone—and then feel better about himself. Mrs. Clinton tended to keep her anger inside. At times she became depressed and listless, at other times she was the Sister Frigidaire of her high-school nickname. But with her own staff, she dealt with adversity by playing the good mother. She would laugh— a deep belly laugh—and giggle and gossip about their boyfriends and visiting celebrities. Her staff sometimes called her the Big Girl in the Big House, and they were very loyal, despite the legal bills they accumulated testifying on her behalf. At a going-away party for Lisa Caputo in August, Hillary toasted her 31-year-old press secretary, noting with some bitterness, "I'm sure you thought you were coming here to work on the issues the American people sent us to take care

of. I'm sure it never occurred to you that people would be so interested in 16-year-old land deals. You never expect a single phone call
will result in $100,000 in legal bills. You get suited up every morn-
ing and you don't know what you're facing. It's not what you came
here for."

Humor was an effective antidote. The day Bob Woodward's
book appeared, with its revelations of the first lady's imagined conversations with Eleanor Roosevelt, Mrs. Clinton told an audience in
Tennessee, "Eleanor sends her best." George Stephanopoulos, a bach-
elor, saw her a few days later and asked if she could set him up with
Helen of Troy. "No problem," she giggled. The gallows humor was
infectious. Her staff joked about opening up a specialty boutique
in Washington called "the Hearing Line." It would sell testimony-
appropriate dresses to female witnesses at court or congressional hear-
ings. For the grand jury, primness was essential. For the Hill, dress
for TV, but never wear red; it clashed with the red cover on Senator
Alfonse D'Amato's witness table.

Hillary also found relief in her role as mother. Her real worry,
her aides said in late summer, was not Whitewater, but the prospect
of Chelsea, now 16, going away to college. The first couple began to
talk more earnestly about adopting a child. Living over the store
meant that the Clintons were able to see Chelsea a good deal, despite
their hectic schedules. Mrs. Clinton would leave the most important
meetings to take Chelsea's calls, or slip away to help with homework;
when she emerged from the residence looking haggard one morning,
she explained, "I was up late working on the Mesopotamians." At
supper, the first family would hold hands and pray. Their intimacy
may have been heightened by a sense that the enemy lurked just
outside the gates and down in the pressroom. Even when Chelsea
had been a little girl in the governor's mansion in Little Rock, the
Clintons had tried to prepare her for the cruelties of the media
by "role playing," acting out what to say and do about unfair scurri-
lous attacks.

The Clintons were fiercely protective. Any aide who suggested using Chelsea as a campaign prop got the Sister Frigidaire stare.

At Sidwell Friends, Chelsea's private school, her classmates were given First Kid sensitivity training. ("Pretend you're Chelsea. Would you want to try out for the school play?") Classroom doors were locked, and students had to knock and give their names. (They soon rebelled and started using passwords instead, such as "Have the lambs stopped crying?" from the chiller movie *Silence of the Lambs*.) Chelsea was never made available for photos or interviews. Remarkably, the press behaved. There were a few nasty skits on TV talk shows and *Saturday Night Live* making fun of Chelsea's teenage looks, but the producers later apologized. *Spy* magazine dropped a story about her, and the worst the *National Enquirer* could do was to consult with beauty experts asking what Chelsea would look like in ten years. (Answer: beautiful.)

Before she died, Jacqueline Kennedy Onassis had given Mrs. Clinton some tips on raising children in the White House. Her advice boiled down to: keep the press away and try to create normalcy. A "normal" childhood was hard in a house with 132 rooms and more than a hundred employees, but the Clintons tried. After a private screening for her friends in the White House theater, Chelsea had to take a broom and sweep up the popcorn. During the summer of '94, Chelsea wanted to go camping in the Tetons, so the Clintons did—and while they slept under the stars, 25 Secret Service agents with night-vision goggles roamed the woods.

Chelsea had looked like a frightened, awkward preteen at the 1992 Democratic convention, especially as she stood next to the svelte, blond Gore children. But when she reemerged in the public eye in 1996 she was clearly a poised, lovely young woman, affectionate with her parents and easy company with strangers. Some advisers wanted to feature her prominently at the convention. The president was furious over rumors that Chelsea would make a speech. But she wanted to ride on "the 21st Century Express," Clinton's whistle-stop train to Chicago, and go to the convention parties, including a bash given by JFK Jr. She got her way.

As the convention planning took shape, some Clinton staffers worried that a major speech by Hillary would revive charges that she was an unelected copresident. Morris suggested that she tape video greetings from various venues around Chicago—the lake, a ballpark, a candy store. Too cute, said Hillary. Besides, she wanted to make a speech about families in response to Dole's dig at her book, *It Takes a Village*, in San Diego. She was nervous when she went to the podium on Tuesday night. She had never spoken to such a large audience, and she was unaccustomed to TelePrompTers. But the audience didn't mind. They roared when Hillary fired back at Dole, "Yes, it takes a village. And it takes a president." She spoke slowly and earnestly in her slightly schoolmarmish way. She mentioned Chelsea six times, including her stay in the hospital for a tonsil operation. (To charges of exploitation, her aides insisted that in a speech about family values, Mrs. Clinton could hardly not talk about her own daughter.)

The speech was a hit with the voters the campaign cared about: working women aged 25 to 50. "She locked 'em up," said an adviser. Her "favorables" with that group soared into the 70s. And her overall favorable rating crept back into the 50s. The message on Tuesday night was exactly what the convention image makers had hoped for: Democrats are pro-family. Through no fault of the Clintons, that theme was about to get a rude jolt.

Mike McCurry, the president's spokesman, got the call aboard "the 21st Century Express" on Wednesday afternoon as the train approached Michigan City, Indiana, on the last leg of Clinton's whistle-stop tour to Chicago. It was Dick Morris with some awkward news. The next day—the day of President Clinton's speech—a tabloid was going to run a story alleging that Morris had solicited sex with a prostitute. "How should we handle this?" Morris asked nervously.

We? thought McCurry. He said, "You know how these tabloids work, Dick." They don't always have the evidence to back the allegation. Morris started to fill him in on the lurid details. "Stop,

Dick," said McCurry. He didn't want to hear the details. The less he knew, the less he would have to confirm or deny. McCurry had once joked that his job entailed the art of "telling the truth slowly." But Morris was getting frantic. What would Clinton say?

The president was told later that evening as his limousine headed for the helicopter to take him to Chicago. He was weary after four days of nonstop campaigning. He knew, from painful experience, the damage a tabloid story could do. He instructed his aides to be careful, not to jump to conclusions. But if the story was true, said the president, "it's not tolerable."

Meanwhile, Morris was telling the other consultants about the story. He was now in full denial. "This thing will blow over," he said. "The president and I have never been closer." Morris at the moment was about to host a dinner for his closest aides in Suite 3331 of the Chicago Sheraton. It was supposed to be a victory celebration, a coming-out party of sorts. Morris's face was on the cover of *Time*, and he was the subject of a front-page *USA Today* profile. He was finally getting the credit he deserved.

Morris and his wife, Eileen McGann, were composed as the guests arrived. There were toasts and laughter, and a glorious sunset over the lakeside skyline. Waiters proffered platters of shrimp and flutes of champagne. Morris played the benevolent pasha, presenting a young assistant with a chocolate mousse birthday cake. At 8:30, he showed his guests the door. The vice president was speaking in an hour and a half. "Folks, there's a show tonight," Morris exclaimed. "Go to the convention! Have a great time!"

Shortly after ten, there was a knock on Morris's door. It was Erskine Bowles, a courtly, patrician southerner who was both a top aide and close friend of the president (their wives had been classmates at Wellesley). Bowles suggested that, in view of the *Star* revelations, Morris take a leave of absence from the campaign. Morris wasn't listening. "Why am I not hearing from the president on this matter?" he kept demanding. At 1:30 A.M., Bowles called in Jack Quinn, the tough-minded White House counsel. Quinn coolly asked Morris if he had a right to cast a shadow over the campaign. Morris insisted that he was not the issue. The question was whether the campaign would stand up to yellow journalism. Morris seemed convinced he could talk his way out of the jam.

The White House pair persisted. You will become the issue, they said. It's not fair to the president. Do the right thing, Dick. Morris finally relented, but he spent the next few hours haggling over ways to save face as he made his forced exit. He wanted no announcement of his resignation until he was airborne (Eileen was terrified of being ambushed by reporters). Morris and Morris alone would write his resignation statement. No one from the White House or the campaign would comment on the substance of the *Star*'s allegations—not now, not ever. The campaign still owed him $100,000 from August ad commissions. He would have to be paid.

Quinn, the White House counsel, listened patiently, but he was disgusted with the way Morris was playing the victim. Morris's resignation statement compared himself to a Christian being tossed to the lions. Quinn told Morris his draft went too far, especially the part about being "deeply honored to help this president come back from being buried in a landslide." It was insulting to the president, said Quinn. It's my resignation, Morris yelled back. He couldn't understand why he was being bullied by mere underlings. "Why am I not hearing from the president?" he demanded once again.

Morris did not sleep. At 7:30 A.M., his fellow consultants began arriving, paged for an "emergency meeting." Morris was red-eyed and uncharacteristically disheveled. Eileen was distraught. Morris showed his resignation statement to Hank Sheinkopf, a friend and fellow consultant. "Hey, Dick," said Sheinkopf, trying to lighten the moment. "You're a Jew. Can the lion shit." Morris punched at his laptop. He substituted, "I will not subject my wife, family, or friends to the sadistic vitriol of yellow journalism." Eileen, standing amidst the suitcases, talked to the early arrivals. A professional litigator, she seemed more furious than sad. "Clinton gets away with this shit all the time," she said. "Why should Dick have to go?" Morris was still despondent over Clinton's silence. "I would have hoped my friend would have at least called me," he said.

By 8:15, Morris's team, a score of pollsters and admen and assistants, was assembled, perched uncomfortably around Morris as he slumped in a plush chair in the corner of his suite. "I wanted to say good-bye to all of you," Morris said, his voice cracking. "To thank you." His voice broke. "I'm having difficulty speaking," he croaked. He reached for his laptop and typed furiously. He turned the screen for the group to see. "TO MY FRIENDS WITH WHOM I HAVE SERVED," it began. "I have loved being part of our joint, thrilling effort." He had listed his colleagues one by one ("Mark Penn, thank you for your mind. . . . Bob Squier, thank you for your wisdom and experience. I should have talked to you more. . . ."). He asked that his staff be allowed to continue working with the consultants, "not with the wolves at the White House"; he asked for "any financial arrangements" the others could make, a suggestion that struck some of the other consultants as a request for kickbacks on their future commissions (Morris stood to make at least $1 million from the campaign, depending on how the advertising commissions were divided up); and promised to "treat each of you generously and fairly in anything I might say or write. I truly love what we have been together."

Embarrassed and shocked, the consultants filed out. Morris and Eileen made for the elevator, shielded by aides. The first person they saw in the hallway was Chelsea Clinton. Morris shrank back. In the lobby, after his aides hustled Morris into his car, they ran into James Carville, the ubiquitous former campaign strategist from 1992. "Hey y'all," Carville smiled. "What's goin' on?"

In the pressroom of the Chicago Sheraton, reporters were already pawing over copies of the *New York Post*, which had reprinted excerpts of the *Star*'s "Love Diaries." The reporters had been in a surly mood. The Democrats, like the Republicans in San Diego, had larded the convention schedule with treacly confessionals and true-grit testimonials—Christopher Reeve for the Democrats, victims of rape and AIDS for the Republicans. This was the year that both parties made the leap into Oprahland, when the convention was drained of conflict and content and transformed instead into talk TV. The 15,000 reporters in town felt like extras milling around a soundstage. The Morris debacle came as journal-istic deliverance.

With hoots and guffaws, the reporters read that the president's chief campaign adviser got turned on by standing in his underwear whistling a sort of "Popeye, the Sailor Man" tune while snapping off a salute. That he called the president "the Monster" and the first lady "the Twister" (Stephanopoulos was "Stumpy"). That he let a hooker listen in while he talked to them on the phone. Gobbling jelly donuts, passing around well-thumbed copies, the reporters bayed, "Where's McCurry?" One reporter joked, "This is finally starting to feel like a Clinton campaign again."

Upstairs on the 31st floor, Clinton was exasperated. "Do I need this today?" he irritably asked his advisers. Here he was, worn out and hoarse from four days of stumping on a train, about to give the most important speech of the campaign. He had been hawking family values like a preacher and now all the talk-show hosts could talk about was foot-fetishists. He read Morris's farewell screed. It sounded like something O. J. Simpson might write.

Hillary was fearful that Morris might try to kill himself. She instructed her husband's staff that no one was to gloat over his down-fall. Dick, she said, needed help, not condemnation or ridicule. No one mentioned the name on all of their minds. "Can you imagine if anything had happened?" said a White House aide a few weeks later. "It would have been Vince Foster all over again. You can just hear it: Why didn't anyone see it coming? What secrets did Morris take to his grave? Who took his files?"

That afternoon, Hillary and the president, as well as Vice President Gore, called Morris to express their concern and support for him during his "ordeal." Other friends and colleagues called the next day. One was a little taken aback to hear him giving instruc-tions to a photographer in the background. It seemed that Dick and Eileen where posing for the cover of Time magazine. "It's a bit hectic now, I'll call you back later," said Morris. It soon came out that Morris had signed a $2.5 million book deal. Over the weekend, he agreed to be interviewed by each of the three networks—if they agreed to hire him as a political commentator for the elections. Two weeks later, he showed up in a chauffeured limousine at the *New Yorker* magazine in Manhattan for a breakfast performance before the magazine's advertisers with Harvard professor Henry Louis Gates. The topic: politics and ethics.

White House staffers rejoiced at Morris's departure. At the next meeting of the political group in the Yellow Oval, Panetta gave a brief, polite appreciation of Morris's contribution to the campaign. Then he sat down in Morris's chair. Mark Penn stood up to report on the latest polls. The convention bump had pushed Clinton's lead back into double digits. Morris's scandal didn't appear to be hurting the president. If anything, the contrast with his fallen adviser made Clinton seem more presidential. Gore joked that he hoped the other consultants would be available to get into trouble if the president ever dropped behind.

In a real sense, Morris had been only half of a strategic team. The other, less flamboyant half was Mark Penn. Whereas Morris wore pinstripes and Italian loafers, Penn looked like a high-tech Pigpen, shambling along with beepers, cell phones and laptops, his shirttails flapping. Though he sometimes spoke in dense pollsterese, droning on about "persuadables" and "message clusters," he was adept at framing the right message. Clinton loved to talk to him, and in particular loved his optimism.

Penn was particularly excited about one of his new findings. Americans were becoming optimistic about the future. For the first time in Clinton's presidency, more people said the country was on the right track than the wrong track. When Penn had first started polling for Clinton in the spring of 1995, "wrong track" had led "right track" 56 percent to 32 percent. By the second week of August 1996, 43 percent of voters said the country was on the right track, 42 percent wrong track. The last president to have a "right track" majority, Penn knew, was Ronald Reagan.

13 ■ PLAY IT AGAIN, ROSS

oss Perot had been the biggest surprise of the 1992 election. At both Clinton and Dole headquarters, there was much concern that he would play the role of spoiler in 1996. Instead, the Perot campaign turned into a slightly wacky sideshow. The reason had less to do with the dynamics of the race or the state of the body politic—there were still plenty of angry voters looking for a third way—than with the curious character of Ross Perot.

Perot once described himself as an "albino monkey" who could draw crowds to the circus. His theme song in 1992 had been Patsy Cline's "Crazy." The Dole and Clinton campaigns weren't quite sure what to make of the diminutive Texas billionaire. Dole's advisers worried that Perot would siphon more votes from their candidate, and some of Clinton's advisers welcomed Perot into the race for precisely that reason. The week after Perot announced the creation of a new political party, Dick Morris called Perot's adviser, pollster Gordon Black, and asked if Perot needed any help gathering signatures in order to get onto the ballot in California. But both sides were wary of an unpredictable, stubborn and extremely rich man who had fantasies of rescuing America from a political process he described as "sick." The real question was whether Perot's megalomania would lift his new Reform party or sink it.

In his own mind, Ross Perot had nearly won the 1992 election. Officially, Perot finished with 19 percent, while Clinton won with 43 percent and Bush got 38 percent. But exit polls on Election Day asked voters how they would have cast their ballots if they "believed Ross Perot had a chance to win." In this hypothetical contest, Perot had won 40 percent of the vote, against 31 percent for Clinton and 27 percent for Bush. As Perot saw it, he should have been elected president. He blamed the Republicans, who urged voters not to "waste" their votes on Perot, and the media, which tried to make him seem like a crackpot. The networks hadn't even bothered to report the exit polls showing the what-if preference for Perot.

Still, Perot thought his $65 million investment had been worth it. He was someone to be reckoned with; Congress and the president could not ignore his preachments about deficit reduction. It's fair to say that Perot's 19 percent was a crucial factor leading to the tax hike on the wealthy in 1993. When Perot called, leaders on both sides of the aisle had to listen. On one day in March 1993, his daily schedule looked like a royal progress: while Perot testified on Capitol Hill, aides had a morning meeting at the White House with the president's chief of staff and senior policy adviser; a late-morning meeting with Senate Republican leader Bob Dole; a lunchtime press conference at the National Press Club; and an early-afternoon meeting with Speaker Tom Foley. In the late afternoon, Perot and his aides had a meeting with Senate Majority Leader George Mitchell. "This thing is working so well it scares me," Perot chortled.

Perot liked the feeling of having arrived. He was less enthusiastic about the process of getting there. Modern campaigning was all about "character assassination," he said. "War has rules. Mud wrestling has rules. Politics has no rules." Perot saw dirty politics everywhere. In July 1992 he had believed a con man's report that the Republicans were trying to smear his daughter; the exposure of this plot as a fraud on CBS's 60 Minutes had made Perot look foolish and paranoid in the final days of the campaign. In the summer of 1995, Perot told friends that if he ran for president again, he'd be "so bloody and beaten" that he'd be useless as a candidate.

But Perot wasn't about to give up his national stage. His organization, United We Stand, America, had slowly imploded after

Perot's failed attempt to block the NAFTA treaty. Still, there were enough of the faithful to form the core of a new political party. Perot warmed to the idea of a permanent third party. As usual, his motives were a mixture of idealism and egotism. A true "reform" party would keep the pressure on the Republicans and Democrats to heed the issues Perot cared about, like deficit reduction, fair trade and campaign-finance reform. Perot thought a new party might attract some well-known but disaffected Democrats and Republicans, former senators like Lowell Weicker of Connecticut and Bill Bradley of New Jersey. Perot even encouraged David Boren, the former Oklahoma governor and U.S. senator, to run for president on the Reform party ticket. He insisted—to some scoffing—that the new party was "not about me," and he was in fact ready to step aside if someone of Boren's prominence had been willing to take the plunge.

Creating a new party had the added virtue of allowing Perot to wait until the last moment to declare his own intentions. He believed, with good reason, that American presidential campaigns had become ridiculously long and expensive. Perot wanted a simpler, cleaner process. No negative ads, no spinmeisters. In the Reform party, the candidates would lay out their platforms in speeches carried over cable TV. Then members of the party—anyone who signed a petition—would be able to place a secret call-in vote before the party held its nominating convention, at Valley Forge, Pennsylvania, on the weekend after the Republican convention. Perot thought he could afford to wait until Labor Day to begin campaigning actively for president. In 1992, after quitting the race in July, he had stood at 2 percent in the polls in the beginning of September. Yet after he got back in the race in early October, he was able to move up sharply, bypassing the press and talking directly to the people through the presidential debates and his TV "infomercials." If he hadn't been sandbagged by 60 Minutes, Perot figured, he might have outrun President Bush.

The new party, as Perot saw it, was his "gift to the American people." Perot liked the line from the movie Field of Dreams: "If you build it, they will come." But they didn't. The only nationally known figure who showed any interest in the Reform nomination was former Colorado governor Richard Lamm. And his candidacy only brought out the worst in Perot.

Lamm was a contrarian, a well-intentioned Democratic maverick who seemed almost perversely determined to offend. He referred to President Clinton as an "amicable windsock." He had been called Governor Gloom for his obsession with American decline. He worried that older generations were robbing the future from their children. Lamm liked to feel the weight of the world; at the top of the stack of books in his bathroom was one called *Who Will Feed China?* He had "unbelievable guilt," said his own daughter, Heather. Beaten in a run for the Senate in 1992, Lamm was teaching (a seminar called Hard Choices) and writing, but he wasn't getting much of an audience for his jeremiads. Defeating Perot, he hoped, would get him one.

At first, Perot and Lamm coexisted reasonably well. They were sufficiently quixotic and idealistic almost to like each other. Typically, however, Lamm had to make life difficult for himself and, as it turned out, for Perot. His first act, even before he decided to run, was characteristic: he wanted Perot to do some opposition research—on him. Lamm called Russ Verney, a former air-traffic controller turned political consultant who had been installed by Perot as head of the Reform party, and announced, "You ought to find out what is in my background. You ought to be asking me questions and find out about my affair with the movie stars and the drinking problem and if I'm a secret gambler." Verney said he wasn't interested. "We're tired of all this negativism," he said. Lamm pressed: "It's a valid issue. The press is sure as shit going to look into it. You should. Somebody's gotta ask, 'Have you had some affairs?' " Verney waved him off. "It's just too negative."

Verney's indifference confirmed to Lamm what he already suspected: Perot was just using him. Ross was not seriously worried that Lamm would win the Reform party nomination. He just wanted some token opposition to make the party appear more legitimate.

Lamm suppressed his doubts for a short time, but in mid-July he went public with his suspicions, accusing Perot of trying to rig the party's odd nominating process. No one would give him a list of party members. The Reform party hierarchy and the Perot campaign were one and the same. Some of Lamm's concern was genuine enough, but he also discovered that stories playing up Perot's secretive and overweening habits made excellent copy. When Lamm talked about Perot's "autocratic" style, it made the papers. His musings on entitlement reform did not. Lamm's people quickly learned that the press was entirely sympathetic to his underdog quest and were eager for dirt on Perot.

Perot, understandably, was infuriated by Lamm's grandstanding. When Lamm complained publicly about secrecy, Perot privately grumbled that Lamm's tactics were "politics as usual." On the same day Lamm gave a press conference announcing that he would challenge Perot to debates, Perot gave Lamm a lift on his private jet. Lamm never brought up the subject of debates. "Why didn't he ask me?" Perot griped a few days later. The angrier Perot and his people became, the less patience they had with Lamm.

As a result, the challenger's complaints became self-fulfilling. The party sent out a mailing urging members to vote in the call-in balloting in August, but the card was called "a message from Ross Perot" and had his picture on it; Lamm's name wasn't even mentioned. Lamm raised another fuss when the party failed to mail him a ballot. Perot anxiously tried to patch things up. He called the former governor six times before 9:30 A.M. one day promising to get him (and his daughter) ballots and even sent a postal inspector to his house. Perot explained that the party hadn't been able to decipher Lamm's handwriting on the petition. But Perot's anger finally overcame his eagerness to please. "You're the cause of all the doubts about the election," Perot charged. "There's no problem with the voting. It's only your people who are making a mountain out of a molehill. Do you realize how hard I've worked over the last 10 months to give this gift to the American people?" He was ranting. "Nothing we do can satisfy you people." When he hung up, Lamm exclaimed, "Jesus Christ, you can't even talk to him."

Lamm and Perot tried again just before the party's nominating convention in Valley Forge on August 18. Lamm told Perot that the election between them was not credible. "Why don't we both withdraw?" Lamm said. "I'll withdraw and you withdraw and we'll pick someone else to run."

"Who are you fronting for?" Perot demanded.

"Fronting?"

"It's obvious that you're fronting for somebody."

Lamm assured him that he wasn't. He tried out some names of possible Reform candidates. How about Sam Nunn, the Georgia senator who had decided not to run again? But Perot would have none of it. He hung up. The two men never spoke again until after the election. Lamm's charges and Perot's equivocations were a disaster for the Reform party. Instead of presenting a new, clean approach to politics, it made the "race" for the Reform party nomination seem like papal politics in the 15th century.

With the nomination safely won, Perot still had to find a running mate. He had been hurt by his choice in 1992, the brave but foggy Admiral James Stockdale. Back in October of 1995, he had asked pollster Gordon Black to come up with a list of possible veeps. Black had sent him 14 names rated by their "willingness to get involved." Lowell Weicker, former Minnesota congressman Tim Penny and Maine governor Angus King were rated "very high." David Boren and New York mayor Rudolph Giuliani were rated "high." It was a list built mainly on vain wishes. Perot wanted people to come forward, but at times seemed to actively discourage prominent politicians from joining his party. When Black tried to entice a few well-known former Democrats and Republicans, including Weicker, to come speak to the Reform party in California in 1995, Perot stopped him. "What are you trying to do with these guys?" Perot demanded. "Trying to get some people out there to help," said Black. "They'll just get in the way," scoffed Perot.

In August, when he was running out of time, Perot finally approached Boren, whom he had earlier asked to run for president, and Congresswoman Marcy Kaptur, a feisty blue-collar protectionist. Both turned him down. The search became comical when Linda Smith, a freshman congresswoman from Washington, announced that she, too, had told Perot no. But had she actually been asked? Well, there had been "persistent rumors," she allowed, which she wanted to scotch. The truth was that Smith was in a tight race to keep her seat and just needed some publicity.

Desperation began to set in. Perot asked Gordon Black himself, who had been conducting the search, if he would accept the nomination. ("Are you sitting down?" Perot's emissary, his son-in-law Clay Mulford, had inquired when he called Black to make the pitch.) Finally, Pat Choate agreed to run. A Washington gadfly, Choate had attracted notoriety with his book *Agents of Influence*, attacking former U.S. officials for lobbying for foreign interests. But Choate had no governing or political experience, and his nomination was greeted largely with snickers and yawns.

In September, Perot was stuck at about 5 percent in the polls. He had spent much of the year in the 15–20 percent range, but his coy behavior and tired routine had made him stale—and that was a fatal quality for any insurgency. Yes, there were flashes of the old flair. He imagined what it would be like if political consultants had controlled earlier campaigns. George Washington would be out (those wooden teeth); so would Abe Lincoln (too tall, too ugly—and that beard). Winston Churchill would have to buy a toupee and lose 60 pounds and the cigar. But Perot had lost some of his bounce and feistiness. He thought that he had become more politically astute. "I understand how the game is played now, see?" he would say. But he had also become timid. Though he chastised Dole and Clinton for trying to buy the voters with "candy," he was very unspecific about the cuts he would make to balance the budget. In 1992, 11 million people had watched his first infomercial. In September 1996 only about a third as many tuned in. Ross Perot had begun to seem like just another politician.

14 ■ THE OTHER WOMAN

During the spring and summer, whenever the news media began to question him about the sagging state of the campaign, Dole would shrug dismissively. The polls don't mean much, he would say. There's still plenty of time. Voters don't start paying attention until Labor Day. Dole had long since learned the virtue of patience; he preferred to bide his time, keep his options open, decide only when absolutely necessary. It was a good posture for a legislator, but not for a presidential candidate trailing by 15 points in the polls. Labor Day came and went with the Dole campaign still floundering in search of a clear message. For all its careful orchestration, the GOP convention had failed to sell Bob Dole. Voters knew him better; no longer did a sizeable minority think he was an heir to the Dole pineapple fortune, as one GOP poll had discovered that spring. But voters were skeptical of Dole's tax-cut pledge, and the campaign had done nothing to build momentum since San Diego.

If the campaign could not persuade voters to be for Bob Dole, then it was necessary to persuade them to be against Bill Clinton. But going negative held real risks. Well aware of his hatchet-man reputation, Dole did not wish to fulfill expectations by reprising the role of Mean Bob. The very swing voters he sought to reach—moderate middle-class women, the soccer moms—hated negative campaigning. And so, as the "real" campaign began in the fall of 1996, faced with a dilemma: how to attack without offending? this riddle would have taken a very adroit candidate backed by a ewd strategist. The Dole campaign had neither.

At Dole headquarters, infighting and paranoia prevailed. Dole's campaign manager, Scott Reed, was not a strategist. The former windsurfing instructor had no illusions about his analytical ability or long-range vision. He was as amiable and seemingly uncomplicated as Dick Morris was calculating. Nor was Reed a fast-talking front man like James Carville; you would seldom, if ever, find him posing for the camera or glad-handing in the hotel lobby (Dole disliked grandstanding by his aides). Reed wasn't even a particularly good manager. The Dole campaign seemed to have more than its share of gaffes and glitches, from last-minute scheduling snafus to the appalling sight of Dole plunging headfirst off a stage because an advance man had failed to nail down the railing. Mostly, Reed was a survivor. He was someone who managed not to get fired, which in a Bob Dole campaign was no small feat.

Don Sipple, the campaign's chief image maker, hadn't much use for Reed. He compared the Dole campaign manager to Eddie Haskell in *Leave It to Beaver*: obsequious around the adults, but capable of terrorizing the Beaver when Mrs. Cleaver wasn't looking. (Reed's allies called Sipple the "brat" behind his back.) Sipple's partner at New Century Media, Mike Murphy, also regarded Reed and the rest of the Dole staff as minor leaguers, politics "Lite." "God, they're idiots," Murphy groused to Sipple. Murphy thought Dole's staff might be of more use if they went off somewhere to stuff envelopes and let him take charge. "I'm just a dictator by nature," said Murphy. "I'm not good when I'm not in charge." He was especially disdainful of John Buckley, the campaign's communications director, for courting the "beltway echo media." Buckley, a nephew of conservative writer William F. Buckley, was an "east coast elitist," according to Murphy, a college dropout who considered himself better connected to Joe Six Pack. Murphy wanted to take over the campaign communications shop and squeeze out Buckley. Before San Diego, he wrote a memo he entitled, "MURPHY LET'S WIN THE ELECTION." In a list of "what to do," he declared, with puzzling syntax but unmistakable intent, "Fire some people after the convention. We need a bit of a shake-up, it says 'new campaign.' Change. Ugly, but needed." He had Buckley in mind.

The backbiting peaked in San Diego, threatening a public blow-up. "You guys have got to get along," begged Scott Reed. After the convention, Dan Balz of the *Washington Post* got wind of Murphy's sniping at Buckley and called Murphy for comment. At that, Murphy and Sipple trooped down the hall to Buckley's office and leaned over his desk like a pair of mob goons. Murphy was furious that Buckley had already talked to Balz. He picked up Buckley's phone and made him dial the *Post* reporter's number. Buckley was turning crimson. Murphy reached Balz: "On the record, there's no problem. We're great friends. We love each other. We're a happy team." He glared at Buckley.

For all their bravado, however, Sipple and Murphy didn't have much to show in the way of effective ads. The campaign had no money to buy airtime and little agreement on what to say. Dole's formal nomination in San Diego finally freed up $62 million in federal funds, but the image makers quickly fell to squabbling over the right message. Obviously, the campaign had to sell Dole's 15 percent tax cut. But Dole's pollster, Tony Fabrizio, insisted that the ad include a line about balancing the budget as well. Sipple hated that idea. Don't muddy up the message, he argued. Murphy, who had successfully sold tax-cut messages for two governors, Engler of Michigan and Whitman of New Jersey, thought the psychology was all wrong if you mixed in a balanced-budget pledge. It was like putting a fat guy in a Diet Coke ad. Voters would be confused. "Shoving these two somewhat conflicting messages together in a 30-second unit is telling them not to believe us," Murphy wrote to Scott Reed.

Sipple hated going through Fabrizio, who wanted to test all the spots in focus groups. Sipple was not against market research, but he thought Fabrizio relied far too much on specific dial readings. What difference did it make whether somebody turned his dial to 30 instead of 20? Sipple contemptuously called Fabrizio's method "painting by the numbers." Sipple was an artist; he trusted his instincts. For their part, Reed and Fabrizio were frustrated with Sipple and

Murphy. The offices of New Century Media adjoined those of the Dole campaign, but they might as well have been in a different city. Reed complained that he would get a script, but when he called over to order some changes, he'd learn that Sipple and Murphy were already at the studio cutting the spot. He was also fed up with Sipple's standoffish manner; Sipple didn't seem engaged in the campaign. The ad maker flaunted his disregard for Fabrizio's numbers, relying in his memos on polling from the newspapers.

Reed decided the time had come to make some changes. On September 4, he called Sipple into his office. New Century's contract was being terminated, he said. The two men could still make ads, but they had to work directly for the Dole campaign.

"We need to have it all in one tent," said Reed

"Why?" asked Sipple. "We're only down the hall."

"There are barriers."

"What are you talking about?"

There wasn't enough "integration" and "communication," said Reed. It just wasn't working right.

Sipple said he'd think about it, but he didn't have to think very hard. He and Murphy knew that this was all about control, and they were about to lose what little they had left. He and Murphy decided to leave.

Dole was not pleased to learn that Sipple and Murphy were out. He, too, had not particularly liked their ads. He hadn't been getting any positive feedback when he worked the crowds on the stump. At one point, he was shown an ad that proclaimed: "Bob Dole. Cut taxes. Fight for what's right." Dole had growled to Sipple, "I don't know what that means. It doesn't say anything." Still, Dole was uncomfortable with staff purges, which reminded voters of his reputation for being coldhearted.

The real problem, though, was not Reed or Sipple or Murphy, or the others who had come before or would come later. The problem was Bob Dole. He was a poor boss. There was, in Washington, a large alumni association of former Dole aides who all told the same story. Dole was a good man, but he was difficult to work for. He was mysterious and uncommunicative, often biting and rarely encouraging. He almost never told anyone everything that he was thinking. They had to guess, searching his countenance for a hint. When John Buckley was arguing with Murphy over when to announce the economic plan, each one believed Dole was signaling him that he agreed. (Buckley thought he had caught Dole nodding at him; Murphy thought he saw Dole wink.) Neither one expected Dole actually to say anything. When Dole was angry, he could be equally indirect. His gaze was like a laser, but it was often aimed at the person just next to the person he was really mad at. Thus, when he was angry at Sipple for making a lackluster convention video ("That was a total failure," he growled), Dole looked at Tony Fabrizio and political director Jill Hanson, who were sitting next to the real target.

Dole would often assign different staffers to do the same job—without telling them. He liked to have competing power centers in the campaign and would play off one against the other. He knew, for instance, that Reed would often sit on Sipple and Murphy's advice. So Dole would summon the two admen himself, usually on some pretense, and then invite them to second-guess the campaign manager. During the convention, Dole called the pair up to his sunbathing perch on the roof of the Hyatt, ostensibly to ask them which tie he should wear to make his acceptance speech (Dole is color-blind). But he also had a more significant question: The staff wanted Jack Kemp to stay behind in California after the convention and campaign alone. What did Sipple and Murphy think of that? Bad idea, they both said. Kemp was dangerous on his own. He was on the wrong side of two wedge issues in California, affirmative action and immigration. Dole needed to be with Kemp to keep him under control, as well as to bond and show off the running mates as a team. Dole, as usual, just listened. But later at a staff meeting, Reed announced that there had been a change of plans. Kemp was no longer slated to stay on in California alone. He and Dole would leave San Diego together. Reed never said anything, but it was obvious that his original decision had been undermined by Dole's back-channeling.

Scott Reed could hardly be blamed for feeling a little insecure. If he appeared weak and bland, perhaps that was the way Dole wanted it. Dole was, in effect, his own campaign manager. He didn't want to be "handled" like Ronald Reagan—or for that matter, like almost any modern candidate for high office. Dole listened to plenty of advice—too much, perhaps, from too many sources—but the really major decisions in the Dole campaign were made by Bob Dole. Alone.

When he was in the Senate, Dole had been able to manage the heavy burdens of majority leader—herding senators, shepherding bills, negotiating compromises—without much help. He did it by working incredibly long hours, by listening, and by keeping it all in his head. He had a small but utterly devoted staff: people like Sheila Burke, Rod DeArment and Bob Lighthizer. But a presidential campaign cannot be a solo voyage. It is the ultimate endurance test, even with the best and most faithful staff. Lacking a strong staff, possessed of political instincts better suited to passing bills than electing presidents, Dole was adrift.

To celebrate the launch of the fall campaign and the success of the San Diego convention, the Dole campaign held a dinner at the Four Seasons, a Washington luxury hotel, on September 7. The bonhomie was a little forced. The elder statesmen in attendance—men like former senators Howard Baker and Paul Laxalt and super-lobbyist Bill Timmons—resented the fact that the staff didn't seem to listen to their advice, and the campaign staffers thought the graybeards were meddlesome. At their regular monthly meeting just the day before, the Wise Men had been querulous and demanding. Why were there so few ads, and such weak ones? "We've fired those people," answered Scott Reed, who hated these dog-and-pony shows. There was also tension between supply-siders and deficit hawks, between Senate staff and campaign staff, between Kempians and Doleites.

After the salmon and steak, Tom Korologos, Dole's old friend, tapped his wineglass. "Okay, now we're going to have speeches," he said in his gruff, jovial manner. There were loud boos. "But the speeches are going to come from the next president of the United States," added Korologos.

"Jack Kemp," quipped Bob Dole. He was, as ever, mordant about his predicament. On the stump, he liked to mention that Elizabeth, as head of the Red Cross, had visited many disaster areas, "not including my campaign." Dole's dry humor masked his discomfort with the campaign's direction. He would have to go negative, he knew, not because he wanted to, but because there was no place else to go.

The key to winning, according to the guru of negative campaigning, Arthur J. Finkelstein, is to "polarize the electorate." Voters are confused and overwhelmed and usually bored. The trick is to find one issue that will make them pay attention, and then hammer away. Forget the positive; always accent the negative. Spending on political organization, Finkelstein believes, is a waste of money. Almost all campaign resources should be devoted to negative or, as consultants prefer to say, "comparative" ads. The classic model was Finkelstein's 1980 campaign to unseat Senator Jacob Javits of New York, a Republican moderate who, unbeknownst to most voters, suffered from a degenerative nerve disease. Finkelstein's one ad, repeated over and over, concluded: "And now, at age 76 and in failing health, Javits wants six more years." Finkelstein's client, an obscure Queens pol named Alfonse D'Amato, came from 60 points behind to win.

Fifteen years later, in the winter of 1995, Senator D'Amato, chairman of the Banking Committee and close adviser to Bob Dole, strongly urged Dole to hire Finkelstein to run his campaign. But Finkelstein insisted on total control, and he was too malevolent for Dole's taste. The answer was no.

Dole didn't get Finkelstein, but he did get many of his most apt pupils. Finkelstein's progeny had become prominent in the upper reaches of political consulting. Pollster Fabrizio was an old protégé. He was an early expert at identifying the "peripheral urban ethnic" vote—read, blue-collar Catholics—and making them into Reagan Democrats by playing to their dislike of criminals, blacks and homosexuals. Like most Finkelstein alums, Fabrizio liked to posture as a bad boy. He taped his nickname, "The Rat," onto his nameplate at Dole headquarters. Alex Castellanos, a cigar-smoking Cuban who was one of three admen brought in to replace Sipple and Murphy, was also proud of his Finkelstein heritage. "Most of us think like him," he said of the Finkelstein men at Dole headquarters. "Or at least we hope we do." Castellanos was rubbing his hands at the prospect of designing an ad campaign aimed at the president, whom he referred to as "Tubby."

In his never-ending search for a campaign strategist, Scott Reed turned in late August to Paul Manafort, a hardball political consultant who had run the San Diego convention with an iron hand. Manafort's strategy boiled down to a single sentence that employed Finkelstein's favorite pejorative term: "Clinton is a liberal." As Castellanos explained it, "It's out of the old playbook. It's like what we did to [Jim] Hunt [who ran against Finkelstein's client, Jesse Helms, in 1984]. First we call him a liberal. And when he says, 'No, I'm not,' great. Now you're a lying liberal and we call him a liberal and a liar. That is how you ease into the character issue."

Manafort emphasized that Dole would have to be "razor-focused." For a while, Dole tried, growling "liberal, liberal, liberal" every time he mentioned Clinton on the stump. But the charge sounded tired to many voters—and somewhat contrived, given the fact that for months, the Dole campaign had stressed that Clinton was a waffler who stood for nothing. As she toured the country, Elizabeth Dole had mocked Clinton's ideological swings with a prop, a little rocking chair that rocked left-to-right instead of backward-and-forward. To suddenly describe Clinton as a deep-down lefty did not ring true. Not even to the master himself: privately, Arthur Finkelstein disavowed the Dole campaign as a botch.

Actually, the Dole campaign had the worst of both worlds: Finkelstein's cynical negativity without his focus and discipline. Once again, as the campaign neared its end, the Dole camp proved incapable of sticking with a consistent message. Part of the problem was Dole. He seemed oddly passionless, as if he didn't really mean what he was saying. Voters could sense Dole's capacity for genuine rage; it lurked there, just beneath the surface. But he seemed to be going through the motions when he attacked Clinton. At times, he appeared to be winking to his audiences, signaling his sense of the absurdity of it all. At other times he just seemed sullen and insincere.

By September, the campaign was having trouble getting voters to pay attention at all. Crises in the Middle East dominated the
headlines. Watching Clinton play the president, somber and statesmanlike as he acted the peacemaker or ordered missile attacks, Tony
Fabrizio chain-smoked Merits and agonized. "My God," he wondered
aloud. "How do we break through?" In early September, the disagreements over message bumped into a squabble over geography. For
weeks, the staff had quarreled over the best places to focus Dole's
time and money. Dole hated the idea of writing off any section. But
Manafort and Fabrizio argued persuasively that Dole was going to
have to concentrate somewhere or risk losing everywhere. But which
states? Fabrizio came up with two maps, a Western strategy and an
Eastern strategy. If the campaign wanted to focus on California, it
should go sharply negative. California voters are moved by hot-button
issues like affirmative action and immigration. On the other hand,
if Dole wanted to make headway in the East—Pennsylvania, New
Jersey and Connecticut—he needed to win over the soccer moms
who found him too harsh. That meant running positive ads stressing
his trustworthiness. Go high road to the East, or scorched earth to
the West. It was a coin toss. Scott Reed hesitated. Instead he ordered
up a third map: go everywhere.

The Dole campaign was paralyzed by more than geography.
In August, the campaign learned that two major news organizations—
the *Washington Post* (owned by the same company that owns *Newsweek*)
and *Time*—had interviewed a woman who claimed to have had an
extramarital affair with Dole in the late '60s, in the waning years of
his marriage to his first wife. The campaign sent a lawyer, Doug
Wurth, to talk to her. At a meeting at the Willard Hotel in early
September, she told Wurth that the relationship had begun in 1968,
when she was 35 and Dole was 44, and had ended after Dole's
divorce in 1972. Wurth made no attempt to challenge the woman's
story, which seemed credible (the woman had date books and other
documentation to support her claim).

The prospect of such a news story was a source of growing
uneasiness in the campaign. Disquiet turned to major anxiety when
Bob Woodward of the *Washington Post* called on September 13, want-

ing to talk to Scott Reed and Nelson Warfield, the campaign press secretary. Woodward was a legendary reporter, the man who had helped bring down Bob Dole's hero, Richard Nixon, and he had per- suaded the woman to talk on the record after *Post* reporter Charles Babcock tracked her down. Dole's advisers feared the story would wreck the campaign. "It was a mortal threat," said one aide. The campaign's last hope was to show that Dole was more trustworthy than Clinton. "It's the one thing we have—the fact that he is an upstanding guy with high morals." The woman's story, if published in the *Post*, "wipes it all out."

On September 20, Mari Will and Nelson Warfield went to the *Post* to meet with Woodward and the paper's top editor, Leonard Downie. Will and Warfield had good relations with Woodward; they had been primary sources for his campaign book, *The Choice*. They made an impassioned case to the *Post* editors not to print the story. The alleged affair had happened 28 years ago in a dying marriage, they argued. Why bring up something so old? Was there no chance for redemption? The *Post* editors listened respectfully, but they gave no assurances. On *Meet the Press* back in January 1994, Dole himself had said that the personal lives of politicians—including marital infidelity—are "fair game." Besides, hadn't the Dole campaign been claiming that Dole's character was superior to Clinton's? Dole's aides argued that they had been talking about public acts, not private ones. "We never made the argument that Dole was a saint and Clinton was a sinner," said one of them.

Gloomily, the campaign began preparing for damage control. Dole had seemed baffled when his friend Bob Ellsworth first told him in late August that the woman was talking to the press. The rela- tionship had not been "that intense," he insisted. "If this comes out it will be my word against hers." But denying the story would be hard. There was some talk of trying to preempt the *Post* by going public in an interview with some friendly and sympathetic TV reporter (Dole liked several, including CNN's Candy Crowley and NBC's Lisa Myers). An old rule of campaigning is to announce your own bad news. But communications director John Buckley argued that the campaign could not very well argue that the affair was irrelevant and then break the story itself.

A better response, the aides agreed, would be to wait for publication and then attack the *Post* for indulging in trash journalism. Campaign aides began making lists of people to rally if the story ran. They would gather senators willing to express outrage, and call on former presidents Bush and Ford to make statements of support. They scrutinized the travel schedules of Elizabeth and Dole's daughter (by his first marriage) Robin to make sure they would be available. One plan was to hold a press conference with them at Dole's side. Dole would neither confirm nor deny the story, but rather castigate the press for wallowing in sleaze. Plans were laid to phone Ralph Reed, Gary Bauer, Henry Hyde and other stalwarts of the religious right to make sure no one "said anything stupid," as one aide put it. In the worst-case scenario, Dole's right flank would collapse as Christian conservatives chose to stay home (or vote for Ross Perot) rather than choose between adulterers. As a result, the GOP might lose not only the presidency, but control of Congress as well.

The staff braced for the story to appear in the *Post* on Sunday, September 22. Dole himself had remained remarkably cheerful that week, even though he had made a baseball gaffe that placed him in an earlier generation (he referred to the "Brooklyn Dodgers") and plunged headfirst off a reviewing stand in Chico, California, when a railing gave way. On Friday, the *New York Times* ran a story marveling at how "calm, unflappable, even chipper" the candidate remained in the face of pratfalls and low polls. But beneath the surface, Dole was beginning to boil.

Dole rarely lashed out when angry. More commonly, he grew very, very quiet. On Sunday morning, as he flew to a rally in Illinois, Dole maintained an ominous silence as he read the *Washington Post*. The story was not the one the campaign feared, but rather a piece quoting anonymous aides as saying that Dole planned to write off Illinois, the very state where he was headed. The next morning, at the 10:30 staff meeting, Dole's ire finally spilled out. "I don't know who the imbecile was who leaked this," he began in a cold, flat voice, glaring in the vicinity of Scott Reed. "We must look like a bunch of idiots sitting around putting our strategy in the newspaper where Clinton can read it." Dole had long been angry about leaks. "This campaign leaks like a sieve," he told a friend.

Dole was also sore about the campaign's handling of debate negotiations. Dole had wanted four presidential debates, the last to be held as late as possible in the campaign. Instead, he had wound up with two, neither of them late. The campaign was so obsessed with the potential *Post* story that some advisers felt its negotiators had caved in quickly rather than try to bargain in the middle of a breaking scandal. Dole was mad, too, that he had been tagged with excluding Ross Perot. When staffers tried to soothe him, he would have none of it. "Perot's not attacking you, he's attacking me," Dole told them.

Reed hastily adjourned the meeting, but word quickly spread through campaign headquarters, which was already buzzing with rumors about the anticipated Woodward article. Staffers close to Dole were convinced that his real anger was not over leaks about strategy, but rather the still-unpublished *Post* story. Some felt a strange sense of relief, that the tension building for weeks had finally been released. Others just felt depressed, sensing that it was the beginning of the end.

The story continued to be expected any day. Scott Reed pleaded with Woodward, "You guys have got to give us 24 hours' notice." Woodward asked why. "I've got to get the candidate's wife and daughter ready for the fact that this may be in print," Reed explained. "I understand," said Woodward, without making any promises. On September 24, the campaign was told by a *Post* reporter that the story "won't be tomorrow." The next day, the message was repeated. The following day, Dole flew to his condo in Florida, partly to practice for his debates, but also to be cloistered in case the story broke. The staff figured there was a better chance to keep the press at bay if Dole was in his 12th-floor condo rather than out on the stump. A rally on the way reminded Dole how much he had to lose. A dark, sparsely filled auditorium in West Palm Beach had been decorated with banners made by schoolchildren that read: "Morality is an issue"; "Choosy Moms Choose Dole"; "Integrity Counts"; "Character Counts." The stage was flanked with two large posters of Dole, each emblazoned with the word "trust."

Dole basked in the sun and perused his briefing books, but he was distracted. Elizabeth was very upset by the prospect of the *Post*'s story. She called the paper's publisher, Donald Graham, to plead for restraint. But with her usual extraordinary discipline, she also filmed two 30-second spots that touted Dole's trustworthiness. In one, sitting in a yellow blouse and looking imploringly at the camera, she declared, "Honesty, doing what's right, living up to his word . . . Bob Dole doesn't make promises he can't keep." She was talking about his 15 percent tax cut, but the awkward circumstances hung heavily over the Dole staffers as they watched. In a second spot, she praised his small-town virtue, "The truth. First, last, always the truth."

In the *Post*'s newsroom and executive offices on 15th Street in Washington, a fierce debate raged over the ethics of printing the story. Many of the reporters, including Woodward, wanted to publish. They argued that Dole had made trust and character an issue, and thus adultery, even from the distant past, was relevant. Most of the editors, however, accepted the distinction between public trust and private actions. The *Post* and its owners, the Graham family, did not want to get into the business of investigating the dalliances of presidential candidates.

By Thursday, October 3, the *Post* had decided that it would be unfair to print the story just before the first debate, scheduled for that Sunday night. Informed by Woodward, the campaign was hugely relieved. Dole's staffers believed that the closer they got to the election, the harder it would be for the *Post* to publish such a sensational article. According to a close friend, Dole was finally able to push the story to the back of his mind.

15 ■ GOING NEGATIVE

In September, after the Democrats' feel-good convention, Bill and Hillary Clinton were "not rejoicing" over the president's lead in the polls, said a close adviser. "Neither one wants to tempt fate." Clinton's whole career had been a series of wild rides; an easy finish in this race, Clinton's last, seemed inconceivable. The first couple remained hostile to the media, still suspicious that reporters, in their determination to add suspense to the horse race, would dredge up some ancient or petty scandal. Clinton still believed, said this aide, that there was a "tacit conspiracy between the press and the Washington in-crowd, which has always believed that Clinton is a rube, and that it is their duty to bring him down." Around his staff, the president made little attempt to hide his anger and resentment against the press. "They're screwing me," he would insist, even after Whitewater had largely vanished from the front pages.

Clinton worried as well that Dole would launch a campaign of character assassination against him. He feared that the Republicans, desperate to catch up, would try to drag him down by harping on Whitewater and hinting at Clinton's personal indiscretions. His advisers tried to reassure the president that the voters didn't care, that polls showed the public had grown indifferent to all that.

But Clinton was insistent. "There still has to be a defense of the man," he would protest during the weekly meetings in the Yellow Oval. In early September, he summoned pollster Mark Penn, who had succeeded Dick Morris as the main campaign strategist. The president was lining up golf balls on the White House putting green when Penn found him. Clinton told Penn that he had heard rumors that the Republicans were planning to launch a series of ads on character. Ordinary citizens would praise Dole as a war hero and a man of the people—damning the president, by inference, as a draft-dodging elitist. "Kind of like Harry and Louise," said Clinton. In 1994, Clinton had been infuriated by ads showing a fictional TV couple criticizing Hillary's health-reform plan as a Big Government boondoggle. Clinton hated being portrayed as hostile to the middle class. "How should we respond?" asked Clinton.

Penn knew that Clinton loved ads that showed real people talking about how his policies affected them. He thought it would be best to respond with testimonials extolling Clinton's character. The spots should feature people with compelling stories that emphasized Clinton's public achievements. Penn mentioned Jim Brady, who had been grievously wounded in the assassination attempt on President Reagan and become a major advocate of gun control. At the Democratic convention, Brady had moved the viewers, along with Clinton's poll numbers, by limping from his wheelchair to the podium and praising Clinton's record on gun control. Another candidate would be Marc Klaas, the father of California murder victim Polly Klaas and a big supporter of Clinton's crime bill. Linda Crawford, the widow of anti-tobacco activist Victor Crawford, could praise Clinton's record against the tobacco industry.

"Hillary ought to hear this too," said Clinton. He walked Penn over to the White House pool, where the first lady was resting in a cabana chair. Hillary was intrigued by Penn's proposal, but skeptical. She had bad memories of Harry and Louise, but she wasn't sure Jim Brady was the answer. Wouldn't average Americans be better? Penn told the Clintons he would do some research and get back to them. Surveys of mall-goers, Penn's favorite research technique, showed that Brady had enormous appeal, especially with swing voters. In October, Bill Knapp, the campaign's chief ad maker, and filmmaker Marius Penczner cut an ad called "Forever." The 30-second spot began with a chilling, slow-motion sequence of the 1981 attempt on Reagan. As the camera focused on Brady lying face down in a pool of his own blood, the voice-over began, "It was over in a second but the pain lasts forever." In a halting voice, Brady praised Clinton for passing the Brady Bill. "When I hear people question the president's character, I say, 'Look what he's done, look at the lives the Brady Bill will save.'" The ad ended with a shot of Clinton striding past the columns of the White House with the words PROTECTING OUR VALUES emblazoned on the screen. The ad was put on the shelf, to be ready as soon as Dole launched any character attacks.

The Clintonites had another insurance policy. Through leaks from the *Washington Post*, the campaign knew about the still-unpublished story detailing Dole's extramarital affair from the late '60s. When Clinton began his usual complaints about the press's assaults on his character, George Stephanopoulos reminded him that the press was ready to unload on Dole. "They have stuff on him," Stephanopoulos told Clinton. "And if he oversteps, they'll run it." The Clintonites surmised that the *Post* story was holding Dole in check. Dole had been careful so far to limit his attacks on Clinton to his public actions; he was avoiding any mention of Clinton's personal life. "That's the reason they're going so far to drive a Chinese wall between the public attacks and the personal stuff," Stephanopoulos said. "They know that if the wall cracks, they're in big trouble. They want to make this whole campaign about trust."

As the campaign entered its final month, Dole was widely expected to "go negative." Almost every day, front-page stories would play out the debate within the Dole campaign, quoting some advisers as vowing to hit hard and others counseling caution. Dole himself seemed to waver on the issue. One day he attacked; the next day he backed off. The public handwringing served mainly to remind voters of Dole's hatchet-man reputation, and to highlight the penchant of his advisers, especially the Finkelstein alumni, for taking the low road. The irony—indeed, one of the great underreported stories of the 1996 campaign—was that the really effective negative campaigning had been done all along not by the Republicans but by the Democrats. The assertion that "Dolegingrich" was out to cut Medicare for seniors, repeated again and again in paid advertisements and by Democratic politicians, was far more lethal than anything Dole could say about Bill Clinton. In Florida, a state that no GOP presidential candidate had lost since Gerald Ford in 1976, Dole trailed by five points in early October. "Why are you cutting my Medicare?" asked an elderly lady in a wheelchair when Dole visited a nursing home. Dole was exasperated. "Mediscare! Mediscare! Mediscare!" he bellowed at the rally at West Palm Beach. "Why don't you be honest with Florida's seniors? Why don't you tell the truth, Mr. President?" To the great despair of Dole's pollsters, the Democrats' agitprop was getting a free pass. When Bob Ward's mother complained to him that the Dole campaign was airing too many negative ads, Ward tried to point out that Clinton was run-ning plenty of them, too. His mother replied, "Yeah, but they don't seem negative."

And the Democrats didn't let up. Surveying his polling data in mid-September, Penn could see that Dole was actually making a little progress. The Clintonites were determined to keep Dole's favorable rating below 50 percent, but he had crept up into the mid-50s. Dole was becoming "a likable old man," said Bill Knapp. "We were concerned that he might trip over the line into becoming a likeable, effective old man. Our goal was to prevent that." Knapp designed an ad campaign intended to portray Dole in a harsher light: not as Bob Dole, war hero and plainspoken man, but as Senator Dole, hypocritical, antediluvian, lifelong legislator.

The spot was dubbed "Dole through the Ages." It opened with pages flying off the calendar in big red numbers across the bottom of the screen. "Let's go back in time," said the announcer. "The 1960s. Bob Dole's in Congress." Cut to a black-and-white shot of Dole wear-ing a skinny '60s tie. AGAINST CREATING STUDENT LOANS is stamped across his forehead. As the decades speed by, Dole's sins mount. AGAINST MEDICARE. AGAINST A HIGHER MINIMUM WAGE. AGAINST THE BRADY BILL TO FIGHT CRIME, even AGAINST VACCINES FOR CHILDREN.

By 1995, he has acquired an evil twin, Newt Gingrich. Photos of "Dolegingrich" float over the Capitol as the tinkly horror music swells. WRONG IN THE PAST, WRONG FOR OUR FUTURE flashes across the screen.

"We wanted an ad about his long, long, long, long career in the Senate and how he has a long, long, long, long record of being wrong," said Knapp. Without any fanfare, Clinton's team relentlessly drove home the message, as Knapp put it, that Dole was "too old and too out of it to be president."

For Clinton, the key to the last six weeks of the campaign was to remain "presidential." It was important for him to float above partisan wrangling, just as Dick Morris had counseled with his "triangulation" strategy. During the winter and spring of 1996, while the Republicans were scuffling in the mud of New Hampshire, Clinton's handlers had tried to create images that were suitably above the fray. At speeches, White House and campaign photographers tried to capture him standing alone on the stage, the captain on the bridge of the ship of state. The plan was to stage Clinton in the Rose Garden or the Oval Office in the morning doing "presidential" things—signing bills, meeting with foreign leaders—while trying to hold rallies later in the day, preferably after early press deadlines.

The presidential debates threatened to drag Clinton back down into the arena. The risk was that Clinton, defensive and thin-skinned, would lash back or engage Dole in lawyerly and tendentious debate that would be at once demeaning and dull. Clinton's debate preparations, at the old summer colony in Chautauqua, New York, were designed above all to make Clinton remember that he was the president—and to act like one.

Clinton's sparring partner was former Senate Majority Leader George Mitchell, a dry and disciplined onetime federal judge. As he came out of the Athenaeum Hotel in Chautauqua on the Friday after their first practice session, Clinton told reporters, "He beat me like a drum." At the time, reporters figured that Clinton was just spin-ning, trying to lower expectations. But in fact Mitchell had clobbered Clinton in their mock debate. In the role of Dole, Mitchell bore in on Clinton's greatest vulnerability. "The issue is trust," Mitchell began. "Where are the files? Will he pardon his friends and associ-ates? How can you trust the president and his record?" Mitchell, who said later he had felt squeamish attacking a president he admired, was biting at times. He called Clinton "an embarrassment to the presidency" and methodically ticked off his ethical problems. Clinton was unable to stay cool, even in practice. He became frustrated and testy. He would wallow in the details, delivering point-by-point re-buttals. At one point, he protested that Mitchell had an unfair ad-vantage. "Of course he's done well, he's got his notes in front of him," the president spluttered. In the role of moderator, White House spokesman Mike McCurry adopted the sneering tone of journalists. Clinton got mad. "That's just the way the press sounds about these things," he huffed, instead of answering the question.

Clinton wasn't sounding presidential. More ominous, Mrs. Clinton arrived in Chautauqua on the final day of debate prep in a difficult mood. "She was jumpy and nervous and had the capacity to blow it all up," said an aide. After taking a sunset walk around the resort grounds with her husband, Hillary decided to stay at the hotel and watch a football game on television instead of attending the final run-through. Watching made her too nervous, she said. Clinton's trainers had tried all weekend to lighten things up. Paul Begala, a veteran of the '92 campaign, worked up a mock training schedule in the style of Erskine Bowles, the former deputy chief of staff who never tired of trying to impose order on the White House: "8:15 A.M.: Undermine confidence. 9:30: Nitpick. 10:15: Second guess. 1:30 P.M.: Overload with facts." Charged with coming up with Morris-type mini-policy initiatives, Bruce Reed and Rahm Emanuel jokingly proposed a federal sock-matching registry aimed at elimi-nating the greatest household headache of soccer moms everywhere. The dorm humor had its effect. By the second night, Clinton wanted to stay up for hours after the mock debate, in order to practice being calm.

Dole had always hated preparing for speeches and debates, and he was worried that Clinton, already a superior debater, would use his incumbency to advantage. It seemed to him that Clinton had brought along half the executive branch to his training camp in Chautauqua. On the first weekend of October, Dole had only his old Senate chief of staff, Sheila Burke, and a few aides in the Crystal Ball Room at the SeaView. "Clinton's up there with hundreds of the finest minds and I'm here with you," he snapped after reading accounts of Clinton's extensive practice sessions. "We have no strategy for this debate. We have no strategy at all," he groused. Burke mentioned that Tony Fabrizio had written a memo. "Never saw it," said Dole. (Fabrizio wanted Dole to pledge never to cut Medicare.)

Media consultant Alex Castellanos had also sent a memo suggesting that Dole take advantage of his perceived weakness as a debater. Dole should play a Jimmy Stewart character. America loves the story of a little guy battling long odds, he said. During the debate, Dole should respond to Clinton's slick answers by saying that he "was never going to match your gifts as a political salesman." Emphasizing Clinton's abilities would make voters identify with Dole. "Last time I checked, Americans hate politics, especially the phoniness of it," Castellanos wrote. It was all good advice: the only problem was that Dole was a 30-year veteran of Washington, not Mr. Smith.

To play Clinton, the Dole campaign had drafted Senator Fred Thompson, the former prosecutor and movie actor. (Typically, the campaign kept Thompson waiting an hour and a half at the airport when he flew down to Florida.) In rehearsal, Dole kept wandering off and exceeding the time limit. Nelson Warfield, who was playing moderator, would anxiously interrupt, "Thank you, Senator." Dole practiced for ten hours over two days, but never for the full 90 minutes, and he refused to watch tapes of his performance. Worried about Dole's snappish streak, his advisers encouraged him to relax. "Your smile looks great, Bob!" gushed Elizabeth. To keep Dole smiling at the debate, she planned to sit beside Senator John McCain, who also had a famously big grin. Both would show as many teeth as possible, hoping that Dole would see them beaming in the audience. To distract President Clinton, the campaign gave a prime seat to Billy Dale, the former head of the White House Travel Office and now an embittered witness in congressional probes. It was a devilish taunt with a major flaw: Clinton had no idea what Dale looked like.

Shortly before 9 P.M. on Sunday night, in a curtained-off room at the Hartford Civic Center, Dole's top aides and senior "surrogates," governors and other notables who would be launched into "spin alley" after the debate, sat stiffly in armchairs before six TV sets. Scott Reed sat behind a table with three telephones. He looked pale and nervous, as if he might be sick. "He's out of his mind," said another aide. "Outta his mind." Most of the men in the room doffed their jackets. Reed kept his on. There was absolute silence until Dole started cracking jokes, making even Reed smile. The campaign manager leaned back and took a swig of Poland Spring water. Dole's advisers tried not to notice the images on the split screen: as Dole spoke, Clinton looked amused. As Clinton spoke, Dole appeared to scowl.

At 10:15, with 15 minutes remaining, the aides started distributing the basic spin to the surrogates. Clinton was "uptight and on the defensive"; Dole was "relaxed and humorous." As the instant analysis began, NBC's Tim Russert declared that this was a Bob Dole many people had not seen before. "Yes!" exclaimed an aide. But another confessed soberly: "I don't think we popped him enough."

Dole was scheduled to take a victory lap through New Jersey the next day on a bus. The portents were not good. Somebody forgot to bring Dole's specially fitted lectern on the press plane (affectionately dubbed the "Bullship"). The crowds were mostly anemic, though a large bunch of schoolchildren turned out at Tom's River High after being given the choice of a Dole rally or algebra class. In Red Bank, Dole pointed out that he had voted 13,836 times in Congress, thereby helping the Clinton campaign portray him as an aging Washington insider. That night, Dole headed back to New York City for a fund-raiser. His motorcade, which the candidate compared to a "funeral procession," arrived at the Lincoln Tunnel at rush hour, tying up traffic for miles. As Dole's bus motored past stranded commmuters, several gave him the finger.

Dole usually shrugged off such embarrassments, but he was tired and cranky when he returned to headquarters the next day. He thought he had won the debate—everyone had told him so—yet the crowds and energy were lacking. Dole liked to keep moving, to keep going forward. There had to be a way out; there always had been, no matter how deep the hole. The candidate announced that he wanted to bring in some experts to help find the "silver bullet" that would help win the campaign. He had hammered drugs and taxes, he had denounced Clinton as a "liberal," but nothing seemed to be catching on.

There was an awkward pause around the table. "Look, senator," said Paul Manafort, the campaign strategist, "there is no silver bullet." Dole looked at him. It was early October, he had been campaigning for over a year, less than a month remained until Election Day, and no one could see a winning scenario. Dole was not angry. He was, in a rare moment of openness, realistic about his fate. "It sure would have been nicer to run against this guy in '94," he sighed. "I guess I missed my moment."

Yet the next day, Dole did get some good news. The campaign learned that the *Post* had decided not to run the story about Dole's extramarital affair. At least now Dole could dare to talk to reporters. He had not given a lengthy interview to a major news organization since mid-September, partly because he was naturally wary of the Diane Sawyers and Sam Donaldsons, but partly because he feared that he would become trapped discussing a 25-year-old indiscretion. Dole also felt freer to attack Clinton's character. True, Dole still had to be careful not to make an issue of Clinton's private life. A *Post* editorial had made a distinction between character attacks that involved public ethics, like campaign spending or scandals in office, and the candidate's personal affairs. The campaign knew it had to stay on the right side of that line or risk provoking the *Post* into running its story. There was tremendous consternation when Bill Bennett hit the trail on October 11 and began talking about how he wouldn't mention personal issues like "philandering," while doing just that. "This was so incredibly dangerous," said an aide. Bennett, he said, was unwittingly "playing with nitroglycerin." The campaign hastily went on background with reporters to assure them that Bennett had been speaking for himself. Scott Reed leaked a campaign memo on "the character issue," making it clear that "personal issues" were out of bounds.

The memo also made clear, however, that the Dole campaign intended to accent the negative from here on out. The decision to take a tougher line helped resolve the basic debate over strategy that had been roiling the campaign since early September. Dole had cratered in the East, where the soccer moms had apparently opted for Clinton. But in California, Dole seemed to be closing the gap a little. Two polls shown him down by only 10 points. Manafort wanted to make a concerted run at California, hitting the "wedge issues" of immigration and affirmative action.

Going after California was bold but risky. It was probably too late to mount an effective campaign, and Dole would surely have to play rough. John Buckley begged his colleagues not to make Dole's "last mission" look like a racist attack. "It would mean us losing ugly," said Buckley. California, he said, "is the biggest, shiniest piece of fool's gold in history."

On the morning of Saturday, October 12, Manafort and the campaign staff presented the California strategy to Dole.

"Where are we in Ohio?" Dole asked.

"Eighteen points down," said pollster Tony Fabrizio.

"Can't be," said Dole. He had just returned from a two-day bus tour of Ohio, seen the cheering crowds. The foolishness of the whole exercise struck him. "Why did I just spend two days on a bus tour of Ohio if you're planning to pull the plug on it?"

His aides anxiously tried to get Dole focused on the California strategy. But the candidate wasn't buying. "Gotta play in Ohio," he said. No Republican had ever won the White House without winning Ohio.

The boundless enthusiasm of Jack Kemp had provided Dole with a much-needed lift in San Diego and given all the Republicans a shot of optimism. But by October, Kemp merely seemed tiresome to some of Dole's advisers. Ever the enthusiast, the vice-presidential nominee believed that no voters were out of reach. Eager to make African-Americans appreciate the virtues of the free-market economy, Kemp courted voters in Harlem and at a housing project in Memphis, Tennessee. "We're gonna win 25 percent of the black vote," he insisted to Tony Fabrizio. "If that's true," the pollster replied, "then this race is over." Kemp and his campaign manager, Wayne Berman, also hoped that stumping in the cities would attract soccer moms by countering the GOP's image of racial insensitivity. One problem was that Kemp tended to improvise, advocating tax breaks that were not in Dole's economic plan. Dole's campaign aides humored Kemp for a while, before suggesting that he reach out to some voters whom he might actually win over, like Catholics.

The Dole campaign did not have high hopes for Kemp's debate against Al Gore, who was stiff but smart and disciplined. Normally, handlers watching a debate backstage in the holding room persuade themselves that their man has won, or at least done a credible job. The scene backstage in St. Petersburg on the night of October 9 was a little more realistic. As the debate began, Haley Barbour, the chairman of the Republican party, said to Ed Feulner of the Heritage Foundation, "Hey, Ed, you're Kemp's right-hand man. Don't you think Kemp would approve if you kept one of these TVs on the Braves game with the sound off?" (The baseball playoffs were on.) Eight minutes into the debate Barbour yawned over Gore's robotic answers. "Jesus, an hour and a half more of this," he muttered. When Kemp floundered on a foreign-policy question, Barbour sighed and swore. When it was over, the party chief said to no one in particular, "I told you we should have kept the ball game on one channel." Kemp had broken out in a Nixonian sweat under the glare of the lights and at one point had even been buzzed by a fly. When he saw Feulner back at the Don Cesar hotel after the debate, he said, "I never want to do that again."

The second debate between Bill Clinton and Bob Dole had been over for 40 minutes, but the president was still talking to questioners. He discussed health-care reform with a cardiologist, welfare reform with a young man, policy issues large and small with anyone who hadn't been able to ask a question during the hour and a half on camera. Clinton listened intently, smiled earnestly, empathized deeply. He gave them the famous handshake, gripping their sweaty palms with his big right paw, cradling their elbows with his left. He bathed them all in the full, profound and soulful attention of the president of the United States. Some of the citizens invited to the "town hall" debate looked like they were about ready to head home. But Clinton was not about to let go, not until he had answered every question, won each and every vote.

Backstage, Bob Dole fumed. He had fled the stage after a few grip-and-grins and now half-listened to his handlers pretend that he had won the debate. He wanted to go to a campaign rally, but he was stuck. By the protocol arranged with the Presidential Debate Commission, the president's motorcade left first.

Finally, Clinton wandered backstage, to a burst of applause from his aides. Like a schoolboy seeking affirmation, he asked, "Did I do okay? I couldn't really tell out there." Pollster Mark Penn handed the president the results of his quickie poll rating the candidates' answers to each question in the debate. Clinton had won all 20, most by wide margins. The networks were showing polls that awarded the president the match by 20 or 30 points.

Clinton would never be satisfied until the last vote was counted, but everyone else in his entourage was in a state of rapture. Gloating is not too strong a word to describe the atmosphere backstage in the president's holding room. Remembering the camaraderie of the "war room," veterans of the '92 campaign—Stephanopoulos, Paul Begala and James Carville—were schoolyard cocky. Straddling their chairs turned backward before a row of TV sets, they had high-fived, fist-pumped and whooped throughout the 90 minutes. More refined Friends-of-Bill like Erskine Bowles and superlawyer Vernon Jordan kept up dignity acts, and other aides tried to maintain a suitable White House hush, but no one could believe their good fortune. The audience—undecided voters selected for the Presidential Debates Commission by the Gallup organization—had lobbed softballs. A young man asked the president to elaborate on his plans to expand the Family and Medical Leave Act, Clinton's most popular piece of legislation. Carville leaped out of his chair and started doing an end-zone dance. "Did Gallup pick this audience? Or was it Central Casting?" asked speech coach Michael Sheehan. As Dole drifted aimlessly from updating the baseball score to trying to explain the difference between Medicare "cuts" and reducing the rate of growth, Stephanopoulos muttered, "He's speaking Chinese." "Yeah," said adman Bob Squier, "really bad Chinese." With 15 minutes to go, Stephanopoulos jumped up to head for the spin room. "That's it," he crowed. "It's over."

During prep sessions, Sheehan had urged Clinton to "dominate the space" on the stage. Clinton repeatedly and deliberately stepped out from behind his podium, claiming no-man's land between the two lecterns. Dole seemed unsettled when Clinton ambled toward him. "Let me move out of your way," he said at one point, provoking a round of chortles backstage. To the camera, it appeared that Clinton was peering benevolently over Dole's shoulder, winking at the audience with a "I'll straighten this out for you folks in just a second as soon as he's done fussin'" nonchalance. At one point, Clinton leaned jauntily against the podium with his ankles crossed, as though he were waiting for a cold one to come sliding down the bar.

The insouciance was carefully rehearsed. "Dole wants you to lose your temper," Mark Penn wrote in a memo to Clinton during the debate prep. "He wants you to be drawn into the mud. These are the only two ways he can touch the President of the United States. He may not even attack you, he just wants to get you mad." There was very little left to chance in any of the debates. Gore's most clever zinger of the night had come in response to Kemp's boast that "trickle down" economics in the Dole-Kemp administration would seem like "Niagara Falls." Gore shot back, "The problem with your plan is, it would put the American economy in a barrel and send it over the falls." It was totally canned: the Niagara line, a favorite of Kemp's, had been anticipated. Backstage, Gore's staffers chanted in unison as Gore uttered his "spontaneous" remark. (Other Gore lines the American people didn't get to hear included a response to Kemp's familiar boast about "growing the pie": "The problem with your scheme to grow the pie is that it's full of half-baked ideas that will leave the American people with crumbs.")

There was, in the Clintonites' celebrating, a touch of condescension, even pity, toward the Dole campaign. Some of Clinton's advisers thought Dole's performance was so bad they should have loaned him the briefing book they prepared for George Mitchell, Clinton's practice foe. When Dole had tried to compare Clinton to his dead brother "Kenny the exaggerator," there were hoots in the Clinton holding room. "I wish I'd been in on that strategy session," deadpanned Begala. "Hey, Senator, I've got a great idea. You can compare Clinton to your dead brother. That'll stump him. Yeah, that's it." Actually, Dole's reference to his dead brother was one of the very few lines he had made up on his own.

The election was starting to look like a sure thing, even to the candidates. Pumped up after trouncing Kemp, Gore exulted to his young chief of staff, Ron Klain, "Am I in great shape or what?" It had been their running gag line during debate prep. Klain told his boss, "If we lose this election, we're the stupidest people in American political history."

Clinton tried not to crow. He preferred what Stephanopoulos called the "gold watch strategy": heap praise on Dole for his years of service and let the voters figure out that he had served long enough. Clinton continued to marvel at Dole's ineptitude at campaigning. While his aides were hoorahing after the debate, Clinton stood in the hallway with political director Doug Sosnik, quietly critiquing Dole's performance. The president thought Dole was "clever" to introduce the character issue in his opening statement, but he couldn't understand why Dole had failed to sustain a more coherent argument. "It just kept coming out in little bits. That makes it harder to follow," explained Clinton, as if he were teaching a class.

The prospect of a landslide created a strategic dilemma for the Clinton campaign: was it time to share the wealth and spare a few million dollars to buy ads for struggling congressional candidates? Leon Panetta and Sosnik, loyal veterans of the House, wanted to, but they were practically shouted down by the consultants. Clinton had already done enough to help the Democrats, they argued; better not remind voters of the Democratic-controlled Congress so resoundingly rejected in 1994. Clinton wanted to keep the money for his own campaign, though he was obviously eager to see the Democrats win back Congress. He wanted to do something other than cast vetoes in his second term, and he was more than a little worried about Republican-controlled investigating committees.

The fear of scandal always hung over the Clinton campaign, and charges of shady political fund-raising from foreigners threatened to open a whole new front after the election. But the dread that had once gripped Clinton's aides had worn off. A few days after the debate, George Stephanopoulos was sifting through his in-box when he gave a yelp. He pulled out a subpoena from Congressman Clinger's House subcommittee. "I don't believe this," he said. "Now it's subpoena by in-basket." Stephanopoulos laughed. He passed off the subpoena—his 20th or so, he wasn't sure—to an assistant. "When I got my first subpoena in March 1994, I was heartbroken, nauseous," he allowed. "Now it's no big deal. This just shows you can get used to anything."

16 ■ ENDGAME

Until the very end, Dole could not quite believe that he was going to lose to Bill Clinton. He respected Clinton's skills as a campaigner, but he couldn't understand why voters would want Clinton to be their president. "This is serious business," Dole would proclaim, like a mantra. Sooner or later, Dole felt certain, voters would see through Clinton's act. George Bush had believed the same thing in 1992.

Presidential candidates live in a cocoon on the stump. Nelson Warfield, Dole's press secretary, did not show Dole the harsher attacks in the press, and the advance team cranked up loud music after every event so that Dole could not hear all the reporters shouting questions. Dole could tell himself that the cheering crowds, even the squealing schoolkids avoiding algebra class, represented a groundswell. Dole said he wanted to see the polls, but Dole's pollster, Tony Fabrizio, wasn't sure that campaign manager Scott Reed was showing the candidate Fabrizio's daily tracking report. Before the convention, Reed had said to Fabrizio, "Don't pay any attention to the polls." "But I'm the fucking pollster!" Fabrizio exclaimed. At a meeting on October 12, Fabrizio handed Dole a map showing him trailing in most states. Dole glanced at the map and then up at Reed. "Hmmm, guess you've only been telling me the good news," Dole said.

Reality finally began to sink in after the second debate. Dole's handlers told him he had won; every media outlet in the country told him he'd lost. Dole's response was characteristic. He was way behind. There was no one to help him. His campaign advisers didn't have any ideas, and Republicans were grumbling that Jack Kemp was running for the year 2000. Dole had once half hoped, half expected that the media would finish off the Clintons, but now reporters seemed bored with Whitewater and unable to untangle the new scandal over the Democrats' foreign fund-raising. Dole was alone, again. It was up to him to convince the voters that Clinton was unworthy.

The sight of Bob Dole pounding on a lectern, shouting "Wake up, America," was almost pitiable, but it was all he had left. As he wandered the country in the last days of the campaign, Dole threw away his prepared speeches and began riffing, offering up a strange pastiche of fractured metaphors, old lines from his primary speeches and whatever else floated into his mind. He compared the White House to a "laundromat" and accused the president of cheating at golf. The diatribes struck some of the reporters on the press bus as oddly good-natured. Dole seemed to be having fun, in a dark sort of way.

But the outbursts just scared off more voters. Ross Perot, largely forgotten until then, was threatening to break out of single digits, capitalizing on some of the voters' disgust with shady campaign fund-raising. At the staff meeting on Sunday, October 20, Reed asked Fabrizio if Perot could pull 15 percent of the vote. "No," said Fabrizio. "Best-case scenario, it's probably 50 (Clinton), 40 (Dole), 10 (Perot) nationally. Could be worse." His prediction was greeted with dead silence.

Depressed, Dole's top advisers sat around Reed's office at campaign headquarters, trying to think of something they could do. The scene reminded one adviser of the story of a test pilot in Tom Wolfe's *The Right Stuff,* radioing the tower as his plane plummeted earthward. "I've tried A," the pilot said. "I've tried B," he said. "I've tried C," he said. Then he crashed.

There was one last maneuver to try. For some time, Dole had been toying with the idea of asking Perot to drop out of the race and cast his support to Dole. It was a long shot, but Reed figured the time had come to try. Maybe, Reed suggested, Perot would be looking for a chance to save face. Reed asked the others what they thought. Fabrizio was skeptical, but the rest argued there was nothing to lose.

Reed's "secret" trip was a fiasco. It leaked before Reed had even met with Perot. Although Reed believed Perot was expecting him, Perot hadn't known he was coming until his press secretary heard it from an AP reporter while Reed was airborne. In a hangar at Love Field, Reed tried to persuade Perot to drop out. But Perot was irked that the news of the meeting had already leaked. Reed said that if Perot persisted in siphoning off votes, Clinton would "sneak in again through the back door." In a second term, "there will be a constitutional crisis," predicted Reed. "This will be like Watergate." Perot listened politely. Then Dole himself called Perot to make the pitch by phone. "If I'm gonna win this thing, it's gotta be me and Clinton," Dole told Perot. At first, Dole thought Perot might be receptive. The Texas billionaire did not want to see Clinton reelected, and he did not dismiss Dole's plea out of hand. "We'd have to have a strategy," Perot told Dole, who was speaking by phone from a weight room at a Florida high school where he was campaigning. That evening, Dole made a second phone call to see where things stood, and this time he concluded that Perot was unlikely to cooperate. When Dole suggested a meeting between the two of them, Perot demurred. The next day, Perot publicly scorned the Dole campaign's overture as "weird" and delighted in the publicity.

That same day, the campaign learned that the story of Dole's long-ago extramarital affair was finally reaching print in the *National Enquirer*. Now Dole was really angry. He called on voters to "rise up" against the national news media. To a reporter along the rope line who asked Dole about the story of his affair, he snapped, "You're even worse than they are." He was hoping to send a signal to editors everywhere to stay out of the gutter. Meanwhile, the staff braced for the adultery story to go up the usual media food chain, from supermarket tabloid to city tabloid to CNN and the rest of the mainstream press.

To their surprise, the sleazefest never happened. The *New York Daily News* did run a short item, and the *Washington Post* made the merest mention of its own reporting, buried deep in a routine campaign story. But most editors across the nation figured that Dole was too far behind, Election Day was too close at hand, the alleged affair was too remote and only arguably relevant. In retrospect, the Dole campaign had been overanxious, although it's hard to say what would have happened if the story had broken in a close race with more than a month to go. The concern over the *Post* story had taken its toll. While Dole never liked to give interviews, communications director Buckley believed that the threat of scandal made him extra wary. Among the shows Dole declined in the last two months were a joint *Meet the Press* appearance with Kemp, interviews with Jim Lehrer and Katie Couric, and requests from *Larry King Live* almost every week.

Newt Gingrich had long since given up hope of orchestrating a "team effort" by the GOP. Dole campaign aides had stopped coming to his meetings. They publicly blamed the unpopular Speaker for dragging down the Republican ticket. Gingrich had sincerely wanted to help Dole, whom he admired. But by autumn, he realized that he would have to distance himself from Dole if the Republicans' House majority was going to survive.

Gingrich's moods had swung wildly throughout 1996. Over Memorial Day weekend, he had returned to the lavish Palm Beach home of his GOPAC patroness, Gay Gaines. This time, there were no giddy parties and sing-alongs. Alone, pensive, Gingrich slowly walked around the pool, reading aloud from *The Five Books of Moses*, a new Biblical translation. At the GOP convention, Gingrich seemed almost manically high again, but at a gathering with *Washington Post* reporters, he had started softly crying when he talked about Jack Kemp's close bond with his children. In September, Gingrich was in a state of rage. There were times, during the endgame of the budget negotiations, when Gingrich had seemed aware of his own shortcomings. But now the only error he could see was failing to anticipate the monstrous treachery of his enemies. He had been the victim of a conspiracy, he railed. He denounced the unions for spending "hundreds of millions" on misleading ads ("$75,000 against me personally"). The president, Gingrich insisted, was a "liar" who had been protected by the "liberal elite media."

Gingrich's anger boiled over at a meeting with *Newsweek* editors in early October. An editor asked him if he thought he had done anything to contribute to the culture of scandal in Washington by his own attacks on former Speaker Jim Wright. Gingrich, who had been drinking cranberry juice and chewing the ice, narrowed his eyes. "I am going to hold my breath and count to ten," he seethed. He launched into an attack on the Clintons, comparing them with the corrupt Grant and Harding administrations. Rather than reform themselves, Gingrich said, the Democrats had decided to destroy him, with help from their friends in the media. In a more reflective mood a few days later, Gingrich said that he was able to endure by "reading history." In his grandiose way, Gingrich compared himself to the Duke of Wellington, who had defeated Napoleon at Waterloo. Before that famous victory, Wellington had been criticized for not taking the offensive and then, when he did attack, for taking too many casualties. Like Wellington, Gingrich just had to hang on to survive; ultimately his cause would triumph.

But certain sacrifices would have to be made. After dinner on the night of September 18, Gingrich asked his top political aides, Don Fierce and Joe Gaylord, to join him on his private balcony over-looking the Mall. Bathed in moonlight, Gingrich confided that he was concerned the GOP would lose control of the House. Something had to be done to reverse the party's tracking polls, which showed a steady erosion of support for Republican congressmen. The polls suggested a solution: many voters, it appeared, wanted to split their tickets. They were more likely to vote for Republican congressmen if they felt that Clinton was likely to win. The trick was to encourage them, but not to be too obvious about it. If the press learned that the GOP leadership was plotting, in effect, to dump Dole, it might depress voter turnout, as well as hurt Dole personally.

Gingrich was actually slow to seize on the split-ticket strategy. As far back as June, GOP chief Haley Barbour had begun worrying that a Clinton landslide would bring down the Republican congress. Without telling the Dole campaign, Barbour had been holding secret "what if" sessions with his aides. Through a focus group conducted by the GOP in the fall, he learned that voters were worried that Hillary Clinton would be back in charge in a second term. As one housewife explained it, "She would do to welfare what she did to health care." Barbour geared the entire RNC get-out-the-vote effort—from television ads to nearly 73 million pieces of direct mail—around a message that was subtle but effective in exploiting that fear: "Don't Give Clinton a Blank Check."

At the same time, Gingrich was strongly urging Dole to go on the attack against the president. Negative campaigning might turn off the soccer moms, but it would "energize the base," stir up the right-wing Clinton haters to turn out on Election Day. In early October, Gingrich persistently lobbied the Dole campaign to hit Clinton, and he took personal credit when Dole finally did. Watching Dole lay into Clinton during the second debate, Gingrich turned to some friends and asked, "Did I miss a personality transplant?" As he left Dave & Busters, a cavernous sports bar in Marietta, Georgia, where he had watched the debate, munching potato skins with bacon bits as Dole and Clinton jousted on the big-screen TV, Gingrich was asked if he had anything to do with Dole's newly aggressive persona. "What do you think?" he asked and smiled wickedly. Gingrich was not at all sorry to see Perot rise in the polls in late October. Although Perot was siphoning off voters from Dole, Perot voters were more likely to vote for Republican congressional candidates than for Democrats. The more Perot voters who turned out, the better.

But in the Dole campaign, nothing seemed to be working. Haley Barbour, the GOP's rotund and folksy chief, groused that the Democrats had completely ignored the campaign-finance laws—this, he said, was the true story of the 1996 election. But the scandal had come too late to save Bob Dole. The overriding factor in the race was the brilliance of the Democrats' attack strategy and the sheer bungling of the GOP. Barbour was defensive about the charge that the GOP had allowed the Democrats to run wild with millions of dollars of unanswered negative advertising, beginning in late '95. In the spring and summer of '96, Barbour protested, he had spent about

$35 million of party money to elect Dole. But the incompetents in the Dole campaign had wasted it on focus groups and consultants who made lousy ads. Barbour shook his head over the vapid bumper stickers dreamed up by Dole's strategists. His personal favorite was OUR GOAL, YOUR SOUL, BOB DOLE. His criticisms didn't get much argument from Tony Fabrizio, one of the Dole consultants who squandered the money. Looking back at the campaign in mid-October, Fabrizio admitted, "We never did one thing well."

Dole's media campaign, never well-conceived or well-executed, collapsed altogether in the waning days. In the early fall, Alex Castellanos had tried to make some lighthearted ads mocking Clinton. He produced a series of spots called "How to Speak Liberal," which purported to translate Clinton-ese. After a clip of Clinton admitting he'd raised taxes too much, an announcer explained, "That's liberal for 'I lied, raised your taxes and got caught.'" (Another spot proposed by adman Sig Rogich showed a pained president holding his head while the voice-over doo-wopped, "You cheated, you lied, you said I could trust you / Ohhhh . . . what can I doooo . . . If I, I can't trust yoouu.") But Scott Reed forbade any reference to "lying" in Dole's ads. Castellanos was exasperated. Dole was going to have to attack Clinton's character, and it would be better to be playful about it. "If you don't do this now, you're gonna find yourself two or three weeks from now with a hatchet in your hand trying to maul this guy in a very violent and graceless way, which you don't want to do," Castellanos argued to Reed. But Reed was adamant.

By the last week of October, Dole was in full-scale candidate rebellion, refusing to approve the travel schedule and canceling a shoot of the last ads of the campaign. The shoot was rescheduled (at an extra cost of $20,000), but Castellanos fell to fighting with the latest consultant to be drafted, Madison Avenue adman Norman Cohen. The two image makers squabbled over the script and camera angle before Castellanos relinquished control. In the final product, Dole looked like he had escaped from a wax museum. At Cohen's insistence, the camera was brought in so close you could see the pupils of Dole's eyes darting back and forth as he read lines off the Tele-PrompTer. Dole wanted to put the ads right on the air without running them past headquarters. "Don't worry about Washington," he said. Staffers there had stopped holding meetings. Instead, they joked that Dole's numbers would sink wherever he ran ads or made a campaign stop.

A week before Election Day, Mort Engelberg, the Hollywood producer who handled much of Clinton's advance work, paced the stage in front of the Clark County government center in Las Vegas. The weather forecast had called for rain and 25-mph winds, but the president stood bathed in brilliant late-afternoon sun. Engelberg was, for the moment, content. He was obsessed with getting the right light. During Clinton's train trip to the Chicago convention, "the 21st Century Express," he would have the train slow down or speed up so it would arrive at the last whistle-stop just as dusk was falling, the time of day that photographers call "the magic hour."

Good light seemed to follow Clinton. The next day, he was silhouetted against the sparkling Pacific, asking a roaring throng of college students in Santa Barbara to "walk across that bridge with me." But the president was in a testy mood. He was furious at the Democratic National Committee for doing an embarrassing about-face, refusing, then agreeing, to release the party's preelection fund-raising report. The flap over Democratic campaign money was starting to cut into Clinton's poll numbers, threatening to drag him below the 50 percent level and spoil a perfect campaign.

Clinton was rattled by Perot's late surge. The protest-vote candidate had denied him a majority in 1992 and now seemed poised to do it again. Pollster Mark Penn tried to reassure Clinton that Perot was taking voters from Dole, not Clinton, but the president just shifted his irritation to the press. "Where is the fairness in all this?" Clinton fumed. "Dole's chief fund-raiser is going to jail and they've outraised us 3 to 2. How come all anyone cares about is the Democrats?" he pouted. (Simon C. Fireman was sentenced to six months' house arrest for making illegal campaign contributions, and the GOP raised $280 million to the Democrats' $140 million.) Mike McCurry tried to reassure Clinton. "You're going to be president and he's not," said McCurry. But Clinton was sure the media would do anything to deny him a good clean victory. "It's one more thing for them to gnaw on," he fumed.

"If I'm gonna lose this, I'm gonna lose this my way," Dole grumbled to Scott Reed a week before Election Day. Dole was now aware that he could lose, as he would put it, "big time." He had seen a *New York Times* poll showing that voters now found him less trustworthy than Clinton. "We'll be lucky if we get 100 electoral votes," he told Reed. "We'll be lucky if we get 50."

Time to get cracking, keep moving. Dole had always tried to stay a step ahead of the dark. On the Friday before Election Day, Dole made a dramatic vow: he would campaign without stopping the rest of the way. So began the 96 Hours to Victory Tour, the last leg of Dole's meandering political death march, a strange odyssey across a sleeping land that seemed, at times, to have forgotten that Dole was even out there.

Before he left, Dole stood on a stage with George Bush in Tampa, Florida, singing Lee Greenwood's "Proud to Be an American." When the song ended, Dole painfully unwrapped the fingers of his left hand, raising the pinkie and index finger as he waved at the crowd. Dole talked about how proud he had been to vote for "Ike" Eisenhower. Dole was the last of America's World War II generation to run for the presidency, and he knew now that he would never join Ike or Bush or his old hero, Dick Nixon, as a winner. As Bush recalled Dole's loyalty and service and told the crowd that he wanted to stand at his side, supporting him in every way, Dole let slip his old envies and resentments and began to cry.

The 96-hour frenzy of Dole's final days had an oddly antic air for a dying campaign. Dole had never been a very vigorous campaigner, preferring to fly back to Washington and sleep in his own bed, and he tried to make sure he got his regular eight hours. For the marathon trip, reporters were issued a small duffel bag containing deodorant and a toothbrush. One of them drew a map of Dole's final itinerary on his laptop. In script, the wandering track spelled out "loser." The media skepticism seemed borne out the first night, when the press plane landed at 4:30 A.M. in Newark, New Jersey, for an expected airport rally. The tarmac was dark and empty.

By Monday Dole had given so many speeches that his voice had been reduced to a croak. But he was buoyant and cheerful, drinking a tea called Throat Coat and gaining strength from surprisingly large and lively crowds that showed up at diners and bowling alleys, high-school gyms and airport hangars. Dole danced with Elizabeth on stage in Lafayette, Louisiana, and choked up in Des Moines when Senator McCain called him the last warrior. Dole's plane got a flat tire on Monday afternoon, so Dole moved onto the Bullship, where he dozed up front while his aides tried to hush the serenades from reporters. By his last rally, at 3 A.M. on Election Day in Harry Truman's hometown of Independence, Missouri, Dole actually seemed to be picking up energy, pumping his fist to the music and dancing on the balls of his feet.

In those final four days, he flew 10,534 miles and touched down in 20 states. Finally he could go home, first to Russell to vote, then to his true home, the apartment he shared with Elizabeth at the Watergate in Washington. Dole seemed cool and calm when he called Nelson Warfield after 7 P.M. and asked "how things look." Warfield told him that Ohio and Florida had gone for Clinton. Dole had long since accepted defeat, but he wanted to hold off on a concession to allow Californians to vote. Typically, someone on the snakebit campaign staff hit the wrong computer button and released a concession statement that was immediately announced on the networks. A sheepish campaign aide had to issue a retraction.

When Dole finally left his hotel suite after 11 P.M. to deliver the speech he had long feared he would have to give, he found the hallway outside lined with old friends. They applauded and shook hands as he moved down the line. In the sweaty, smoky basement ballroom of the Renaissance Hotel, he offered a last gesture of graciousness. "C'mon up," he said to Scott Reed. He would not abandon his beleaguered campaign manager at the end. Reed had been feeling low, blaming himself ("Maybe I coulda won another way," he mumbled), but the self-recrimination was unnecessary. If ever there was a candidate not destined to win, it was Bob Dole.

Newt Gingrich had been giddy again on the last weekend. He believed that the GOP would actually pick up a half-dozen seats in the House and mock the conventional wisdom that demonizing Newt was the way to win. "The average person began realizing about three weeks ago that I am not their congressman," he insisted. But in the early evening of Election Night, the mood turned grim in the "war room" set up by the Gingrich forces at the Cobb Galleria Conference Center in Marietta, Georgia. It was becoming clear the GOP would keep the House, but with a narrower majority. Reporters clamored to see Gingrich. The Speaker, once the most overexposed political figure in Washington, remained hidden inside until 2:45 A.M., after the networks had gone off the air.

Bill Clinton had finally come, after 23 years, to the last speech on the last night of his last campaign. It was 1 A.M. in Sioux Falls, South Dakota, and the president couldn't stop.

Clinton, his voice thick with emotion, wondered aloud how a boy "born in a summer storm to a widowed mother" in a remote corner of Arkansas had become "president of the greatest country in human history." It was easily his most moving speech of the campaign. When he was finally done talking, Clinton hugged a teary-eyed Hillary and Chelsea, and he worked the rope line. Then he bounded back onstage to work the band. Finally pried away, he kept on dancing inside Air Force One as the big plane swung south to Arkansas. Staffers gulped down champagne and mango ice cream in the aisle, watching the president do an airborne Macarena. In Little Rock, he still would not rest. He sat up until dawn in a suite at the Excelsior Hotel with Leon Panetta, Doug Sosnik and Bruce Lindsey, playing hearts.

On Tuesday, after the voting was done, old Little Rock friends found the first couple floating serenely through a party at Senator David Pryor's house. One F.O.B. said he hadn't seen Hillary happier in years. The Clintons had been told that an electoral college landslide was in the making; the only open question was control of Congress. In the last days, Clinton had decided not to travel to the big states, where he might rack up a bigger popular vote, but rather to concentrate on picking up key Senate seats. Hillary, meanwhile, had campaigned for House candidates. Their interest was more than political: both wanted to keep control of the congressional investigating committees out of GOP hands. Hillary tried to be philosophical about it as she chatted with friends. Scandals, she said, were "all politics, all politics, it's all about the balance of power in Washington."

Shortly after 6 P.M. in Little Rock, Clinton had just awakened from a nap when his pollster, Mark Penn, walked through the door. Penn told the president that he had carried New Hampshire and Florida. "If those two states are going our way, it's over, it's over," he said. The president and the pollster high-fived. Hillary came over to hold her husband's hand. Then, as Clinton sat in an armchair chomping on a cigar, the loyal lieutenants lined up to receive the presidential blessing. There were Panetta, Stephan-opoulos, Ickes, McCurry and Terry McAuliffe, who had raised the early war chest. Old friends like superlawyer Vernon Jordan and Mack McLarty came by later, as did campaign manager Peter Knight, who had led a retinue of retainers in an operation that had seemed al-most Nixonian in its efficiency. Missing, of course, was Dick Morris. He was back in New York, living alone in an apartment. There were reports that his wife, Eileen McGann, had asked him to move out of their house in Greenwich, Connecticut, though Morris insisted he was trying to keep his marriage together. Meanwhile, he worked on the memoir that would make clear who was the true architect of one of the great comebacks in American political history.

Inside the Bill Clinton suite of the Excelsior Hotel, decorated with a gilt-framed oil portrait of the president, the first family seemed serene. Hillary played with Clinton's 20-month-old nephew, Tyler. The president's brother, Roger, sliced an apple for the boy and said he felt "bittersweet." He missed his mother, he said, and he was sure Bill did, too. Clinton sat in a wingback chair by himself, his reading glasses perched on his nose, tinkering with his victory speech. Dole had called Clinton to concede at 9:20 P.M.; shortly after 11 P.M. in Washington, Dole came on the television to publicly bow out. Hillary and Al and Tipper Gore gathered round the four TV sets. The presi-dent did not even look up. Just after midnight, the president walked hand in hand with Hillary and Chelsea out of the State House and onto a brightly lit outdoor stage. In 1992 Tipper and Hillary had done a little jig here on Election Night; now they just held their children close by.

Clinton uttered the usual political bromides—it seemed rather like an inaugural address—and one great political truth: "The vital American center," he said, "is alive and well." With keen in-stinct and sheer doggedness, Clinton had found and enlarged that center. He had won with no clear mandate. In the exit polls, the voters continued to cast doubt upon his character. But they had taken him back. Redemption and renewal are peculiarly American graces, and in 1996 Bill Clinton embodied them.

EPILOGUE:
"DID WE WIN THIS THING?"

A month after Election Day, Dole headquarters was a half-empty shell. Computer cables and phone wires lay in a tangle on the floor, the file cabinets were empty, the Secret Service gone. Bob Dole sat alone in his corner office, reading letters of condolence, yet not feeling sorry for himself. After losing to George Bush in the primaries in 1988, he had been unable to sleep for weeks, turning over in his bed with thoughts of bitterness and regret. But this time he felt that he had done his best. He had been "a long shot, we were the underdog," he said to a *Newsweek* reporter in his first interview after the election. Tanned from a Florida vacation, he seemed relaxed and thoughtful as he sat on a cream-color love seat, dressed as usual in a crisp white shirt with French cuffs.

Dole was careful to not cast blame, at least not directly. He acknowledged that the Democrats had successfully paired him with Newt Gingrich. "They ran all these ads, you know, Bob Dole and Newt Gingrich, Dole-Gingrich, Dole-Gingrich. We've been referred to by [Vice President Al] Gore as a two-headed monster. I mean, talk about over-the-edge statements. I think Gore made them every day." It was clear that Dole was stung by these attacks. He produced a letter from one voter who declared that he would have voted for him if not for Gingrich's extremism. But Dole steadfastly insisted that he would not have distanced himself from Gingrich if he had to do it all over again. At moments, he tacitly acknowledged that he had been a less-than-stellar campaigner. He had tried to "stay on message, not talk in the third person," but he knew that he had often failed. "I got to thinking about why do I do that, and that's what we do in the Congress," he said. "In the Senate you never talk first person. In fact, you can be corrected by Senator [Robert] Byrd [the West Virginia Democrat who is a stickler about parliamentary rules]," he explained. Dole was typically mordant about his directionless campaign. "I worked as hard as I could and tried to follow the strategy. If there wasn't a strategy, I tried to follow what there was." He wished that he had been able to banter easily with reporters, as he had during his Senate days. He felt he couldn't afford to "go back there and mix it up" with the press on his plane because there was "always somebody with a gotcha question. Gotcha, gotcha, gotcha."

Dole was proud of his marathon finish. In the final days, he said, he had told Elizabeth, "It's not gonna happen, unless there's some miracle out there." But he felt that he could save House and Senate seats for the GOP by going all-out. Initially, he had wanted to "walk across America" in the final weeks, but opted instead for the 96-hour fly-around when his aides convinced him that the logistics would be simpler. He was not angry that the Republican congressional leaders had, in effect, abandoned him as early as the end of August. The rush of legislation in August, including welfare and immigration reform, had given Clinton a series of bill-signing ceremonies while robbing Dole of some hot-button campaign issues. "That's just the way it works," Dole said, with a shrug. He had been a senator, and he understood the pressures.

The only time Dole displayed any real bitterness was on the subject of the Democrats' "Mediscare" ads. Professionally, he admired the tactic. "It was effective, no doubt about it," he said. But he was angry at the Democrats for portraying "scary Republicans" out to frighten senior citizens. "It really bothered me," he said. He was incredulous at the suggestion that he chair a bipartisan commmmission to reform Medicare. "After the Democrats kill you with it, why should you rush in and say, oh yeah, sure? They must think I have a hole in my head." Dole did not attack Clinton directly for the "Mediscare" campaign ("we get along, we're not unfriendly"). But with tongue firmly in cheek, he twice described Clinton as a "flexible" politician. "That was his strategy," said Dole. "To run as a Republican."

Bill Clinton was strangely disconsolate after his victory. Listening to Bill and Hillary Clinton, said an aide, "you kind of have to wonder: did we win this thing?" The '96 race, Clinton told an adviser, had been like "a dinner party that went on two hours too long." He was frustrated that his perfect campaign had failed to secure him a clear majority. As ever, he blamed the press. If the media hadn't made so much of the DNC's fund-raising flap in the last two weeks, Clinton said, he would have topped 50 percent on Election Day. His vexation grew as he fielded questions at a postelection press conference. Why had so few people bothered to vote? How did Clinton intend to keep his second term from becoming a disaster? What about the Indonesian money? Only two reporters—one Kuwaiti, the other Palestinian—congratulated Clinton. Several days later, the president's spokesman, Mike McCurry, was uncharacteristically bitter. No one should be surprised that the euphoria had been short-lived, he said. "It's basically because the press decided to take it away from Clinton."

Among Clinton's advisers, there was a pervasive world-weariness. "In '92, there was a feeling that we had reached the promised land," said one aide. "Everyone was thinking what it was going to be like to park in the West Wing driveway and have an office in the Old Executive Office Building with a fireplace." The grind of four years had taken a toll, although the constant threat of scandal had, over time, produced more numbness than fear. "It's a little like nuclear weapons in the Cold War," said the aide. "Were you aware that the Russians could push the button and blow us all up in a second? Yes. Did it keep you from getting up and putting your pants on in the morning? No."

The mood was not improved by Clinton's shabby treatment of Harold Ickes, the deputy chief of staff who had worked around the clock for three years to protect the president from his enemies, both real and imagined. Erskine Bowles, the calm, middle-of-the-road North Carolina businessman who replaced Leon Panetta as chief of staff after the election, understandably wanted his own team. The explosive Ickes, a liberal labor lawyer from Manhattan, would not fit in. But Clinton had not bothered to give the news privately to his trusted aide ahead of time. Ickes read about his fate in the *Wall Street Journal*. The only really happy face at the White House after the election belonged to Vice President Gore, who, behind the scenes, had used the campaign to shore up his base of supporters, financial and political, for his own presidential race in the year 2000.

In retrospect, it seems clear that Clinton should have been grateful that the press did not do more to push the "Indogate" scandal. The superb machinery set up to handle Whitewater—the "Masters of Disaster" in their Arsenal of Democracy—had been oddly quiet and passive in October. Mark Fabiani later explained that he didn't really feel that his defense perimeter ran to the DNC and the Commerce Department. He also worried that if he began making too many inquiries, calling Democratic donors or party officials or agency bureaucrats, reporters would think the White House was trying to orchestrate a cover-up. But mostly, Fabiani and his lawyer colleague, Jane Sherburne, were worn out and planning to move on.

The let-it-all-hang-out ethos pushed by Fabiani and Co. began to give way to more familiar stonewalling habits. In October, the White House was worried that Dole would make an issue of the White House trying to cover up a 1995 memo from FBI Director Louis Freeh outlining the administration's lackluster performance in the war on drugs. Fabiani argued to release the memo, but White House counsel Jack Quinn prevailed, insisting that the classified document be kept secret (a leaked version is reprinted in the documents section of this book).

The withdrawal of the Masters of Disaster essentially left no one in charge of scandal control. Into this vacuum stepped Clinton's old confidant, Bruce Lindsey. In October, when the White House realized that Indonesian business tycoon James Riady had in fact met several times with the president, and that policy matters had come up, there was a querulous debate over what to tell the press. Sherburne argued for releasing as much information as possible without characterizing the conversations one way or another. Lindsey, however, insisted that it would be best simply to call the Riady visits "social occasions." As the president's senior adviser, Lindsey set the strategy. Other White House aides, like spokesman McCurry, passed Lindsey's information along to the media, basically praying that Election Day would arrive before reporters dug up anything really damaging.

In fact, the press did not try all that hard. The mainstream publications pursued the story, and the political reporters on the trail yammered at the candidates during rare press availabilities. "Indo-gate," an unsavory blend of potential influence-peddling and dirty money, spiced up an otherwise boring endgame for reporters. Their editors made a half-hearted effort to push the story with big headlines and drumbeat coverage. But after months of boring the public with the arcana of Whitewater, a degree of scandal fatigue had set in. The press also lacked the usual sources to feed the scandal: it hadn't yet moved to the congressional committee or special prosecutor stage, which generally offer such generous opportunities for leakage. Besides, there was no "smoking gun," no clear quid pro quo for the large Indonesian donations.

In the end, Clinton's own pollster, Mark Penn, did not blame the scandal for Clinton's failure to go over the 50 percent mark. After the election, he claimed that Clinton's polls had never showed the president going much above 50 percent. The scandal may have slowed Clinton's momentum, said Penn. But the real reason he finished below 50 percent was low voter turnout and the presence of Ross Perot. About 10 million fewer people voted in 1996 than 1992, and a majority of those, according to Penn, were potential Clinton supporters. Perot started taking swing voters away from Clinton when he regained the public spotlight after Scott Reed's ill-fated mission to Dallas in mid-October. On Election Day, Perot stayed in single digits, but his eight percent was enough to deny Clinton his much sought-after majority.

More than Indogate or Ross Perot, Clinton's biggest enemies at the polls were apathy and cynicism. Ronald Reagan's reelection in 1984 was seen as an affirmation of the man and his worldview. Clinton's mandate was much murkier. Clearly, voters—especially women—were casting votes against "Dolegingrich." But it's far from certain that voters were embracing Clinton or any vision of the future they may have thought he had. After the election, Clinton's communications director, Don Baer, insisted that his boss had genuinely moved to the center, where the voters are. "The centrist stuff comes naturally to him," said Baer. "He's not struggling. This is what he wants to say. He's more sure in his skin." Maybe so, but there was a plaintive quality to Clinton's answer to the question, at his post-election press conference, about why voter turnout was so low. He admitted that he didn't really know and that he was worried about it. George Stephanopoulos, who left the White House after the election to teach, write, and lecture, offered the shrewdest explanation for the 1996 election. "America was acting out its internal contradictions," Stephanopoulos said. "People want less government but they want to be taken care of. They didn't like either extreme, so they struck a balance." Clinton, he said, "captured the center ideologically, politically, morally and culturally." The last politician to do this, Stephanopoulos said, was Richard Nixon. As he begins his second term, Clinton, along with most Americans, can only hope that the analogy stops there.

AFTERWORD:
THE SMALL DEAL
by Peter Goldman

In the aftermath, it was easy even for the most loyal Democrats to ascribe Bill Clinton's victory to anybody or anything but Bill Clinton. It was the economy, stupid, or the hubris of Newt Gingrich, or the Machiavellian whispers of Dick Morris, or, in the most common analysis of all, the woebegone candidacy of Bob Dole. Clinton? It couldn't have been his doing. He was, on the evidence of the polls, neither beloved as a leader nor trusted as a man. His prospects for a second term were shadowed by the scandals of his first. His fellow Democrats avoided using his likeness in their advertising, finding it more useful to run against Gingrich than for him. His average grade as president in a nonpartisan Pew Research Center poll a few weeks before Election Day was a merely passable C. "Look, this election will not be used as evidence for the Great Man theory of history," a leading strategist of Clinton's own party had said on the eve of battle—a judgment as widely held at the end of the race as at the beginning.

What the pre- and postmortems denied Clinton was the recognition due him for his return engagement as the Comeback Kid. Great man or not, he had learned what Jack Kennedy had discovered in his books and Ronald Reagan had intuited from the movies: the presidents who succeed are those who master the part. Jerry Ford never managed it. Neither did Jimmy Carter or George Bush. Clinton did, though it took him two bumpy years of on-the-job apprenticeship; he grew into the office thereafter by reverting to his campaign

mode, the president as performance artist, a role that suited his for-
midable gift for hands-on electoral politics. Frank Luntz, a rising
young Republican pollster and student of public rhetoric, called him
the greatest communicator since Franklin Roosevelt—greater, even,
than the Great Communicator himself. "Reagan was likable," Luntz
said with an air of sad-eyed bemusement. "People don't like Bill
Clinton, and yet they follow him."

They followed him in important part because he seemed
connected to his moment in history—a moment of deep economic,
social and political change. The New Deal and the Cold War, the
organizing principles of our politics for decades, were history. The
baby boomers had come of age, moved to the suburbs, borne children, and planted the seeds of a postmodern political agenda. It had
little to do with the old issues, or with the great philosophic debate
over whether government should be big or small. What people
wanted in the '90s, in the Democratic pollster Geoffrey Garin's reading, was enough government to help them cope with the cares of
everyday life—work and family, schools and doctors, safe streets and
clean water, drugs on the playground and violence on TV.

Both parties had interesting answers to offer, but in the presidential politics of 1996, it was Clinton who captured the music of
his time. Dole by contrast seemed unplugged, an artifact from another era in a nation whose statistically average citizen was a woman
in her middle 30s. He promised a return to a golden age that most of
America knew, if at all, from K-Tel nostalgia albums and Norman
Rockwell townscapes. When the press asked the candidates which
television shows they had liked best in their teens, Clinton said
Bonanza; Dole's reply was that TV hadn't been invented yet. It
mattered less that he was old—his 96-hour finishing kick was evidence enough of his vigor—than that he came from that other country called the past. For a newer, younger America, Simon Rosenberg
of the centrist New Democrat Network said, "Bob Dole was always a
black-and-white movie in a color age."

In the circumstances, the great issues of the day never got
addressed. They rarely do in presidential elections, except in moments

of crisis like 1860 or 1932. Campaigns are about power first; candidates most often seek it by finessing the hard questions until they are safely in office. So it was with Clinton. The state of the economy was good, or good enough for him to brag on in an election year. The quest for a New Democratic approach to its deeper, longer-term weaknesses was accordingly postponed to another day. "I'm not sure we know what the answers are," said Stan Greenberg, Clinton's pollster in 1992, "and if we do know what they are, we know they cost money. This isn't exactly the moment when you want to be talking about $100 billion spending programs."

Neither was it a propitious time to be arguing the proper size or role of government—not, anyway, in the apocalyptic terms proposed by Newt Gingrich in his moment of glory two years earlier. Gingrich's Hundred Days had ended more like Napoleon's at Waterloo than FDR's in the White House. He had mistaken the election returns of 1994 for a revolution, when only 19 percent of the eligible electorate had actually voted Republican for Congress and fewer still understood what it was they were voting for. If they wanted a revolution at all, Joe Trippi, a Democratic media consultant, said after a year's immersion in polls and focus groups, "They didn't want this one. They were literally shocked by what these guys were doing. It was like they were saying, 'I voted for 'em, but I didn't know the gun was loaded.'"

Even Gingrich's choice of the word "revolution" came to be regretted by his party's savvier strategists, among them some who had used it as freely as he until the backlash against it set in. It was as if, having given up his professorship of history to stand for Congress, the Speaker had forgotten its lessons as well. There had been four previous midterm landslides in the postwar era, as the political analyst Kevin Phillips noted, in 1946, 1958, 1966 and 1974. None of them had delivered an affirmative mandate to do much of anything; they were, rather, rejectionist in spirit, driven by anger at the party in power. But the winners had usually divined mandates in the returns just as Gingrich had, in his own epochal tones. His excesses of language and ambition were his undoing; long before the first attack ads against him, he had supplanted Ross Perot as the least loved man in our public life. His party mates barely held on to their majority in the House, surviving in part by skittering away from him. Even his chief propagandist, Tony Blankley, conceded at mid-passage in his assault on the welfare state that the Gingrichians had "probably slightly overreached . . . We may have tried to force the system farther quicker than our base was capable of."

Gingrich could claim to have won the battle of ideas, if not finally the war. He and his comrades-in-arms had forced Clinton to agree to the principle of a balanced budget and finally to concede what once was heresy for a Democrat, that the era of big government was over. The Speaker's man Blankley, for one, doubted that the case for centralizing power in Washington could any longer be successfully argued in more than 20 percent of the congressional districts in the country.

But it was another thing to claim, as Blankley did, that it was the Republican conquest of the Hill in 1994 that had "delegitimized" the idea of Washington trying to do everything for everybody. That issue had long since been settled in the real world, as against the historical pageant Gingrich had brought to the Federal City. It has been reasonably argued, indeed, that a Republican, Richard Nixon, was our last New Deal president—the last, that is, to dare to expand the reach of the welfare state and of government regulation. None of his successors had argued the philosophic case for more government. Clinton pushed the boundaries in practice in his first two years, notably with his and Hillary's health-care plan. Its defeat, and the president's own as party leader in the 1994 midterm elections, seemed to cure him of his edifice complex.

The lesson he took from his losses was the one Gingrich had so grievously missed: that Americans do not like to be governed by abstract principle. Clinton moved accordingly to the unideological soft center, as if, Frank Luntz said dourly, he were seeking a mandate to continue the policies of Gerald Ford. His New Democratic admirers called his positioning "postliberal." The old guard, on the Hill and elsewhere, looked on it as something nearer treason. Clinton alienated traditional Democrats with his serial retreats on the balanced budget, on Medicare spending, and finally on what seemed to them a punitive welfare-reform bill. A Democratic president seemed to be walking away from the core Democratic idea of an activist government, one party strategist who counted himself a moderate complained, when he ought to have been trying to "reinvest" people in it.

His apostasy went down even worse with Old Democratic fundamentalists, though they found it prudent to bite their tongues in an election year; the price of Clinton's victory, in their eyes, was the loss of the party's identity—the sense that Democrats were different from Republicans in kind rather than mere degree. In the autumn of 1995, some had muttered privately in the cloakrooms of bolting to Colin Powell if he chose to run or of snubbing the president if he showed up in their districts. Little happened thereafter to bind them any closer to Clinton, except the seeming inevitability of his success. "Fuck him," one endangered Rust Belt congresswoman told her own reelection strategists, even as the president was opening up his double-digit lead in the public polls. "He's destroyed our party. He doesn't stand for anything."

The old crowd wanted him to be a liberal, that is, at a time when the purer ideologies of the left and right were out of public favor. The safer route in 1996 was to speak the gauzier language of values, not principles; the technicians of both parties understood that, but Clinton and his generals seized the ground first, in the shadow war against Gingrich, and held it till Election Day against the enemy without and the dissidents within. The irony was that Dole was by genetic code an unideological man; in the company of the secular and religious militants of his own party, he looked as if his teeth hurt. He tried catering to them in the run-up to the primaries—pandering was the more common term of art—and ignored them later, when they seemed an impediment to his chances in the general election. Neither tactic worked. The events of 1995 had freeze-framed the Republicans as the ideologues and Dole as their entrée to presidential power.

In the aftermath of his defeat, the crisis of identity was at least as profound for the Republicans as for the Democrats. They had come to take their leasehold on the presidency for granted; their average share of the vote since the death of FDR had been 53 percent until Clinton came along. In the two elections since, it dropped 14 points, to 39 percent, and not just because Ross Perot was siphoning off Republican votes; the contrary case could be made that Perot had hurt Clinton more, robbing him of back-to-back landslides. The returns revealed the fault lines in the coalition that had enthroned Reagan, endured George Bush and recaptured Capitol Hill from the Democrats for the first time in 40 years. "It really doesn't matter who we run for president," Grover Norquist, an antitax agitator and a member of Gingrich's privy council, said comfortably in the winter days when Dole's nomination loomed as a distant but inescapable fact. He meant that it didn't matter so long as the Republican ultimately won. Having tasted defeat with Bush and now Dole, both unvisionary men, the party's sectarian right was unlikely to be so tolerant soon again.

In fact, the president's fall and rise was a lesson in the dangers of doctrinal politics in the 1990s. Clintonism was not an ism at all, if ism implied a system of belief; it was nearer to the eclectic New Democratic platform the president ran on four years ago than to the old New Deal and Great Society traditions. What he offered in 1996 was less an ideology than an assemblage of tactics forced on him by the necessities of dealing with a hostile Congress and of getting himself reelected. In the national conversation of our politics, he changed the subject from grand to homelier concerns: V-chips and school uniforms, breast cancer and tobacco, time off work for family emergencies and longer stays in maternity wards. He was much derided in Washington for running a government and a campaign of tiny ideas, but there was a certain binding genius to them: they addressed the quotidian anxieties of middle-class life without the swollen bureaucracies and the red-ink budget lines of the Democratic past.

What Clinton offered America in effect was the Small Deal, an ad hoc activism that sought to meliorate problems rather than write and staff expensive programs to solve them. If it had a disappointingly Lite taste to older Democrats, it was strong enough for a newer, under-50 generation coming into positions of power and influence in the party. The Republicans had their own schismatic future to look forward to, their own warring tribes to reconcile. They had been getting less moderate with the arrival of the boomers, especially on the Hill; the new bunch typically drew their political economics from the thoughts of Speaker Gingrich and their social values from the deacons of the religious right. The younger Democrats were more often centrists, whether out of conviction or a sedulous reading of the polls. They tended to think and sound more like Bill Clinton than Ted Kennedy, and after the bloodbath of 1994, a Small Deal suited them just fine.

Whether it would sustain the Democrats in office beyond the year 2000 was another question. All politics in America is situational, shaped more by personalities and events than by large ideas. On Election Day 1996, it was Bill Clinton who found himself in the right place, where the people were, at the right time, when moderation was back in vogue. His victory, impressive in the electoral college, was less so in the popular vote. His eight-point final margin was drawn down by the lowest turnout since Calvin Coolidge beat James W. Davis and Fighting Bob La Follette in 1924, another election in which the issues were narrow and the results a more or less forgone conclusion. Clinton's big lead in the polls gave his less ardent supporters license to stay home or to go elsewhere, to Perot, say, or Ralph Nader. Any claim by the president to embody the will of the people would have been as delusional as Gingrich's had been two years earlier; he owed his second chance to the mere 24 percent of the electorate who troubled to show up at the polls and mark ballots for him.

Neither his battered person nor his modest program invited more heroic numbers. His central promise was to keep doing what he had done in his chastened fourth year in office: seeking out lesser good works that could be wrought at low cost—often a few words from the bully pulpit would do—and with the cooperation of the two major parties. The Small Deal was unlikely to qualify him for enshrinement on Mount Rushmore. But as Newt Gingrich could have told him, if candor had been the habit in conversation between the two men, it would be foolish to look at one election and claim a "mandate" for anything more.

DOCUMENTS:
THE CAMPAIGN PAPERS

A NOTE ON THE DOCUMENTS

In more than a year in the field, *Newsweek*'s special election team collected a large number of confidential memoranda, polling reports, meeting agendas and other documents meant for private circulation within the bunkers of presidential politics. Some, but by no means all, were provided by the authors themselves; some came from their comrades—or, occasionally, their adversaries—within the campaigns. All of them seemed to us to illuminate the process by which we select our presidents in fin de siecle America—particularly its heavy reliance on polling, advertising and other modern merchandising techniques and on that new class of men and women, called "handlers," who have brought those techniques into the marketplace of our politics.

We have reproduced a sampling of those documents in the pages that follow. They appear in chronological sequence, the artifacts of moments in time. Practically all have been excerpted from longer originals, sometimes far longer; to publish our collection whole would have required a companion volume equal in size to this one. We have tried in every case to be faithful to the ideas and arguments as the authors meant them to be understood, limiting our pruning to what seemed to us repetitive, arcane, or otherwise of limited interest to the general reader.

Experience with similar collections in past volumes in this series has taught us that a handle-with-care warning is in order. There is a tendency to take the documents of politics too much at face value, as the record of what actually happened in a campaign and which ingenious (or incompetent) handler made it happen. A real-life campaign doesn't work that way. It is, for one thing, a relentlessly gabby business, and some of its best practitioners talk their ideas rather than setting them to paper; thus, some principal players in our narrative are barely represented in these pages, if at all. Campaigns are fluid as well; they define and redefine themselves in motion, reacting to events, circumstances and squiggles in the polls. Sometimes the strategies proposed are— or already have been—adopted by the candidates. Sometimes they are rejected or ignored; our selection of Dole papers, for example, is the record of how much advice he and his managers were given—some good, some bad—and how little of it ever was acted upon in any disciplined way. Sometimes, important actors in the drama are barred by some mix of obligation, loyalty and personal interest from seeing their words in public print; the Clinton campaign, like most incumbent candidacies, was run from the White House, but staffers there were more guarded than outside advisers about publishing work meant principally for the eyes of a president.

The documents below are thus not a certain key to the history of the Clinton and Dole campaigns. They *are* an unusual series of glimpses into the thoughts, inspirations, arguments and anxieties of some of the major players in the two camps, one side constantly spooked by shadows on its march to victory, the other still groping for a rationale down to the eve of its defeat.

DOLE: "SMILE A LOT AND ORGANIZE"

On March 31, 1994, while Bob Dole was still brooding about whether or not to run, his friend and adviser Bill Lacy sent him a memo on what it would take to win. Excerpts:

MEMORANDUM FOR THE REPUBLICAN LEADER
FROM: WILLIAM B. LACY
SUBJECT: RUNNING FOR PRESIDENT

Making the decision to run for President in 1996 is a very personal one you and Mrs. Dole will have to make pretty much on your own. The purpose of this memorandum is to outline what I consider to be some of the factors you should consider.

TIMING

In 1988, we suffered from assembling our senior team too late. There's no doubt in my mind that we can take advantage of your status as a front runner if we start to assemble people soon. This means two things. First, you should allow a few of us to start approaching people on your behalf. Second, you should set a timetable for your decision.

I believe you should make your decision no later than Christmas. If you choose to run and we've done our homework, we could have a campaign team in place in January. That gives us just over a year to put an organization together.

THE CHARGES

Let me spend a few moments on the case the media and our opposition will make about you:

1. *Bob Dole is a dinosaur; he won't match up well with Clinton in terms of age or programmatic leadership.* More a generational and stylistic point, this immediately highlights the general election contrast. If Clinton is still bogged down in Whitewater, or suffering from its effects, the nation will be looking for more mature, proven leadership. If Clinton moves beyond Whitewater and can make some progress on his promises, that makes it tougher.
2. *He's too old.* This is the age/health issue; the media will focus heavily on it, so you should be prepared for it. Luckily for us, Reagan faced the same charge in 1980. Our pointing to him as an example should downplay this issue with Republicans.

3. *He's mean.* Like Mari Maseng said in 1988, smile a lot. Do what you did on Larry King: note that people around you like you. To a large degree, though, this is something that will go away only over time and through winning. It's similar to the "Bush as wimp" argument in '88 and won't be significant *unless we make it so.*

4. *Dole can't organize.* Based on the constantly shifting management of the '80 and '88 campaigns, this will pose a real problem in recruiting. We can overcome this in two ways: first, getting a senior team in place ASAP that you can live with through the campaign, and making that known. Second, be organized from day one.

5. *He's a two-time loser.* Lee Atwater's theory that the more times around the track, the more likely a candidate is to win was correct in 1988 and will be in 1996. The last three elected GOP presidents each ran at least twice nationally before being elected.

6. *Dole must step down from the leadership.* This is more difficult for me, since I'm not a creature of the Senate. From a campaign perspective, I would like you to remain as Republican Leader through March of 1996; if you've locked up the nomination, you should step down. At least until early 1996, the forum and fundraising power you get as Republican Leader outweigh disadvantages.

THE CHALLENGES

In my opinion, the above aren't the real barriers to your nomination. These are:

1. *Lack of strategic discipline.* Legislative victories are won by adroit maneuvering and by maintaining flexibility. Presidential campaigns are won by designing a plan and sticking to it, except as circumstances dictate change.

2. *Lack of organizational discipline.* You must force the senior people in your campaign to get along and for this once to put winning ahead of personal agendas. In 1987, making decisions was virtually impossible because of all the different power centers in the campaign; once we started down a path, somebody would come along and insist we change our approach. Many individuals can provide excellent advice, and you should seek it. But only a few should be empowered to make decisions.

3. *The campaign structure must reflect your style.* I have come reluctantly to the conclusion that a typical campaign structure simply doesn't match your style. It relies too heavily on a tightly structured chain of command. Breaks in the chain undermine and paralyze senior leadership. At one time in 1987, I counted twelve "power centers" in the campaign that I felt I had to consult before making decisions. Because of your hands-on style and accessibility, those "power centers"—which in a normal campaign would work for and report to the campaign manager—in effect served two masters. That's why a traditional structure won't work and shouldn't be tried.

Allow me an analogy from sports. A traditional campaign organization works much like a professional football team, which requires a tight structure based on plays formulated in advance. While a coach often advises players during practice and calls the plays, he would never consider calling a lineman or a wide receiver over during a game and suggesting they deviate from their pre-assigned responsibilities.

In professional basketball, however, players are rewarded for their ability to innovate and respond to unique situations. While teams have to have some plays, and players generally have an assigned role, the ability of the team to win is based on their team orientation, on their ability to play together and on their flexibility and ability to do several things well.

Your 1996 campaign structure should be built this way, like a pro basketball team, with a small number of key people who have assigned roles but also wide talents that allow them to work outside their roles as necessary. They also must have a strong personal commitment to you.

CLINTON: "A CONTRACT WITH THE MIDDLE CLASS"

In the ashes of the great Democratic defeat in November 1994, Mark Penn and Douglas Schoen, who would become pollsters to Bill Clinton, wrote an unpublished analysis prefiguring the main themes of his reelection campaign. Excerpts:

THE NEW DEMOCRAT AGENDA

The 1994 midterm election was a complete rejection of what the Democratic Party has come to represent—bigger government, more taxes, higher spending, more bureaucracy. It was more than just a rejection of Bill Clinton's leadership. After all, Bill Clinton had a 50% approval rating on election day, and unemployment and inflation are at historically low levels.

Rather, the election was an expression of the fundamental national will, which is anti-tax and anti-spending. It was not, however, fundamentally a rejection of government and its role in our society. Rather, it was a rejection of the way the Democratic Party has come to use the resources of government, which is increasingly perceived to be at the expense of the middle class to benefit (almost exclusively) the poor.

The future of the Democratic Party hinges on its ability to develop an agenda which makes government work for the middle class—perhaps even to craft their own Contract with America. More directly, to elaborate their Contract with The Middle Class.

This Contract must stand for the same type of fiscal conservatism embodied in the Republican Contract, yet at the same time present positive programs that acknowledge that most people still believe that government can, and indeed must, play a role in improving the lives of middle-class Americans.

Democrats need to recognize that the needs of middle-class voters, and the issues they care about, were not addressed by Republicans in this election and are not likely to be addressed by them in the future. The Republicans have proven to be the party of "negativism"—reduced taxation, limited spending, smaller government. This message is effective only in the absence of a positive alternative which appeals to the true needs and values of middle-class Americans who feel abandoned by the Democratic Party.

This positive alternative, embodied in our Contract with The Middle Class, should call for tax restraint and recognize that spending programs must deliver tangible results that positively impact on people, not just create more bureaucracy. Thus, the Democrats should embrace anti-government initiatives, like the balanced-budget amendment, the line-item veto, and term limits.

Perhaps there is no better way to demonstrate this renewed commitment than by carrying out Bill Clinton's campaign promise of a middle-class tax cut. But to win back the confidence of the American people, Democrats must do more. They need to assure middle-class America that they have a program to address all the needs they face—rearing their children in a safe environment, obtaining quality education for them. It also entails vocational training, and ultimately assuring job opportunity, providing affordable health care, and a secure retirement. Democrats also need a renewed commitment to family stability, working to increase opportunities for home ownership and expanding retirement savings programs.

In 1992, Bill Clinton promised sweeping changes in the way government worked. He promised to reinvent government to make it smaller and more efficient. He promised the middle class a tax cut. He promised to avoid the irresponsible spending habits of Great Society Democrats, defining instead a more centrist image profile that was pro-business, pro-growth, and pro-middle class.

Bill Clinton was elected on this platform in 1992, and the 1994 election reaffirmed voter approval of that notion. Clinton's, and ultimately the Democrats', problem lay in the perception that they had dramatically failed to live up to that promise. Voters endorsed this agenda, but rejected a Democratic Party that appears to have abandoned it.

The Democratic Party must once again become the party of middle-class Americans. Absent this commitment to the middle class and its values, the Democratic Party will once again be running as the party of big government against the "non-government" Republican Party. Faced with this choice, voters will again opt for negativism—lower taxes, lower spending, and reduced bureaucracy—leaving the Democrats with minority status well into the 21st Century.

DOLE: WORKING ON "THE VISION THING"

On February 23, 1995, Bill Lacy tried his hand at outlining a coherent message for Dole, a set of themes that came to be known as the Three R's. Excerpts:

MEMORANDUM FOR SCOTT REED
                    MARI WILL
FROM: WILLIAM B. LACY
SUBJECT: MESSAGE

I think we all agree, absolutely, on two things:

1. The Senator needs a sound, believable message that he's comfortable with; we don't need any rocket scientists to help us figure it out.
2. Mari has successfully framed three broad themes that work for the Senator and are consistent with national attitudes.

Given this common ground and the work both of you have done on the "vision thing," I have pulled together my suggested wording of the themes we need to put to work for us.

THE MESSAGE FORMAT

Three themes:

1. Reining in the federal government:
    *   empowering people and the states (10th Amendment)
    *   cutting spending and reducing taxes and burdensome regulations
    *   reforming Congress (term limits, cutting committee staffs, etc.)
2. Reconnecting government to our values:
    *   hard work, individual responsibility and community involvement
    *   affirmative action
    *   strengthening families
    *   crime
3. [Reasserting] American leadership abroad:
    *   continuing Reagan "peace through strength" model
    *   key guidepost for foreign policy: does it promote our interests?
    *   standing for freedom

Three other themes/concepts we need to talk about:

1. Leadership
2. Character
3. Change

Obviously, the Senator can talk about leadership (he does all the time) and can make less than direct references to character (largely his bio and the line, "I've been tested, tested in many ways"). We also need him to talk about change.

Everyone wants to give us the "magic message bullet," but I don't think we need one, if in fact it exists, for the nomination fight. We need a solid message we can stick with.

CLINTON: "THE U.S. IS LOSING THE FIGHT AGAINST DRUGS"

On April 11, 1995, the chiefs of the FBI and the Drug Enforcement Agency sent Clinton a scorching secret memo on the state of the war on drugs on his watch and those of his recent Republican predecessors. Their report would become an issue in the fall campaign the next year, with Dole and the Republicans demanding its release and the White House claiming executive privilege. A copy of the memo was obtained by a Newsweek correspondent, Michael Isikoff, and is published here, in condensed form, for the first time:

MEMORANDUM TO THE PRESIDENT OF THE UNITED STATES
THROUGH ATTORNEY GENERAL JANET RENO
FROM LOUIS J. FREEH, DIRECTOR, FBI
AND
THOMAS A. CONSTANTINE, ADMINISTRATOR, DEA
SUBJECT: PROPOSAL FOR NEW ATTACK ON DRUGS

The attached study, created for your review and action, proposes that the Federal Government launch a bold new attack on drug trafficking that has reached such crisis proportions that it now gravely threatens the very national security of the United States.

For decades, the Government has waged what it termed a "war" against drugs. But it has been neither a "war" nor even an effective "battle." Rather, the efforts have failed, and the Nation faces a violent crime and drug emergency of immense proportions.

If firm new action is not taken soon, the dreadful possibility exists that the United States will irrevocably lose the struggle against drug use and drug trafficking, thus allowing to develop a national nightmare that will kill and maim and terrorize our people in perpetuity.

Cocaine and heroin, primarily produced in six countries, flow into America like an invading, all-conquering army. If a foreign enemy using traditional military power created such death and destruction in our country, the United States would fight that foe with every ounce of our energy.

Unfortunately, the United States is losing the fight against drugs. Firm steps must be taken. The attached paper proposes the strategies necessary to win the struggle against drugs and save our country in the process.

Our anti-drug efforts need a new focus, both in the United States and abroad. The command structure in the fight against drugs is now inadequate. In today's grim parlance, it is a loser, and the casualties are all around us.

Our Nation's anti-drug efforts must be revamped and streamlined. There must be a sea-change in efficiency. The flow of cocaine and heroin into the United States must be choked off—and quickly.

Abroad, we must form more effective alliances with nations that will be our staunch allies in the struggle against drugs. The United States must also develop an unprecedented toughness in dealing with those parts of the world that contribute to the flow of drugs inundating our country with violence and death.

It would be a devastating turn of history if the United States lacked the resolve to save itself from drugs and crime in this 50th anniversary observance of the Nation's victory over the other great evils in World War II.

SECRET

AMERICA'S DRUG PROBLEM

For many years, America has had an acknowledged drug problem, principally related to the abuse of cocaine, heroin, and marijuana. According to the Office of National Drug Control Policy (ONDCP), there are currently 2.7 million chronic hard-core drug addicts in America. The National Household Survey on Drug Abuse reveals that there are currently 11.7 million drug users in the United States. (This category refers to individuals who have used an illicit drug at least once during their lives.)

In 1993, despite impressive law enforcement seizures of cocaine and of vast sums of money that its sale generated, cocaine was readily available throughout the United States. The upward trend in cocaine-related episodes seems to have reached a plateau. In 1993, however, cocaine-related episodes were at their highest level.

Heroin, like cocaine, was readily available for users through the United States. Heroin-related episodes have increased steadily since the early 1980s. Violence is associated, to some degree, with the trafficking of drugs at all levels.

PROPOSED SOLUTIONS

Despite the annual expenditure of billions of dollars, a plethora of drug laws, and the valiant efforts of countless law enforcement officers, the United States is not winning the "war against drugs." There has never really been a "war against drugs." Indeed, the United States is not even waging an effective battle.

Within the United States Government, there must be a major realignment of counter-drug responsibilities. In this regard, law enforcement's command structure, which targets the supplier of illicit drugs, must become clearer. America's drug enemies are well-organized and, in many instances, unified in their goals. As with any effort of epic proportions, therefore, it is imperative for American law enforcement to have a unity of command and unity over the control of resources. At the same time, ONDCP's role must be redefined to focus on curbing America's insatiable appetite for drugs. If this effort is to be successful, however, more money, resources and personnel will be needed.

In order to dismantle completely the drug-trafficking organizations that have spread throughout the United States, more law enforcement agents must be assigned to investigate them. To ensure their success, those agents must receive sufficient operational funds. Additional federal prosecutors must be appointed to present the influx of anticipated drug cases. Similarly, more federal judges will be needed to preside over those cases; and more prisons must be built in order to house convicted drug defendants.

Published reports estimate the annual budget for the Intelligence Community to be around $28 billion. Now that the Cold War has ended and America faces a drug-dealing enemy, which is a major threat to national security, a portion of the Intelligence Community's budget should be reprogrammed to finance this effort.

A handful of countries pose a major threat to America's national security on account of their roles as drug source, transshipment, and trafficking countries. If this country is to wage a truly meaningful "drug war," it is imperative that substantial measures be directed against these countries. These measures should feature more energized diplomacy. If that diplomacy fails, however, America's willingness to neutralize the foreign drug threat should not be misunderstood.

The preferred course would be for the United States Government to procure multinational support through one of the international bodies for a range of punishments to be inflicted upon the non-compliant country. These punishments would include travel restrictions, economic sanctions up to an embargo, and the possible deployment of multinational security forces.

The President should also direct the National Security Council to consider whether covert action is a viable option against foreign drug organizations. In this regard, consideration should be given to the destruction of clandestine drug laboratories and the aircraft that the organizations use to ship drugs, while they are on the ground.

CONCLUSION

The current methods that the United States Government uses to attack the drug scourge are not adequate. There must be an acknowledgment that "declaring a war on drugs" and "waging a war on drugs" are two different matters entirely.

If the United States Government does not radically alter its counter-drug efforts, then the effects of drugs and drug-related violence in this country will only grow worse. For the American people, that is not an acceptable option.

DOLE: "MEDICARE IS FOR REAL—BE CAREFUL"

On April 26, 1995, Dole's longtime friend and counselor Don Devine warned the then Senate majority leader against getting caught up prematurely in the Republican effort to cut back on the growth of Medicare spending. Excerpts:

TO: SENATOR BOB DOLE
FROM: DON DEVINE
SUBJECT: MEDICARE

MEDICARE: THE CLASSIC "THIRD RAIL" ISSUE

I'm pretty hard core, but I'm a moderate on Medicare reform (at least until 1997). If there is one issue that can blow our coalition off course, it is Medicare. I have seen the focus groups and polls done by the [Republican National Committee] and the people will turn on us savagely if we cut this too much too soon. Medicare is for real. Be careful.

DOLE: "MEDICARE IS FOR REAL"

On May 9, 1995, a year and a half before Election Day, Don Devine sent campaign manager Scott Reed a worried heads-up about whether Dole's handlers were working him too hard:

TO: SCOTT REED
FROM: DON DEVINE
SUBJECT: DOLE SCHEDULE

1. Dole Tired?
   - I have not noticed it, but several people have mentioned that he looks tired lately.
   - I did see a C-Span speech where he wandered more than he should, but I could not tell if it was fatigue.
   - What do you think?
2. Pacing
   - I know well that Dole is difficult to keep down.
   - But he is not stupid: if he must rest, he will.
   - One good speech is better than one good and two bad ones.
3. Main Danger to Campaign is Ourselves
   - The candidate is the major campaign asset.
   - If Dole gets ill, age will become an issue.
   - Even being tired will be noticed; and mistakes are made.
4. Scheduling
   - First principle must be to keep candidate sharp.
   - Do not overschedule.
   - Everything but the candidate's health and humor can be done some other way.

On June 13, Devine carried his concerns to Dole himself, reporting on a meeting of some of the senator's outside advisers. Excerpts:

TO: SENATOR BOB DOLE
FROM: DON DEVINE
SUBJECT: UTILIZATION OF YOUR TIME

The *unanimous number one recommendation* was that you cut down on the number and length of the events and meetings you decide to accept. You are the number one asset of the campaign, and assets should be used wisely. This group represents a wide range of smart people with your interests at heart.

And they do not even know:

- that your shoulder has hurt since April 14.
- that I have heard indirectly [that] Gramm's only strategy for the summer is to get you to pop off at him (presumably easier when you are tired).
- that the favorable ratings for your Sunday interview shows is less than half that of even a poorly delivered speech.

When all of this is put together, it tells me you should:

- take off all day Sunday to relax and recover,
- cut the in-town schedule to only what is essential, and
- choose only selected big-news out-of-town events.

CLINTON: "IT IS SIMPLY A MATTER OF PACKAGING"

In October 1995, Penn and Schoen reported on what they called a "Neuro-Personality Poll"—a profile of the American electorate reaching far beyond politics into the psyches, the values and the lifestyles of the voters. The objective was to arm the Clinton campaign with the latest techniques of market research as a way to target various subgroups in the population and set them up for the sell with the new language of "values." Excerpts:

NEURO-PERSONALITY POLL

The Penn & Schoen Neuro-Personality Poll includes practical research for message administration and targeting of the electorate. Throughout the report, you will encounter four voter groups that comprise the American electorate. The first group, Clinton Base, is 28% of the electorate. They are most likely to support President Clinton in this election. The second group, Swing I (29% of the electorate), leans towards Clinton. The third group, Swing II (25% of the electorate), is much more conservative than Swing I and less likely to support Clinton. The fourth group, Dole Base (18% of the electorate), shows no interest in supporting Clinton. To win the 1996 election, the Clinton campaign must capture its own base, plus 60% of Swing I voters and 30% of Swing II voters.

ISSUES

Clinton Base voters represent the traditional Democratic voters who want to help the disadvantaged and society at large. They support all sorts of programs— guaranteed health care, helping families take care of aging parents, social and job training programs to prevent crime. They want to raise the minimum wage and impose strict gun control. This group stands behind family programs like Family Leave and strongly opposes more budget cuts of social programs. There is an element of class warfare—a small majority (52%) approve taxing the rich to reduce the deficit and they want to keep inflation down.

  Swing I voters are less concerned with partisan politics and more interested in family-oriented middle-class programs. These voters remain supportive of many progressive causes, but their first priority is programs that will help them feel safe physically and financially. Clinton's middle-class message will be effective in driving Swing I voters back to his camp; if he should fail to develop an effective economic plan, though, these voters will flock to the candidate with the best middle-class economic message.

Swing II voters are disgusted with Beltway politics that have ignored their struggling middle-class needs. They support the common-sense measures of raising the minimum wage, keeping inflation low, creating programs to help take care of aging parents, and calling on insurance companies to cover preexisting conditions and job changes. On social issues, this group's moderate-conservative composition has a low tolerance for a progressive agenda. These people identify with traditional values that match their middle American culture. Overall, this group shows little inclination to support President Clinton and is a primary target of the Republican or Independent candidate.

The Dole Base shows no interest in programs for the elderly or for struggling families. These voters leave no room for compromise with Clinton's policies [and] will support any other Republican candidate. They are interested in a scorched-earth, bare-to-the-bones, isolationist Fort America. Their version of stopping crime is to build more prisons and expand the death penalty. These voters have a strong belief in traditional cultural values and are strongly opposed to the progressive programs of the Democratic establishment.

OBSERVATIONS

Redefining Family Values to include a set of compassionate, values-oriented issues affecting the lives of kids, parents and grandparents appears to be the most responsive set of issues for swing voters. These voters are in no mood for Medicare cuts—they even want to see the problem of aging parents addressed through new government programs.

Policies the Swing I voters want include:

1. New programs for taking care of aging parents
2. Crime prevention programs, gun control
3. Regulation of insurance companies so they cannot deny coverage
4. Raising the minimum wage to $5
5. Strengthening maternity and paternity leave
6. Banning smoking advertising for kids

Swing II voters have similar domestic concerns, but want a much more direct approach to crime, foreign policy and economic issues. They want a tough trade policy with Japan, cut-off of welfare after two years, and wider applications of the death penalty.

PERSONALITY TYPES

The purpose of this analysis is to determine if President Clinton appeals to certain personality types and if it is possible to better relate to the rest of the people. In many cases, people may actually agree with President Clinton on issues but are turned off by his communication style. In fact, voters who share the same personality characteristics as the President are more likely to support him, and those with opposing personalities are less likely to vote for him.

To conduct this analysis, we used a modified Myer-Briggs scheme to classify each voter within four sets of basic traits: extroversion-introversion, sensing-intuition, thinking-feeling, judging-perceiving.

Extroversion: Preference for drawing energy from the outside world of people, activities or things.

Introversion: Preference for drawing energy from one's internal world of ideas, emotions or impressions.

Sensing: Preference for taking in information through the five senses and noticing what is actual.

Intuition: Preference for taking in information through a "sixth sense" and noticing what might be.

Thinking: Preference for organizing and structuring information to decide in a logical, objective way.

Feeling: Preference for organizing and structuring information to decide in a personal, value-oriented way.

Judgment: Preference for living a planned and organized life.

Perception: Preference for living a spontaneous and flexible life.

President Clinton received the most support from *intuition* (51%), followed by *feeling* (48%) and *perceiving* (47%). Grand, future-oriented presentations appeal to these voters.

Swing voters are more likely to be *sensing, thinking* and *judging.* Emotional appeals devoid of facts will not work with these voters. They need tough, detailed policies explained to them. This has enormous implications for the "common ground" theme—the more it is tied to abstract notions of citizenship, the more it speaks to our base. But when the theme is presented as a pragmatic way to break gridlock on key legislative issues, it appeals to the swing voters.

LIFESTYLES

The Lifestyles research provides key insight into how Americans lead their lives—and, more important, what the lifestyle differences are between Clinton voters, Dole voters and the Swing.

There are a number of contrasts between the groups of voters and their likes and dislikes. For example, Clinton voters are more likely to enjoy running or jogging while Dole voters are more likely to be found watching hockey or tennis or enjoying hunting and guns, and Swing voters watch baseball, football, bowling and enjoying the outdoors.

When choosing radio stations, Clinton voters will be listening to Classical, Rap and Top 40, while Dole supporters enjoy Talk Radio and '70s/Classic Rock, and the swing voters turn their dial to News/Sports and '50s Music.

Television is another source of lifestyle differences. Clinton voters are more likely to watch HBO, MTV, Oprah (and similar TV talk shows) and soap operas, while Dole supporters turn to sports and "Home Improvement," and Swing voters watch "Seinfeld" and "Friends."

Clinton voters are more likely to be afraid to walk alone at night, consider themselves overeaters, and visit department stores. The Swing voters are more likely to worry about retirement, work in a technical setting, care for a relative and consider their family important. The Dole voters are more likely to be found in a religious setting, and are less likely to be tolerant of gays.

VALUES

The next election is not just about issues and accomplishments, but about values. The result of voters' cynicism about Washington is that they now tune out the specifics of things elected officials have done and pick apart their programs. If they agree that the candidate is expressing their values, then they believe that, whatever the details of his actual policies are, the details will be in a direction that voters will approve of.

We have related this thesis to voters' view of Clinton as a person and as a leader. We believe that if we can raise the esteem of his views as embodying mainstream values rather than being a maze of hard-to-follow policies, then we can make major vote gains.

Another key piece of data is that white singles (of all kinds and ages) are very closely divided on the election, but once someone has a spouse or a child, they are solidly in the Republican camp. This "family gap," which is closely tied to the values perception, is the second key to closing in on the election. There is a 10- to 15-point gap in favor of Dole among families in the United States, and we have all the programs and positions already in place to help families. Thus, it is simply a matter of packaging them and presenting them in a way that will reach those families.

In voter testing so far, the respondents have consistently chosen the values-based approach. In a world where they no longer believe in the "facts" justifying programs because they believe they are manipulated by each side, they are much more likely to instead trust in their internal barometers of right and wrong. The values approach offers the best hope of hitting a home run both with speeches and with the media.

"Finding our Common Ground" is an interesting value that has been created by emphasis through several key speeches. It ties into the public's belief that compromise and settlement are the best ways to end disputes and get the government moving.

Four [other] values we want to hit are:

1. *Standing up for America.* Every time our actions and words are interpreted as standing up for America, our support grows. This has been true in the trade dispute with Japan, our actions on Oklahoma City, and the First Lady in China. This is not a value we say we are doing, it is one that comes through a series of strong, definite actions that have us standing up to threats in the world from a very U.S. point of view.

2. *Providing opportunities for all Americans.* This is clearly what our defense and expansion of education is all about—giving people the opportunity to make the best of their own lives. Despite all the frustration with government, people are NOT frustrated with their own abilities as long as they and their children are given a chance to get ahead.

3. *Doing what's right even when it is unpopular.* Standing up to the tobacco companies and supporting the assault weapons ban are examples not just of doing what's right, but doing it despite what are perceived as heavy political costs. There is no benefit to a values-based strategy if people say the president is taking the easy way out. Only when they see a cost can they come to admire the actions as extraordinary.

4. *Preserving and promoting families* (helping parents protect kids from the bad in society). In every poll we have taken, this is the top-scoring value. It is made doubly important by the fact that we are so behind with the votes of people with families. We have to change the perception we have of promoting the single-parent family over the conventional, two-parent family by grouping as

many of our programs under a banner of "putting families first." This means that the Family Leave Bill is just a small part of a program that helps kids with their educational opportunities, young people with the new minimum wage, parents with a middle-class tax cut, and our aging parents with their health care. This is an administration helping families on all levels. And parents will be getting some of the help they need to raise their kids with the antismoking initiative and the V-chip.

. . .

[In future Clinton speeches] first we have to define the need to govern with values, talk about the values that are lacking, illustrate how we have lost our values, and then discuss the kinds of programs that represent the return to a values-based style of governance.

General things no speech should be without:

1. A view of the world and what is happening in values terms, not just economics.
2. Putting our accomplishments in values terms, not just economic ones.
3. Putting our new programs in the same terms.
4. Concluding that taking this approach is the real way we can find a common ground and get this country moving.

We are doing something very specific in terms of our rhetoric on balancing the budget. We are taking out the class rhetoric (except to base audiences) and increasing the values component in explaining how we are balancing the budget, but in the right way. And how the "right way" can make a tremendous difference to the families of America.

DOLE: "FIX PROBLEMS, NOT BLAME"

In early November 1995, Bill Lacy wrote a fretful memo to Dole's campaign manager, Scott Reed, on the state of the campaign. Excerpts:

CONFIDENTIAL

I begin these suggestions with two premises:

1. A [Colin] Powell candidacy fundamentally alters the dynamics of this race. This requires a rigorous reassessment, both strategically and operationally.
2. The campaign generally runs well; there have been some notable exceptions. This memo focuses on those exceptions because we can beat ourselves with a major mistake.

I take the Japanese view: fix problems, not blame. This isn't intended as a criticism of anyone—just some suggestions that will improve our performance.

I. COMMAND FOCUS

We seem to do OK when you or I are involved in a project or event. The manager/trouble-shooter model generally has worked well.

And, generally, where something got fouled up, we weren't sufficiently involved. There are simply so many important things going on that we need to make sure we focus on what's important and—frankly—let go of stuff that isn't.

II. COORDINATION

I believe there is a real need for information exchange at the senior staff level of the campaign. In informal discussions, I have found that many people simply don't know what's going on.

I think we need more structure. It will solve the problem overall and prevent the kind of coordination problem that could really hurt us as we get into the primaries.

III. COMMUNICATIONS

We react rather than act. We have no plan. We have very capable people, but we seem to be totally in the business of firefighting rather than fire prevention.

Easy to fix, if we just commit to it:

First, a communications calendar with key speeches and other important media hits.

Second, more daily direction.

Third, integrate research better. They know our record, our vulnerabilities and our lines of attack better than any of us [do].

Finally, reimplement the original—or an improved—speech process. Move up the date when the principal sees the draft. Allow more time for clearance.

WARNING:

- Isn't it interesting that we discuss broadcast scripts out the kazoo and show them to everybody, but none of us knows virtually anything about speeches until a day or so before they are to be given?
- How can we build the principal's confidence when our speeches arrive on such an erratic schedule?

DOLE: "OUR SUPPORTERS ARE SCRATCHING THEIR HEADS"

On November 28, 1995, Dole's communications director, Mari Maseng Will, warned him in a memo that he was doing too much conventional politicking and too little message-mongering in the early primary and caucus states. Excerpts:

MEMORANDUM FOR SENATOR DOLE
FROM: MARI WILL
SUBJECT: IOWA AND NEW HAMPSHIRE MESSAGE STRATEGY

Up until now, your schedule has been dominated by political events to the exclusion of message events. Perhaps this has been necessary, but it has put us behind the curve in our ability to drive home messages likely to energize our supporters, let alone win new recruits among the culture/moral/religious voters I believe are the key in states like Iowa. Since your schedule has consisted [mostly] of endorsement press conferences, headquarters openings and traditional town meetings—a format in which you are least successful in message delivery—it is no wonder our research reveals supporters scratching their heads as to what your message is.

As we begin the crucial run-up to the caucuses and primaries in February and March, we must schedule you dramatically differently. In both Iowa and New Hampshire, and in a pattern that should be repeated elsewhere as the campaign focus shifts, there should be at least one "color" message event per day. These events should be structured to accommodate our new model of three minutes of newsmaking soundbites on a single subject drawn from our "vision" themes. These events should feature local supporters speaking to you about the problems they are enduring. The events should be in colorful, theme-reinforcing settings, which are attractive to cameras and conducive to message-supporting print descriptions. The events should be able to generate local coverage without you saying a word, through the combination of "hot" topics, picturesque settings and local citizen participation. You would make news and "connect" with local voters by just convening the event.

I remain convinced that our supporters are generally in the "low motivation" category. Perhaps our motivation problems stem from the fact that a large chunk of our base consists of moderates who are detached from the "Contract with America" revolution, and economic conservatives who do not feel particularly threatened now that the economy is relatively stable and dramatic economic reforms seem to be rocketing through the Congress. Or perhaps it is because many of them have come to support you out of respect for your tenacity and leadership, or as the result of your name ID, or because they believe it is "your turn." These reasons for supporting you are of low personal impact for voters, and therefore result in low personal motivation.

As you know, I believe it will be the "culture conservatives" who will be bounding out the door that snowy night of the caucuses, for it is they who are motivated by what they see as the real, personally menacing threat of a decaying community, which requires, in their view, redress by the political system. Hence, my focus on culture themes to expand and energize our base, and which are authentic coming from the populist conservative from Russell, Kansas: Bob Dole.

DOLE: CHOOSING A RUNNING MATE

Four days before Christmas 1995, Rich Bond, a veteran Republican operative, wrote a lengthy memo to the campaign on the opportunities and risks involved in choosing a running mate—particularly for a septuagenarian candidate like Dole. Excerpts:

Senator Dole's status as the oldest president ever inaugurated *guarantees that his choice of a running mate will be the most heavily scrutinized in history*. Volumes will be written about Senator Dole's choice, because, actuarially, this individual stands a much better than average chance of being president some day. No confusion, indecision, or mistakes can be associated with this choice. The choice of a running mate will serve as *one of the very foundations of the Dole candidacy*.

It is likely that Senator Dole's candidacy will be weakest, and therefore most at risk, during the April–August 1996 period. This assertion is based on several assumptions:

- That Senator Dole will wrap up the nomination by March 26 and will only have limited funds available until the national convention ending in mid-August.
- That President Clinton will remain unchallenged in the primaries and will have $20 million cash in hand available (plus the powers of the presidency) with which to pound the Dole candidacy.
- That during this period the race will appear to be a two-man race and that Clinton will have a solid lead as Senator Dole's negatives once again begin to rise to dangerous levels.
- That the full hypocrisy of the Beltway intelligentsia and national media will begin to pick over Senator Dole's bones prematurely, and that the House freshmen in general will begin distancing themselves from Senator Dole.

Senator Dole and the campaign will have little means by which to stem this negative tide. One creative option that should be explored is the early (June–July) announcement of a vice-presidential nominee. This would work best if it were a super-personality such as Colin Powell, but the idea still has merit even with a more traditional choice.

The downsides are obvious—an ever greater strain on scarce resources, and a national convention with little or nothing to offer in the way of a surprise (at least a positive surprise). Nonetheless, the idea of an early announcement may be worth exploring if fortunes are temporarily sagging as badly as may occur.

Clinton and Gore (and their wives) appear to the voters to genuinely like each other. This is a huge plus in the media-drenched environment of a presidential campaign, where even the faintest hint of strain between the principals can be blown into a huge press storm.

Senator Dole's acerbic wit and reputation for "meanness" will be points of vulnerability that the media and the Democrats will attempt to exploit to the fullest. It is crucially important that Senator Dole feels personally comfortable with his choice, and does not allow ideology or other ticket-balancing approaches to color his thinking.

The Senator, known for trusting few, must be mindful of fully embracing his understudy in very public ways so that the first image of the ticket burned into the minds of the American people is one of a likable team who are up to the job and have a well thought out agenda for the future. Again, Clinton and Gore serve as a useful example.

Elizabeth Dole's importance in this area cannot be overstated. She too must be part of a "bonding" process with the wife of the vice-presidential nominee and their positive interaction together will be a further signal that the national ticket rests on solid ground.

CLINTON: "PAY CHILD SUPPORT, YOU DEADBEAT SOBS"

In January, after Clinton auditioned his family-values platform in the State of the Union Address, pollsters Penn and Schoen reported on what had actually hit home with voters:

RHETORIC AND IDEAS FROM SOTU

This is a partial list of some of the rhetoric and ideas from the SOTU that tested well:

- Our goal must be to enable people to make the most of their own lives with strong families, more educational opportunity, economic security, safer streets, a cleaner environment and a safer world.
- Give the American people their balanced budget, a tax cut, lower interest rates and a brighter future.
- All families must begin by taking more responsibility for children . . .
- Create movies and CDs and TV shows you'd want your own children and grandchildren to enjoy . . . enable parents to assume more personal responsibility for children's upbringing [V-chip related].
- Welfare reform.
- Fighting the scourge of domestic violence.
- I challenge America's families to work harder to stay together. For families who stay together not only do better economically, their children do better as well.
- Pay child support, you deadbeat SOBs.
- School uniforms.
- Turn off TV. See that homework is done. Visit children's classrooms.
- Buy health insurance policies they do not lose when they change jobs . . . and require insurance companies to stop dropping people who switch jobs, and stop denying coverage for pre-existing conditions.
- FBI—target gangs and prosecute as adults teenagers who maim and kill like adults.
- Executive order—deny federal contracts to businesses that hire illegal immigrants.

CLINTON: "BITESIZES WORK BEST"

On March 20, Clinton's polling team brought him their latest survey research at a meeting in the White House. In one study, they mocked up some possible Dole ads attacking the president and tried them out on voters in shopping malls. In another, they tested ways to respond if General Colin Powell were to join Dole on the ticket. Excerpts from strategist Dick Morris's agenda for the meeting:

HOW TO HANDLE DOLE NEGATIVES ON CLINTON

Mall test results:

1. Negatives against Clinton work well—contrary to previous findings.
   Attacks on:
   promises
   character
   flip flops
   and taxes work well.
2. Rebuttals Work Well—Need to Do Context and Contrast
   a. Context: Needs to set up 1991–92 comparison on economics and make Dole part of 91–92.
   b. Contrast:
      • Generational Contrast:
         1. Dole's old ideas of opposing everything against our positive values agenda.
            a. Republican values are basically negative.
            b. Ratified by physical contrast in age and appearance.
      • Our achievements vs. Dole's opposition.
      • Our agenda for change vs. Dole's opposition.
   c. We look better in comparison.
      • Our achievements become credible in the context of Dole's opposition to them.
      • Our agenda becomes compelling in the context of his lack of agenda and opposition to ours.
      • Our values contrast with his both from budget debate and from opposition to our agenda and achievements.
      • Our character flaws are minimal when we are compared with him, not with perfection.

- By framing the contrast as one about ideas, vision, and values, we move away from ad hominem attacks and toward a comparison which Dole can't win.
3. Which contrasts work best:
    - Bitesizes work best—budget doesn't work as well.
    - We have picked the budget issues clean and already have those votes.
    - Bitesize family agenda works best: immunization, domestic violence, tobacco, day care, student loans, V-chip, family leave, pensions.
    - Crime issues also work well: handguns, assault rifles, crime bill.
    - Economic improvement also works well.

HANDLING POWELL—STRESS DISAGREEMENTS BETWEEN DOLE AND POWELL

A. Baseline vote of 52–38 drops to 48–46 with Powell on the ticket.
B. By showing disagreements between Dole and Powell, we recover it all.

"Bob Dole supports a constitutional amendment to ban almost all abortions, Powell opposes it. Dole opposes bans on assault weapons and waiting periods for handguns, Powell supports it. Dole supports cutting billions from Medicare while Powell opposes these cuts. Given these policy differences, some people say no matter how much you like Powell, Dole would be running the country if he were elected, and we should focus on the policies of Dole, not Powell."

Clinton 54   Dole 41

C. Added element: Powell is a gimmick.

"Some people say Dole is way behind and that selecting Powell, someone whose views are so different from his, is just a desperate political gimmick to try to win votes, and no one should vote for the ticket because of Powell, but instead look at the contrast between Clinton and Dole."

Clinton 54   Dole 40

CLINTON: "MAKE DOLE GRIDLOCK AND NEGATIVE, NOT US"

On March 28, the Clinton team reconvened at the White House to fret over some slippage in his poll numbers and to plan a counterattack on the air. Excerpts from Dick Morris's agenda:

AGENDA FOR MEETING WITH PRESIDENT ON MARCH 28

I. TRACKING—DOLE ON THE MOVE, WE ARE SLIPPING

- Dole's favorability up 55–41.

      DOLE FAVORABILITY

Feb. 28	38–52
March 5	48–45
March 14	52–41
March 19	51–42
March 27	55–41

- Our vote share down to 51–39.

Feb. 11	54–33
Feb. 28	53–36
March 5	53–36
March 14	53–38
March 19	52–38
March 27	51–39

- [Clinton's job] approval down to 57 (after having been at 59 since February 4).
- Favorability down to 58–41 (down from 60 last week).
- Dole's Favorability rise has caused us to yield ground grudgingly, but dangerously.
- Hillary Favorability at 51–46 (up from 46 last week). She bounces back to 50 every time she recovers from a Whitewater assault.

II. EXPECTED DOLE NEG ADS COULD MAKE THINGS WORSE

  Expected ad attack:
  a. balanced budget, welfare, taxes
  b. character through these attacks
  c. flip flop and promises broken through these issues
  d. paid attack on crime somewhat less likely

We need to rebut quickly and harshly.

1. Theory is to air the ambivalences people have about Clinton that they have overcome in recent months and defeat the negatives in plain view.
2. We must use Dole ads to "out" the grumbling about Clinton and show how it is baseless.
3. We must use Dole as a comparative backdrop to show that compared with reality, not with perfection, Clinton is really pretty good.
4. Incidental goal is to raise Dole negatives and stop his favorable march—real goal is to solidify our positives by defeating the negatives people already wonder about.

III. RECOMMENDATION: START COMPARATIVE CAMPAIGN NOW

- Dole Favorability gain cannot be allowed to continue.
- We need Dole as a context and backdrop to sell Clinton positives.
- Expected paid media attack will be effective, and we need a head start on the rebuttal.
- We can avoid blame for starting negatives by framing our ad as a response to Dole's attacks and by making the thrust of the ad positive.

Text of ad:

Begins with Dole film clip: "We gave him a balanced budget and he vetoed it . . . Let's veto Bill Clinton."

The facts?

The President proposed a balanced budget, protecting Medicare, education, environment.

But Dole is voting no.

The President cuts taxes on 30 million Americans.

But Dole votes no.

The President bans assault rifles; says welfare recipients must work.

Dole: No to the Clinton plan.

It's time to say yes to the Clinton plan, yes to America's families.

Reasons for this ad:

a.　Make Dole gridlock and negative, not us.
b.　Bolster President's positives in face of likely attack.
c.　Reinforce budget position.
d.　Set up Dole negatives to attenuate his current climb.

We are mall-testing the ad tonight, as we meet. We request permission to satellite this ad tonight at 2 A.M. so we can get it on the air [the day after tomorrow]. This will give us at least four days in the clear before they start.

DOLE: THE OWL AND THE PUSSY CAT

In May, one of Bob Dole's pollsters, Bob Ward, reported on a series of fourteen focus groups conducted in seven key states during the last week in April. Excerpts:

FOCUS GROUP FINDINGS
VOTERS IN NJ, IL, CA, CO, TN, FL, AND MI
APRIL 24–30, 1996

Key findings:

- Voters lack information about Dole. They know very little about him personally, where he wants to take the country, or his stance on virtually any issue.
- They are looking for an excuse to *not* vote for Clinton. He seems to be saying the right things but he's not honest. Use Clinton's own words to spell it out that he is a fraud.
- We are losing the values (bad word) that made this country great.
- Lack of jobs, unstable economy and crime are inextricably linked to a breakdown in these values.
- Economic anxiety runs strong, despite higher wages and an improved economy.
- We need to stop talking about the election, about bills, about negotiations, and start talking about the world under a President Dole. Get out of Washington and don't come back until Inauguration Day.
- Big business and lobbyists control the agenda in Washington.
- No one believes a politician who says he'll give you a tax cut.
- The world we live in is getting ever colder, darker, and more harsh. The bunker mentality is setting in. The problem is, we are currently *outside* the bunker.

. . .

People want to be able to trust their President. They want someone who is sincere. A presidential candidate needs to be able to convey a sense of direction: tell me where you want us to end up before we hitch a ride with you. The reality here is that although people do not believe Clinton (about anything), they like the fact that he talks a good game. They perceive his vision as a happier place. We need a competing vision of where the country needs to go.

There is no love lost for this president. In all groups, attitudes toward Clinton ranged from disappointed indifference to total contempt. Having said that, Bob Dole is not yet viewed as an acceptable alternative. Over and over we heard the phrase, "It is a choice between the lesser of two evils." At present, the devil they know, Bill Clinton, is the lesser of two evils.

To the extent that the participants knew anything about Dole, they generally cited character traits, most of which were presented negatively. Chief among these were: too old, old school, rigid, intolerant, angry, and lacks vision. The most often cited positive characteristics attributed to Dole were that he is seasoned, experienced and honorable.

THE DOLE CHALLENGE

This void of knowledge about Bob Dole presents an opportunity for *both* camps to define his public perception pre-convention. Clinton, for his part, has started the effort. Now it's our turn.

- *Get out of town.* As more public focus is brought to the presidential election, it will be helpful to define Senator Dole as the man from Russell, Kansas, and not the Senate Majority Leader from Washington.
- *But can you lead me?* Among the attributes that people do know about Dole is that he has experience in Washington—he's a "can do" guy. What they don't know is whether he can relate to their lives, problems and daily experiences. On this measure, Clinton has it all over us.
- *The record needs to speak louder than the primaries.* Dole is also viewed by the public as being rigid, intolerant and too willing to cater to the extreme right wing of the party. In short, he has been defined by some voters by the experiences of the past eight months, rather than the previous 35 years he has spent in Congress.
- *Been there, done that.* The Dole personal story needs to be told. Perhaps the most compelling part of that story is Dole's experience in Russell, Kansas. People are extremely dejected and pessimistic about the future. Almost everyone believes the American Dream is dead. People yearn for the stability of the Fifties, and don't mention that the happy era of Ike was preceded by depression and war.
- *The wisdom of the ages.* There is real potential to turn Dole's age, the most frequently mentioned negative in these groups, into an

advantage by carefully telling the Dole story. If Bob Dole did not live the perfect life, it can be said he lived the quintessential American story.

- *Touch the spirit by talking secularly.* It is important to acknowledge that word choice is critical. When we say "family" it is perceived as code for "religious right" by everyone but our base. Are there ways we can say the same thing using "safe" language? The American character. Virtues that made America great. Citizenship. Ethics.

THE CLINTON OPPORTUNITY

- *How can you tell the president is lying? His lips are moving.* Bill Clinton is a liar. Bill Clinton is twenty points up. You figure it out. The truth is that in group after group, swing voters (heck, Clinton's voters!) think Clinton has a fatally flawed character and are yearning for a reason not to vote for him.
- *Luck be a lady.* There is no love for Hillary, and an immediate stark contrast is drawn between her and Elizabeth Dole, the true role model for working women.
- *Last one holding the bag gets the blame.* Most of Clinton's initiatives were seen [as] dying at the hand of the GOP Congress. We are losing the connection that Clinton had single-party control for two years and failed miserably.
- *Now that's a scandal.* The scandals have little additional legs from the overall conclusion that you can't trust Bill Clinton—they are already there.
- *That's one small nudge for man . . .* Bill Clinton is precariously perched on the streetcorner of credibility. It will take precious little effort to nudge him into the [path of the] oncoming bus that is his record.

. . .

WHAT ANIMAL BEST REPRESENTS CLINTON/DOLE?

As silly as this question may sound, it turned out to be a rather telling measure of how the participants view the two candidates. More often than not, the participants saw Clinton as a harmless but inoffensive animal, often choosing domestic pets to represent him. Those participants who did ascribe animals with a negative connotation to Clinton chose deceptive or sneaky animals. On the other hand, Dole was most often represented with angry, unfriendly and aggressive animals.

Most common Clinton animals:

Pussy cat	Fox
Puppy dog	Ferret/Weasel
Teddy bear	Mouse
Snake	Jackass

Most common Dole animals:

Lion	Tiger
Mule	Panther
Owl	Hawk
Pit Bull	Bull
Dinosaur	Wolf

CLINTON: "DOLE IS ESCAPING FROM THE BOX"

In late May, after Bob Dole surprised the world with his resignation from the Senate, a rattled Dick Morris looked over the latest polling and wrote an agenda for an emergency meeting with the president and his campaign command. Between the lines of his overheated prose lay some of the outlines of Clinton's fall election strategy. Excerpts:

AGENDA FOR MEETING WITH PRESIDENT ON MAY 24,1996

I. TRACKING—DOLE IS ESCAPING FROM THE CELLAR . . . WE ARE LETTING HIM DO IT

> Vote at 54–37—17 points. Up 1 for Clinton, up 3 for Dole from last week.
> Clinton Favorability at 62—a new high.
> Dole Favorability up 50–45—5 point gain from last week's 48–48.
> Clinton job approval at 61 and re-elect at 51—tied with past for record high.

Analysis:

1. Dole has his best week through resignation. While his gains appear modest, the hardest thing to do in politics is switch direction and he did it successfully.
2. Clinton moved to record high due to effectiveness of paid media.
3. Dole is escaping from the box in which we had him and may be getting off the mat. In the face of a virtual [Democratic] monopoly of paid media, he was able to post double digit gains on:
   > Strong Leader
   > Clear stand on issues
   > Balancing the Budget
   > Peacemaker
   > New Ideas
   > Does things cause they're right
   > Flip-Flops
   > Vision for Future
   > Does right thing even when unpopular

> Dole is about to break this race wide open and slash our lead to single digits.

We must not let him.

Recommendation: Run our negative ad "Empty."

. . .

Negative campaigning—Clinton has clear advantage although it dropped a bit. Dole is seen as doing more negative campaigning by 46–22 (compared to 51–16 last week).

We could carry this edge into our grave. This lead in positive campaigning is to [be] spent, not hoarded, to buy us credibility to run negatives we need. . . . Dole is highly vulnerable and let's hit him right now to reshape views about his resignation.

III. OVERCONFIDENCE AND RISK AVERSION—THE CREEPING CANCER OF THIS CAMPAIGN

This campaign is tongue-tied. [It is] bent on the same self-destructive caution that caused the collapse of 1994. White House and campaign must adopt a pro-response bias. We rely on bite-sized jabbing rapid-response replies, which are fine, but [we] need to use counter-positioning by President and VP as major line of counter. We need to put out a message, by the president, every single weekday night except Fridays (no good TV news).

. . .

IV. A DOLE TAX CUT MOVE—THE ONLY WAY DOLE CAN WIN

In going to a tax-cut move, Dole is making his third bid for a breakout—his third long bomb.

A tax cut move that we do not defend can put him right back in the race. When told Dole proposed "major across-the-board tax cut" the head-to-head dropped to 45–45. A 17-point gain for Dole. This represents the first time in the past four months that we found an issue that gets him back to even. Tax-cut moves always do better in reality than in surveys.

We have never had the credibility on the issue of tax cuts that we have acquired on balancing the budget, fighting crime or reforming welfare. Dole wins taxes by 41–45. Therefore, any Dole move on tax cuts must be handled from a pro-tax-cut position. [The president] cannot be perceived as Democratic opponent of tax cut.

Opposition to across-the-board tax cut and support for targeted tax cut must be the linchpin of our position. Tactical response to Dole proposal should be hypocrisy and pandering.

a. Dole has a lot better rating on hypocrisy than we do, argument is uphill.

b. We are seen as taxers, so it is the bad vs. the hypocrite even if we succeed.

c. Hypocrite is a short-term, limited-gain, harassing response to Dole's tax cut, NOT the key to winning the issue. We can fight all election season on the BIG issue of targeted vs. across-the-board tax cut. The argument is played on their side of the field, how best to cut taxes, so gains come out of their hide. This argument permits us to address Democratic goals—education, etc.—with Republican tools—tax cuts—and leaves us in perfect positioning. We must seek to make this the big issue over which we fight the election. It inoculates us against their best charge: that we are high taxers. If we are always debating how to cut taxes, it is hard to sell that we want to raise taxes.

V. FEAR OF CLINTON SECOND-TERM LIBERALISM

A very potent issue and they are onto it.

Will Clinton be too liberal in second term?

Concerned—56   Not concerned—41

Will Dole be too conservative in second term?

Concerned—59   Not concerned—36

The answer: raise fears of Dole's first term to overshadow Clinton's second term.

"If you knew that Dole's agenda included: Medicare cuts, assault-weapon repeal, environmental cuts, eliminate Department of Education":

Less likely vote Dole—74   Much less likely—52

WE MUST USE DOLE'S OVERT AGENDA TO OFFSET FEARS OF CLINTON'S HIDDEN AGENDA.

DOLE: FIGHTING THE "WHATEVER" FACTOR

In early June, Dole's Manhattan-based speech coach, Jack Hilton, sent his dour pupil a list of ten reminders and urged him to tape them to the side of his refrigerator where he would see them every day:

1. First-rate, world-class speech *material.*
2. *Same* TelePrompTer operator on all occasions from now to November. (Facilitates smooth delivery.)
3. Practice, practice, practice—mostly to gain good familiarity with the *contents.*
4. Head *up!* (This is *why* you need good familiarity.)
5. Soften facial expressions—i.e., *smile*, grin, laugh. (Warmth.)
6. "I"—*not* "Bob Dole." (Personalize!)
7. Use *humor.*
8. *Slow* the pace. Neither you nor your audience is double-parked!
9. No false starts; no unfinished sentences.
10. No "whatevers."

DOLE: "MOVE THE AGENDA OF THE ELECTION TO TAXES"

On June 5, Mike Murphy, a member of Dole's constantly shifting media team, faxed a memo to headquarters staffer Kevin Stach pushing for a tax cut as the centerpiece of the campaign. Excerpts:

FAX MEMO
TO: KEVIN
FROM: MIKE MURPHY
RE: A FAX ON TAXES

My experience on the tax cut issue comes from running three tax-cut-centered challenger campaigns: [Michigan Governor John] Engler in 1990, [New Jersey Governor Christine Todd] Whitman in 1993, and Mike Harris for Premier of Ontario in 1995. All three came from behind to win, shocking the experts.

Right after you announce a big tax cut, here is what always happens: The "echo chamber" hates it and the media covers it as totally irresponsible. Allies on your own side mutter darkly about it and complain on background to the press. One or two showboat and publicly denounce it. They are praised as courageous. Expert pundits say you've blown the election with a single move. "Voters" interviewed and polled by newspapers (and your campaign pollster) say they do not believe you will ever really cut taxes. *You actually do go down in the polls.* Half the campaign panics and there is a lot of talk about restoring "credibility" (translation: abandon the tax cut).

Then, a few months later—after sticking with your tax cut and fighting for it—you come from 25 points behind to win the election. Everyone is shocked.

How come? Tax cut agendas unify the base, and more importantly, *move the agenda of the election to taxes.* That is a big victory. The election discussion becomes [one] about your philosophy of cutting taxes (to create good jobs) and your opponent's terrible record of raising taxes. Voters are finally convinced that, at least, you will not raise taxes, while the opponent who has done it before may indeed raise taxes again. That agenda leads to victory.

A big tax cut plan will initially be unpopular and badly reviewed. It will be labeled a huge political mistake. The candidate will be under *incredible pressure* to backtrack (the worst thing to do; you admit your opponents and the press are right—you *are* an irresponsible hack). But, *if you stick to your guns*, the agenda of the election will change to a focused discussion which the Republican is likely to win.

DOLE: "STEADY, DEPENDABLE LEADERSHIP"

*In June, with the Dole campaign still struggling for a tradable message, Don Sipple—
Lacy's replacement as strategist—dropped a memo into the suggestion box. Excerpts:*

TO: SCOTT REED
          DON RUMSFELD
          TONY FABRIZIO
FROM: DON SIPPLE
RE: MESSAGE/THEME

I've been thinking about a theme that reflects the truth, the facts, the record and the real Bob Dole. I believe the theme should be descriptive of Bob Dole and what he stands for as well as implicitly setting up the contrast with Clinton.

I propose:

STEADY, DEPENDABLE LEADERSHIP TO SECURE AMERICA'S FUTURE

Let's discuss.

DOLE: "CONNECT THE DOTS FOR THE AMERICAN PEOPLE"

In June, Sipple, the Dole strategist and media man, proposed that the Republican National Committee run a tough ad attacking Clinton's ethics. Excerpts:

TO: HALEY BARBOUR
          SCOTT REED
          TONY FABRIZIO
FR: DON SIPPLE
RE: RNC ADVERTISING

I propose we do a spot on the constellation of ethics problems facing Clinton and his administration. It should be credibly presented using headlines etc. and should include his own quote, "We will have the most ethical administration in history . . . " There might be an FBI files piece, Whitewater convictions, eight cabinet members under investigation, and Travelgate. The purpose of doing this ad would be to connect the dots for the American people —to demonstrate a pattern of behavior. Additionally, this is a spot that [Dole For President] shouldn't get to until late (if at all, in advertising). And it may have the benefit of picking up these stories and moving them along as they may ebb in news coverage.

Let me know your thoughts.

DOLE: "YOUR CREDIBILITY IS AT STAKE"

On June 25, Pete Domenici, the chairman of the Senate Budget Committee, wrote a letter to his longtime friend and fellow deficit hawk Bob Dole, warning of the perils of going forward with his proposal for a 15-percent across-the-board cut in income taxes. Domenici swallowed his doubts only on the assumption, encouraged by winks and nods from his old chum, that Dole as president would do whatever it took to wrestle down the deficit and balance the budget. Excerpts:

The Honorable Robert Dole
810 First Street, NE
Suite 300
Washington, DC

Dear Senator Dole:

As you develop your economic plan, you are aware that your credibility is at stake. If you propose something that results in the media and the Clinton administration criticizing you, you could lose some of the high credibility that you have built in this area over the years. The Clinton administration is surely looking to shift the issue of credibility off them (Whitewater, FBI files, etc.) and onto you.

I am somewhat skeptical about the feasibility of a 15 percent marginal tax cut. Your panel of economists does not believe that a 15 percent tax cut could be enacted without altering your commitment to a balanced budget. Neither of us over the years has been able to produce credible spending cuts of the magnitude that would be required to balance the budget by 2002 and execute such a tax plan. Furthermore, be aware that, correctly or incorrectly, any across-the-board tax cut will be judged by many as unfair—favoring higher-income over middle- and lower-income individuals.

I think it is very important that your economic plan emphasize overall reform. In my mind, there are three crucial issues which should be given equal weight: (1) tax reform; (2) balanced budget; and (3) education/ retraining reform. While seemingly separate issues, they are all geared toward one objective—raising US investment and thus boosting the level of long-run growth by as much as 0.5–0.6 percent annually if enacted together.

The US is in great need of tax reform. We must adopt a system which is simpler, flatter, lower and consumption-based. If the three-pronged plan laid out in this letter were adopted, the boost to yearly growth could produce cumulative budgetary savings of $175–$210 billion out to 2002. If one looked out ten years, this figure would obviously increase significantly. This would provide room for tax cuts within the overall package.

Any Dole economic plan must not give up on the goal of a balanced budget by the end of the first term of a Dole presidency.

Sincerely,
[signed] Pete

PS Let's stay in touch.

DOLE: THE MATHEMATICS OF ANGST

On June 26, pollster Fred Steeper warned the Dole campaign and the Republican party against putting all their chips on economic issues at the expense of other concerns. Steeper's unspoken worry was that Clinton had staked out the moral crisis in America as his thematic centerpiece, and the Republicans were letting him get away with it. Excerpts:

MEMORANDUM
TO: HALEY BARBOUR
          CURT ANDERSON
          TONY FABRIZIO
          WES ANDERSON
          BOB WARD
FROM: FRED STEEPER
RE: U.S. NATIONAL JUNE 20–23 RESULTS

ECONOMIC DISCONTENT AS A THEME

The results to our economic questions support making the economy and the economic "angst" of the voters one of our major themes, but they do not support making them the overriding or central theme of the campaign.

The results to [some] questions are certainly seductive to making pocketbook concerns a central theme: over 80% agree, mostly strongly so, that it is harder today than in the past to pay for a house, college, etc., that Americans are working longer for less pay, and the government is taking too much out of people's pockets. A 69% majority reject Clinton's assertion that the economy is the best it's been in 30 years.

The problem with these questions is they have no history. We don't know if we are measuring unique economic discontent or everyday financial grumbling that one would have heard in 1988, 1984 or 1964! (Anyone have parents who did *not complain* at the dinner table on how tough it was to make ends meet?)

I raise this caveat because another set of economic questions in the survey present a more positive picture of the economy. The one question we did ask with a history shows that voters are less negative about their family's financial situation than they were in the 1992 election cycle. In December 1991, one in three registered voters said they were "worse off" financially, compared to four years ago. Today, only one in five voters say they are worse off compared to four years ago.

There are opportunities on Clinton's handling of the economy for us, but they are not overwhelming. We should address the voters' pocketbook angst but not to the major exclusion of other themes and messages.

To be sure, Americans are troubled, beyond their normal financial complaints, by the necessity to have two wage-earners and the negative consequences that has for families and child-rearing. However, this social problem has been with us at least for two decades. If we so chose, the 1996 campaign would be the first to try to tap into this systemic economic problem; as the first to try, both the gain and the risk (in not having a credible program to solve the problem, for one) would be very high.

DOLE: "WE HAVE TO MAKE A CASE FOR CLINTON'S REMOVAL"

In early July, Don Sipple sought inspiration in a published newspaper poll—a slap at the Dole campaign's own polling team—and tried once again to frame a coherent message. Excerpts:

TO: SCOTT REED
        DON RUMSFELD
        JILL HANSON
        TONY FABRIZIO
        JOHN BUCKLEY
FR: DON SIPPLE
RE: THEME & MESSAGE

As a preface, I'd like to make a couple of points about the Big Picture:

1. This election will be a referendum on Clinton. The voter equation will be roughly two-thirds satisfaction/assessment of Clinton and one-third perceptions of Dole.

2. Currently, somewhere between mid-fifties to low sixties say that the country is seriously off on the wrong track. Yet Clinton's approval (positive) is roughly low fifties to low forties. Those numbers cannot remain incompatible until election day; something's got to give . . . and it will be Clinton.

3. According to the polling there are three major components to the pessimistic mood: economic anxiety, moral decline, and frustration with Washington and both political parties (the fuel for Perot).

4. Absent war, recession, or major scandal, we do not have the luxury of an electorate ready to *fire* their incumbent. Instead, we, in the campaign, have to make a case for Clinton's removal. The burden of proof is on us. Currently, Clinton receives relatively good marks on his performance. However, we can defeat Clinton if we focus on two things:

    a. *Poor performance*—We offer proof that Clinton's performance is worse than they believe.

    b. *Values Disconnect*—Offer proof that Clinton does not share "your" values.

Thus, the challenge in this campaign is to harness current voter dissatisfaction ("wrong track") and link it to Clinton's values disconnect and poor performance. Both offer us the added opportunity to assail his credibility/trustworthiness as well.

It is now urgent that we come to agreement on a rationale for [Dole's] candidacy, a theme and the message/Dole Agenda:

    A. *Rationale for Candidacy*

        Setting the stage for America's renewal in the 21st Century.

    B. *Theme*

        Leadership you can trust to make America work again.

    C. *Agenda*

        1. *Putting our Financial House in Order*
- smaller government
- lower taxes
- ending wasteful Washington spending
- reducing the deficit

        2. *Ending Decades of Social Decay by Rediscovering the Difference Between Right and Wrong*
- drugs
- juvenile crime
- replace welfare with work
- (illegal immigration)

        3. *Economic Growth and Opportunity*
- tax reform and tax cuts
- creating and attracting the best jobs in the world

    D. *Message*

        1. End Wasteful Washington Spending

        2. Replace Welfare with Work

        3. Stop Drugs and Violent Juvenile Crime and Gangs

        4. Higher Incomes . . . Lower Taxes

We will utilize a mix of network television, statewide television, cable and radio. We are planning that two-thirds of our messages be aimed at Clinton. These ads would reinforce the "wrong track" perception and tie [it] to Clinton's performance and/or values disconnect.

DOLE: "WORRY, WORRY, WORRY, WORRY"
On July 22, Don Devine sent a chin-up memo to his friend Bob Dole. Excerpts:

SENATOR BOB DOLE
FROM: DON DEVINE
SUBJECT: WHERE WE ARE

- *Worry, Worry, Worry, Worry.* Everyone is in a panic. But there is no reason. I remember all the campaign and media talk about Ronald Reagan being too old and making "gaffes" daily but it did not matter. The speeches are sound. The slogan "The Better Man, For a Better America" is good as are the themes—more economic opportunity, smaller government, and stronger, safer families. Do not let them get you down. It will all work.

- *Congressional Panic.* The panic on the Hill is manifest. After over a year of predictably foolish strategy, now it is everyone for himself on welfare, health, spending, etc. Columnists are writing about Congress taking the lead away from you. Ridiculous. They are too frightened. They bolted when the message on core issues was confused. You can calm them down by going back to base issues and staying on them.

- *Back to the Base.* If you: (1) keep steady with the [party] base the next two weeks, (2) deliver a strong platform, (3) pick a VP who does not explode the Convention, (4) give a solid nomination speech and keep giving it, (5) limit media access, and (6) have strong ads, you will win. Clinton will be like Carter in 1980—it will be late but support will fall quickly.

DOLE: "CHANGE—UGLY BUT NEEDED"

In early August, a worried Mike Murphy proposed shaking up the assumptions—and the command—of the Dole campaign. When the shakeup came a month later, Murphy himself was among the shakees. Excerpts:

LET'S WIN THE ELECTION

We need a theology of how to win this race. Here it is:

- It's about Clinton.
- Post Labor Day is the ball game.
- Taxes/Wages and Right vs. Wrong/Better Man are the Issues.
- We want them to know this: "Bob Dole will CUT TAXES, GROW THE ECONOMY, FIGHT FOR WHAT'S RIGHT, TELL THE TRUTH." That's the mantra.
- Policy hit-a-day thinking is fragmented, voter-irrelevant and wrong. Repeat the big themes.
- Dole's instincts are defensive; that's a weakness. We need to control and fight that.
- We need to outspend Clinton on paid media to win. The old model is not appropriate to our situation. Less travel, less staff, less polling crap, less of everything that is not voter contact. A few more million on the air means a few more states and the difference.
- Our communications mindset is all wrong. Print is dead. (Bob Dole has been in the national print press for 30 years and no voter we need knows a damn thing about him.) The Beltway echo media is not our friend and not our answer. We should care about TV news; network and local and local print and radio. We need to change our emphasis away from the weekly newsmagazines, the [New York Times], the [Wall Street Journal] and the pundit crowd. The hell with *George* magazine.
- We don't have to debate. If we do debate, we want two.

WHAT TO DO:

We push pictures on the road. Dole gets one good soundbite a day. Light days that are well-prepared for look. Less travel is OK. (Travel wastes money and makes wrong news.)

- We make tax cut news every week. Even if it is just a mantra: "Lower taxes for everybody, higher wages for America." Don't fall for the phony Dole has to make "news" or we will not get covered. Just redo the theme day in and day out. The national news (media) will bitch. We shouldn't care. The tax/wages stuff will get local coverage and that counts more.
- Fire some people after the convention. We need a bit of a shake-up, it says "new" campaign. Change. Ugly, but needed.
- Primary is over. Steve Forbes has Newt-level negatives. Kemp is yesterday/'80s. Get 'em away from us. Let Govs carry the tax plan. Now.
- Ad campaign will be about Better Man Bob and push Clinton [as] the Wrong Track (bad wages, highest taxes ever, weak president who cannot tell the truth).

DOLE: "WE ARE LOSING THE SPIN BATTLE"

On August 9, with the Republican convention just four days away, Dole's pollsters looked at their latest tracking numbers and set off an alarm about Dole's problems in selling his tax-cut package. Excerpts:

CONFIDENTIAL MEMORANDUM
TO: DFP SENIOR LEADERSHIP
FROM: TONY FABRIZIO AND THE POLLING TEAM
RE: NATIONAL TRACKING

* * * ALERT * * *

We have a serious problem in communicating our economic plan. Only 38% of the country says they know either a great deal or some about Bob Dole's tax cut and economic-growth plan. Among these voters, Dole trails Clinton by 2% (42%–44%). Understand, these voters are more likely to be Republicans than not. Among the 60% unaware of the plan, Clinton leads by 28% (30%–58%)

More people oppose our plan than favor it. Even among those most aware of it, the plan is viewed negatively. Overall, 34% favor the plan while 38% oppose it. Among those who say they know a great deal or some about the plan, 41% favor it, while 46% oppose it.

We are losing the spin battle.

Five very important points to stress: 1) the plan will balance the budget and it is not a gimmick; 2) it will benefit the lower and middle class families; 3) elements of the plan beyond the tax cut need to be highlighted; 4) the plan needs to be related to tangible, everyday benefits, and 5) we need to be offensive.

We are still at our own lowest point that we have tracked in the campaign. We are now down by 18%, with Dole at 35%, Clinton at 53%.

DOLE: "WE ARE NOW AT OUR STRONGEST POINT TO DATE"

On August 19, Tony Fabrizio and his polling team sent forward a memo celebrating the great success of the Republican convention—and warning that it could go away. Excerpts:

CONFIDENTIAL MEMORANDUM
TO: DFP SENIOR LEADERSHIP
FROM: TONY FABRIZIO AND THE POLLING TEAM
RE: CONVENTION TRACKING SUMMARY

We are now at our strongest point to date. The tasks we needed to accomplish—restore our base, improve our image and deteriorate Clinton's job approval—were accomplished. It is important to understand what did not catalyze this advancement. It was not our attacks on Bill Clinton. Clinton was almost a non-factor in our resurgence.

More than any one thing, it was Jack Kemp's selection, and the resulting re-focus on our economic plan that brought us where we are today. Secondarily, our greatest advancements came among GOP moderates—suggesting our outreach to the middle, whether through the image of Kemp or the effects of our convention, was successful.

Dole's ballot position has increased nine points from our all-time low of 30% to our high point of 39%. We are in a statistical tie with Clinton at 42%, Dole at 39%, and Perot at 9%.

Dole's image underwent a dramatic change during the two weeks of tracking. When tracking began, Dole had a net negative image, with a 39% favorable rating and a 48% unfavorable rating. The final two nights, Dole had nearly reversed those numbers with a 48% favorable rating and a 42% unfavorable rating. Dole's favorable rating is the highest we have seen since our research began in April.

Over the two weeks of tracking, Clinton's job approval rating dropped nine points from a high of 60% to 51%. Consequently, his disapproval rating rose 8 points from 34% (an all-time low) to 42% (an all-time high).

Despite our much improved position, we still have a lot of campaigning to do. We are only a strong second to Clinton after the most positive two weeks of media we have had. We can expect some of this excitement to fade, so we must be diligent in building on the convention momentum.

CLINTON: "I TRULY LOVE WHAT WE HAVE BEEN TOGETHER"

In late August, Dick Morris wrote two farewells to the campaign he was obliged to leave in the thick of a seedy tabloid sex scandal. The first, defiant in tone, was for public consumption:

STATEMENT ON RESIGNATION
Richard Morris
Aug. 29, 1996

Last night, I resigned as campaign strategist for President Clinton. While I served I sought to avoid the limelight because I did not want to become the message. Now, I resign so I will not become the issue.

I will not subject my wife, family or friends to the sadistic vitriol of yellow journalism.

I will not dignify such journalism with a reply or an answer. I never will.

I was deeply honored to help this President come back from being buried in a landslide and to make it possible for him to have a second chance at a second term.

He is a great president and a great man. He truly can unite the country around the partnership of opportunity and responsibility. It is the message for our times.

I want to thank the President and the Democratic Party for allowing me to return. I hope I have served them well.

Politics will remain for me what it was to Robert Kennedy, an honorable adventure.

Morris's second statement was private, a mawkish valedictory pecked out on his laptop computer when words failed him at his last meeting with the campaign team:

TO MY FRIENDS WITH WHOM I SERVED

I have loved being part of our joint, thrilling effort.

Thank you for the privilege of working with each of you.

Mark Penn, thank you for your mind.

Doug Schoen, thank you for your sense and your ballast.

Bob Squier, thank you for your wisdom and experience, I should have talked with you more.

Bill Knapp, thank you for your judgment and your ability.

[Ad man] Hank Sheinkopf, thank you for your loyalty and love.

[Filmmaker] Marius Penczner, thank you for your creativity and your gentleness.

I ask two things if they are possible:

First, please see that those of my staff who wish to remain can do so working with you, not with the wolves of the White House.

Second, if you feel that it is appropriate, I would appreciate any financial arrangements you care to make. I will be grateful if you do, understanding if you don't.

Finally, I will always treat each of you generously and fairly in anything I may say or write. I truly love what we have been together.

DOLE: "RAISE THE STAKES OF THE ELECTION"

Just before Labor Day, the latest in Dole's parade of chief strategists, Paul Manafort, drafted a limited-distribution memo—only six numbered copies were struck—offering the latest in a series of attempts at a game plan for a troubled campaign. His advice, with just two months left, was to sell Dole in September and attack Clinton in October. Excerpts:

TO: SCOTT REED
FROM: PAUL MANAFORT
RE: DOLE CAMPAIGN STRATEGY DOCUMENT

INTRODUCTION

The key to a winning Presidential Campaign is defining the race and then running that campaign. Currently, Bill Clinton is defining the Presidential contest.

The challenge to the Dole campaign is to raise the stakes of the election. We need to seize the agenda immediately. Time is passing and each day is critical if we are to regain our footing and dominate the campaign in the manner that is necessary in order to be victorious. There is little room for error.

The purpose of this document is to lay out a strategy for the remaining nine weeks of the campaign.

STRATEGY

Opening Moves

The Republican and Democratic National Conventions provided the first major opportunities for the two parties to reposition themselves vis-à-vis their opponents. Given the fact that the Democratic Convention was last, they have some momentum moving into September. We must recapture the momentum that Senator Dole received coming out of the Republican Convention.

The Democratic Convention and the Rose Garden bill signings sought to undo what we accomplished. Their goal was to associate President Clinton with the people and to continue to show him as compassionate, caring and with a program that did not cause major disruptions.

The second objective of the Clinton convention was to define Bob Dole as radical, disconnected, and a man of the past. The result of their convention was to dramatically affect Bob Dole's favorable image and to improve President Clinton's job approval.

Critical to any analysis is the fact that the hard vote for Clinton and Dole is still relatively close, Clinton at 33% and Dole at 22%. The softness of the remainder of the vote is an indication of how volatile the election is. It is vital that we recapture some of the vote that we gained from our Convention which has slipped away as a result of the Democratic Convention. This is our first target.

Proposed Strategy
The starting point post–Labor Day is to reaffirm and solidify the foundation that the Republican National Convention set down. The message that we need to communicate during the month of September is two-fold. First, we need to build out who Bob Dole is. We cannot sell the Dole vision in a "winning" way until we have resolved the issue of "who is Bob Dole, the man."

a. Who is Bob Dole?
It is important that Americans feel that their President understands their problems. (If anything, this is something that Clinton has been very effective in communicating, even though his programs do not reflect his rhetoric.) Our speeches, as well as events, need to identify Senator Dole with the problems that voters feel they are faced with. This includes issues such as earning more, taking home less; struggling to send kids to college; fear for personal safety; no time to spend with the kids to teach them values.

Currently, the data indicate that Bob Dole is perceived as lacking compassion. Whether it is because of his Washington image or the negative connotations of the Republican Congress as branded by President Clinton, the fact is that we need to tell a story different from the current image. We need to have him perceived as "in touch," "understanding" and "caring."

The third element regarding personal characteristics deals with leadership and trust. The American people need to understand that Bob Dole is a man of his word. Once they know this fact, it is easier for them to accept his vision, including his economic plan.

b. The Dole Agenda for America
Given the time constraints facing the campaign, we must begin to lay the case for the Dole agenda simultaneous with explaining who Bob Dole is. The choice between Dole and Clinton cannot be viewed the way a voter would choose between two candidates running for Congress. They must come to understand

that the nation is at a fork in the road, and that going one way with Dole will have a significantly more important outcome than going the other way with Clinton.

In raising the stakes to this historic dimension, this part of the campaign must focus on issues, not personalities. The time for the presentation on the hard choices on issues is the month of September.

All of [our economic proposals] were favored by over 60% of the electorate. Yet most of the people who favor these issues are not following their positions with their ballot support. The results demonstrate that our campaign has not drawn a contrast with Clinton. The average voter does not know that Clinton opposes many of the things they strongly favor.

c. Economic Plan

The initial presentation of the Dole agenda is the economic plan. The emphasis of this effort must focus on the fact that Dole has a plan, the plan can work, and who the plan will benefit. The latter point must focus on relief for the middle class, showing a sensitivity to working women and the impact it has on families.

The significance of the September presentation is to establish the historic significance of choosing the Dole plan of action vs. the direction Clinton wants to go. Clinton's approach in his acceptance speech was to attack the Dole plan as one which will trigger a new deficit crisis while benefiting the rich and risking future economic instability. He is crafting the historically significant argument. Dole must create a similar frame of reference which creates the basis for selecting his approach.

d. Crime and Drugs

The second phase in September needs to focus on the crisis in America. This crisis is in the moral dimension.

Currently, Clinton is beating us badly on crime and drugs. It is his core issue when reaching into our base. 25% of the Republicans believe that he is better on this issue than Dole. We must severely attack his failures.

Clinton very deftly laid out a Republican agenda in this area during his acceptance speech. What has gone unnoticed is the fact that he has been president for 3 ½ years and has not dealt with the problems. We must demonstrate that Clinton does not have the resolve to deal with these issues and that his election-day conversion is no more reliable than any of his other promises.

In October, we begin to wage the real battle. Using the debates and paid media, we must drive home the consequences of four more years of Clinton.

TACTICAL GAME PLAN

Message

In order to run a successful campaign, we need to integrate the paid and earned media. We have not been efficient in integrating the two. National tracking indicates that after two months and $17 million behind our paid media, the Dole campaign is six points down from where we were. While a part of this can be attributed to the Clinton convention, the fact is uncontested that our paid media efforts have tended to lag behind our earned media. Every significant movement in our tracking can be tied directly to the earned media in the campaign—the resignation from the Senate, the economic plan, the Kemp announcement, and the Republican Convention.

All major speeches should be built around a simple format which says the following:

- The present situation isn't working because . . .
- Life can be better
- Here is how

Finally, in October, when we are exposing the Clinton record, it is important that we build our speeches around a core section which talks about Clinton's broken promises, his embracing Republican ideas as his own, and misrepresenting the facts and his failures.

Additionally, the discussion on Clinton's record must focus on the course of future events if we continue on the Clinton path. The future of social security if it isn't cured, of taxes if they aren't cut, of government spending if unchecked, and what will happen to the deficit in a second Clinton term.

The conclusion of this exposure is to show that the bridge will not reach the other side. That the new promises are being made just to get re-elected. The key to this is to tie his future promises to his past failures and broken promises.

It is imperative that our paid media reinforce and push the message of our earned media. The messages need to be crisp. It is easy to use clichés in order to make a point. Given the cynicism of the American people, it is very important that we not fall into this trap.

During the first phase of our paid media program in September, we need to have the following messages:

1. A spot defining Bob Dole, the man.
2. A spot defining Bob Dole's economic plan vs. Clinton's record.

3. A spot defining the drug problem as a crisis affecting America.
4. A spot defining Bob Dole's drug program.

The second phase of the paid media program (the end of September) needs to turn its focus towards Bill Clinton. Our media plan must define America under Bill Clinton . . . an America of higher taxes, higher crime, higher drug use, failing educational standards.

Debates

A successful Dole candidacy must include successful performances in the debates. It is the means by which the American people will measure Bob Dole against Bill Clinton. It is also the opportunity for Senator Dole to clearly articulate his message.

The goals for the debate should include the following:

1. *"Why Bob Dole wants to be President."* This needs to definitely be a part of our strategy for our first debate. We need to make the case that the election is historic, that there are real choices, and depending on which selection is made on November 5, America will go in a different direction.
2. *Humanize the image of Bob Dole.*
3. *Demonstrate to America that Bob Dole has a plan.* We need to play to the hope of the American people. "Restoring the American dream" provides that unifying theme.
4. *Tie Clinton's record to broken promises.* We need to show what Clinton has done vs. what he has promised to do, and then talk about his [broken] promises, the cost of his programs, and relate them to his future broken promises. This becomes important especially in the second debate.
5. *Create a unified slogan to cite Clinton failures.* Just as the slogan "There he goes again" was used by Governor Reagan to characterize Carter's comments and criticisms, we need to create a slogan which will symbolize the excessive and/or broken promises of President Clinton.

There are a series of tactical issues that we need to address.

Are we better off in a two-man debate or should we include Perot? The preliminary data from our research indicate that a two-way debate is best for us. Given the fact that the Commission has rules that can exclude Perot, we should review how we might seek to make this a two-person race. Obviously, if Perot is to be discussed, we should put Nader on the table as well. We want the Clinton campaign to reject Nader, or at least get some of the blame for Nader not being involved, in order to motivate that group.

The timing of the debates is also very important. While some might argue that a late debate helps Clinton because it allows him to appear Presidential and presents a forum in which he may visually look better than Dole, I don't believe this should be a driving force. The value of a late debate is to keep voters undecided until they have seen our full campaign. It allows us to use the full two months to communicate our message. It also provides a protection against an "October Surprise." Finally, it allows us to throw a "long ball" if the campaign is behind.

While the safe course is not to have a late debate, a winning campaign requires one. If the rest of the campaign has been successfully executed, the late debate allows us to win the election (not unlike the 1980 Reagan vs. Carter situation).

STRATEGY

While it is too late to do a variety of new things, there is still time left to win this campaign. It is very important that our strategy for September and October be finalized. As soon as the conclusion is reached, the discipline of executing the plan needs to be asserted. Having a strategy that no one pays attention to or is changed based on circumstances is to have no strategy at all.

DOLE: "MAKE THIS ELECTION ABOUT BIG AND BASIC THINGS"

On September 2, Don Sipple urged moving moral as well as economic issues to the center of the Dole campaign. Three days later, Sipple was gone, one more exile from Dole's unstable media operation. Excerpts:

TO: SCOTT REED
         DONALD RUMSFELD
FROM: DON SIPPLE
RE: "MORAL DECLINE IN AMERICA" THEME

As you know, I've been a strong advocate of introducing a second theme in the campaign: Moral Decline in America.

It is clear we are set to switch gears in mid-September and move from the Economy/Taxes theme to a period where we focus on drugs and crime. How we frame that period is important.

The reason for the umbrella theme of moral decline over these issues is threefold:

1. A majority of the electorate believes there is a moral crisis in America.
2. The backdoor of the moral decline theme is the character issue, which we will want to focus on in October.
3. It is an opportunity to employ new and meaningful language in relation to a set of issues that oftentimes are treated as clichés. Given that Senator Dole currently is perceived as better-equipped to promote strong moral values as President, I believe this theme will serve to make his generational status more as a positive.

Proposed Mission Statement:

There is a moral crisis in America:

- One out of every three babies born in the U.S. today is out-of-wedlock.
- Teenage drug use has doubled in the last four years . . . the use of cocaine and LSD has nearly tripled.
- Crime is more random, more violent, and criminals are younger and meaner.
- The Moral Fabric of America is not strong enough because the difference between right and wrong is not clear enough.

- The United States is the greatest country on the face of the earth. A great country and a good people should not accept this level of illegitimacy, drug use, and crime.

The role of Senator Dole in leading this national discussion is not that of a Preacher, but of a Patriot. Bill Clinton, and his minimalist agenda, seeks to marginalize the Presidency of the United States. Senator Dole by and through his campaign must make this election about Big and Basic Things.

DOLE: "CROWD SAYS . . . A LIBERAL!"

On September 24, with Dole running thirteen points behind Clinton, Tony Fabrizio's polling team sent one in a series of daily strategy messages to the road-show command on the campaign plane. Excerpts:

TO: MARGARET TUTWILER
FROM: TONY FABRIZIO AND THE POLLING TEAM
RE: DAILY STRATEGIC INFORMATION BRIEFING

MESSAGE:

Continue with liberal theme: [Clinton's] liberal perception among voters jumped last night, and we win by 22% among those who think he is a liberal. Among those who think he is moderate or conservative, he wins by 45%.

Tomorrow's headline should read, "Dole Offers Proof That Clinton Is a Tax and Spend Liberal."

VISUALS:

The picture on television should be the people who are going to be helped by Bob Dole's economic plan, and who have been hurt by Clinton's tax-and-spend liberal policies. We need to communicate that real people will benefit from our program. These people should be represented by families, working women, small business owners and seniors.

CROWD DYNAMICS:

It would make for good TV if we could get Senator Dole to work the crowd in the following manner: *Bob Dole* . . . "Bill Clinton says he's not a closet liberal. But what do you call someone who broke his promise and gave us the biggest tax increase in American history?" *Crowd says* . . . "A liberal!" *Bob Dole* . . . "What do you call someone who thinks that $20 million of midnight basketball is the way to fight crime?" *Crowd says.* . . "A liberal!" *Bob Dole* . . . "What do you call someone who tried to take over our nation's health-care system and had government bureaucrats run it from Washington?" *Crowd says* . . . "A liberal!" *Bob Dole* . . . "What do you call someone who thinks the way to fight drug use is to eliminate DEA agents and appoints a surgeon general who considered legalizing drugs?" *Crowd says* . . . "A liberal!" *Bob Dole* . . . "What do you call someone who proposed 489 new spending programs for things like Alpine slides in Puerto Rico and sweet-smelling toilets?" *Crowd says* . . . "A liberal!" *Bob Dole* . . . "Mr. President, you're right. You're not in the closet— you're out of the closet. Because you can't hide the fact that you are a . . . " (leans ear to the crowd . . .) *Crowd says* . . . "A liberal!"

DOLE: "WE ARE THE WHITE GUYS WHO CAN'T JUMP"

On September 25, one of Dole's new media consultants, Alex Castellanos, laid out a strategy of attack against Clinton. Excerpts:

MEMO
TO: THE DOLE TEAM
FROM: ALEX
RE: MOMENTUM & POSITIONING

There is a perception out there that Bob Dole cannot win this race. The numbers say 75% of Americans believe Bill Clinton will win. As we close the gap, [in the] next few weeks, that perception will begin to change, of course. But if this were a football game, how would we get the fans in the stands rooting for us even though we are behind, late in the game?

We have an opportunity to do exactly that in a way that also does four other important things:

- attacks Bill Clinton as a phony and therefore a liberal
- makes Bob Dole's plain-spoken honesty a decisive strength and contrast
- softens the Dole image and drives up his favorables
- and robs Bill Clinton of his strength as a political performer—in fact turns it against him as a weapon.

America has seen this race before. Many times. We all have: It's in every bookstore and Blockbuster Video. If Hollywood were to make a movie of this race, and wanted Bob Dole to win, how would they set it up to get the audience on our side?

Remember the movie "Hoosiers"? A bunch of short white guys from America's heartland who play honest, fundamental basketball, can't jump, and take on the biggest, baddest, tallest team in the state. That's who we are: the white guys from the heartland who can't jump. Right now, the press and America thinks that's our weakness—Bill Clinton's better at this stuff than we are.

Let's make it our strength.

In this movie, and in countless others like it, America knows who to root for. They root for the little guy. The "one of us" battling Goliath. Think of Harry Truman and Jimmy Stewart.

It is not hard to change the dynamic of this race, to set it up so America asks, "Can the short white guy from the heartland who plays honest ball beat Goliath?"

Take Bill Clinton's great strength and turn it against him. Nail him as a political phony, the fraud he is. Make America look at the messenger instead of the message. In effect, we should make Clinton's most powerful moments working against him by always following them with this message: "Is this guy good at this phony bull@*"^, or what?" Then get into our theme: The truth is he's liberal.

A million different ways to do it, out on the stump or in a debate:

- "Mr. Clinton is so good at politics and campaigning. He's unbelievable."
- "President Clinton is good. *Real* good. It's going to be tough to beat a political salesman who is as talented as he is."
- "Look, I know this is going to be hard. Bill Clinton may be the best we've ever seen, the best there ever was when it comes elections and campaigning. True, I think he's better at *running* for President than *being* President, but how am I going to beat a candidate like that? All I can do is call 'em the way they really are."
- "All I can do is tell the truth in honest, plainspoken words, and trust the American people to look behind shallow surface of politics at what's important."

Bill Clinton *is* politics. Last time I checked, Americans *hate* politics, especially the phoniness in it. Bob Dole's great strength is that he is honest, plainspoken. Let's use that. Real vs. phony is a battle Bob Dole wins.

Objections: Someone, I'm sure, is going to say that we should not "praise" Bill Clinton or "give him anything" by saying he's *good* at anything. That is very old thinking. First of all, we are not giving him anything. The American people already think he is a great political salesman. We are only confirming something they already know. Secondly, saying someone is "a great politician, a great political salesman, the best we've ever seen," is not saying something good. *It's another way of calling someone the best con man on the planet.* And it turns the race into an IQ test: Are you, the voter, smart enough not to be conned by Clinton.

We are taking no risks by doing this. This story, the battle against long odds, the journey against the tide, is a story as old as time. It's already been road-tested. It has already been focus-grouped in a million novels, stories and movies. We are set up to tell this story. And when Bob Dole says he is battling long odds, the listener thinks this is also *his* story, his life's journey. *If we have a concern that Bob Dole sometimes comes across as too dark and we want to hu-*

manize him (I hate that term) *and drive up his favorables, this is a way to do it, to get voters to identify with Bob Dole.*

The point: I would like to suggest that Senator Dole start framing the battle this way on the stump. Now. It sets expectations exactly the way we want for the debates: "Boy, it's going to be tough to beat this guy. He's good. Real good. But the American people have honored me all my life. So I will speak and fight in the plainspoken words I know, the honest words I've always had."

America knows who to root for in that battle. Go Hoosiers.

By the way, in the movie, the short white guys who can't jump and play honest, fundamental basketball win.

DOLE: "GET CLINTON'S BOOT OFF OUR NECK"

In October, campaign manager Scott Reed decided against using a tough new Alex Castellanos commercial called "Talking Liberal" and ordered a slightly milder version instead—one that didn't go quite so far as to call Clinton a liar. The ruling brought a sharp protest from Greg Stevens, Castellanos's colleague on the new Dole media team. Excerpts:

CONFIDENTIAL MEMORANDUM

TO: SCOTT REED
FROM: GREG STEVENS
DATE: 10/3/96
RE: "TALKING LIBERAL" SPOT

You may not like this memo but I feel a strong obligation to let you know my views regarding Alex's "Talking Liberal" spot. I totally disagree with your decision not to use Alex's version that incorporates the lies charge. This probably goes without saying, but today Clinton has a boot on our neck. We have no credibility, no ability to deliver a message—very few ways to dig out of the hole we're in. Every morning I see vivid evidence of how hard Clinton has hammered us virtually since last spring. Every morning I see vivid evidence of how hard Clinton has hammered us right now.

The American people know Clinton's a liar—they don't like it. But if we don't say it and point it out—as Alex so cleverly has done in an *acceptable* way—in my view, we have very little chance.

In the last three weeks since I have been on board, I have been heartened by our strategy: draw the contrast on crime, draw the contrast on spending (our issue), draw the contrast on taxes (our issue). Close the sale and turn the election on Clinton's enormous ethical moral deficiencies—his utter lack of trustworthiness.

Why are we afraid to use this tactic? What can we possibly lose? We need to get Clinton's boot off our neck. Without a very strong, attention-grabbing move like this very soon, we lose.

I urge you to reconsider and suggest you release Alex's original spot tomorrow. This will go a long way toward putting Clinton on the defense going into the all-critical debate.

DOLE: "REMEMBER NIXON"

On October 9, with the first debate over and the second a week away, Don Devine pressed Dole to attack Clinton's character in the rematch. Excerpts:

TO: BOB DOLE
FROM: DON DEVINE
SUBJECT: NEXT DEBATE

You Must Raise Character in the Second Debate. I know you are concerned with the media hitting you for being mean. But you have no choice—people will not believe there is anything there unless you say there is. Remember, Nixon won more votes than any Republican this century and he was perceived as mean and the media hated him (and cut him up badly). But he won.

After a face-to-face meeting that day, Devine scribbled Dole's reaction in the margins of his own copy of the memo. Excerpts:

10/9 Met with Dole personally, for 20 minutes this morning. He said he would do.

He doesn't want to use character—but he will. The Nixon reference really hit with him.

DOLE: DRAWING THE LINE ON CHARACTER

In mid-October, the Dole campaign was in a strategic bind: how to keep going after Clinton on character issues when several news organizations were poking into the tale of an amour in Dole's own long-ago past. The answer was to draw a bright line between public ethics and private morals—a distinction set forth in a memo by campaign manager Scott Reed and leaked by design to the press as a signal that the attack on the president wouldn't get personal. Excerpts:

MEMORANDUM TO DOLE/KEMP '96 LEADERSHIP
FROM: SCOTT REED
              CAMPAIGN MANAGER
SUBJECT: THE CHARACTER ISSUE

From day one of this campaign, Bob Dole and Jack Kemp have made it clear that they would not make personal attacks on the President or Mrs. Clinton or discuss the ongoing Whitewater investigation. Those subjects have been and will continue to be off-limits, and we will not address them.

By character, we do not mean innuendo and name-calling, but the ethical character of the Clinton White House, something we believe is a legitimate, appropriate, and vital issue in this campaign. The aspects of presidential character that govern one's decisions and are reflected in one's actions—things like keeping your promise, standing up for what's right, not abusing the power of your office, and demanding the highest level of ethics from your appointees—are all fair points for discussion.

Those are important—and fair—issues for the American people to consider as they make their presidential choice this fall. These are not personal attacks, or decades-old allegations of impropriety. They are current issues that go to the very core of Bill Clinton's presidential character.

THE CAMPAIGN: BY THE NUMBERS

From August 7, during the run-up to the Republican convention, until October 10, when the money was diverted to other needs, Tony Fabrizio and the Dole polling team conducted a tracking poll charting the daily ups and downs of the race. Major public events during the campaign season, indicated by numbers in parentheses, are listed in the notes below; it usually takes at least a day or two for the full impact of such events to register in the polls.

	THE RACE			FAVORABLE/UNFAVORABLE		JOB RATING
	Clinton	Dole	Perot	Clinton	Dole	Clinton
August 7 (1)	48	32	13	56–37	38–48	60–34
August 7–8	48	32	12	55–37	37–49	60–34
August 8–9	46	33	10	54–38	36–50	58–35
August 9, 11 (2)	45	33	12	53–39	38–49	56–35
August 11–12 (3)	48	39	11	54–39	42–45	55–36
August 12–13 (4)	42	37	11	50–42	45–41	51–40
August 13–14 (5)	42	38	10	48–45	46–42	50–42
August 14–15 (6)	43	40	9	47–46	47–44	51–42
August 15–16	—	—	—	48–45	48–42	51–42
August 19–20 (7)	46	36	8	52–41	49–40	53–41
August 20–21 (8)	43	39	9	51–41	49–39	54–41
August 26–27 (9)	43	39	10	53–41	51–38	53–41
August 27–28	46	37	9	53–42	49–42	54–39
August 28–29 (10)	49	35	9	56–37	44–46	58–36
September 3–4 (11)	49	33	6	62–33	52–39	63–33
September 4–5	51	31	7	60–35	47–41	63–33
September 5, 9–10 (12)	47	35	7	54–37	47–43	61–34
September 10–11 (13)	45	35	8	57–38	47–45	60–33
September 11–12	46	34	8	58–37	46–46	60–33
September 16	49	35	7	57–36	45–44	59–35
September 16–17	49	35	7	58–36	47–43	59–36
September 17–18 (14)	47	35	8	59–36	47–44	60–35
September 18–19	45	34	9	58–36	43–47	61–34
September 22–23	47	34	7	56–37	45–44	62–33
September 23–24	46	36	6	55–37	46–43	59–35
September 24–25	46	34	9	57–36	45–44	60–33
September 29–30	47	37	7	56–38	47–45	61–35

(continued)

	THE RACE			FAVORABLE/UNFAVORABLE		JOB RATING
	Clinton	Dole	Perot	Clinton	Dole	Clinton
September 30–October 1	47	34	8	57–36	45–45	61–34
October 1–2	49	32	9	56–37	42–48	60–34
October 7 (15)	45	35	7	54–40	45–45	57–37
October 7–8 (16)	47	34	7	55–39	44–46	58–36
October 8–9 (17)	49	33	8	55–37	41–49	58–34
October 9–10	46	35	8	52–37	44–44	57–36

A key to the major events: (1) Dole had announced his tax plan on August 5. (2) Dole selects Jack Kemp as his running mate on August 10. (3) The Reform party opens its two-part convention in Long Beach, California. (4) The Republican convention opens in San Diego on August 12. (5) Elizabeth Dole's Oprah-style speech steals the show at the convention on August 14. (6) Dole accepts the Republican nomination on August 15, offering himself as a bridge to a happier past. (7) Perot had accepted the Reform party nomination in Valley Forge, Pennsylvania, on August 18. (8) As the poll shut down for much of the week between conventions, Clinton signs three major bills— a minimum-wage increase, a health-insurance package and welfare reform— in three days, August 20–22. (9) The Democratic convention opens in Chicago on August 26, while the Clintons journeyed toward the site by train. (10) Clinton delivers his acceptance speech on August 29—an event clouded by Dick Morris's forced resignation early that morning in a tabloid sex scandal. (11) Clinton orders two waves of missile attacks on Iraq on September 3. (12) Clinton's onetime business partner Susan McDougal is jailed in Arkansas on September 9 for refusing to answer questions in the Whitewater inquiry. (13) Perot names Pat Choate as his running mate on September 10. (14) Dole takes a televised fall off a platform at a rally in California on September 18. The same day, a House committee charges Clinton with having abused his power in the purge of the White House travel office. (15) Clinton and Dole met in the first of two presidential debates on October 6; the second would be held on October 16. (16) The story of the Asian connection in Democratic fund-raising, first reported by the Los Angeles Times in mid-September, becomes a campaign issue with stories in the New York Times on October 7 and the Wall Street Journal on October 8. (17) Gore and Kemp met in the vice-presidential debate on October 9.

On November 5, Clinton won reelection with 49 percent of the vote, to 41 percent for Dole and 8 percent for Perot.